Recovering Landscape

RECOVERING LANDSCAPE
Essays in Contemporary Landscape Architecture

James Corner, Editor

Princeton Architectural Press

Published by
Princeton Architectural Press
37 East 7th Street
New York, NY 10003
212.995.9620

For a free catalog of books, call 1.800.722.6657
Visit our website at www.papress.com

Cover design: Alexa Mulvihill
Interior design: Alexa Mulvihill and Adam B. Bohannon
Project editor: Beth Harrison
Copy editor: Madeline Gutin Perri

Cover photo © Alex MacLean/Landslides, 1999

Special thanks to:
Eugenia Bell, Jane Garvie, Caroline Green,
Therese Kelly, Clare Jacobson, Leslie Ann Kent,
Mark Lamster, Anne Nitschke, and Sara E. Stemen
of Princeton Architectural Press
—Kevin Lippert, Publisher

Library of Congress Cataloging-in-Publication Data
Recovering landscape: essays in contemporary landscape architecture /
James Corner, editor.
p. cm.
ISBN: 1-56898-179-1 (alk. paper)
I. Landscape architecture. I. Corner, James.
SB472.R385 1999
712—dc21   98-047386
               CIP

ISBN-13: 978-1-56898-179-6   eISBN: 978-1-56898-842-9

Contents

A landscape is a space deliberately created to speed up or slow down the process of nature. As Eliade expresses it, it represents man taking upon himself the role of time.

J.B. Jackson

Preface

James Corner

There has been a remarkable resurgence of interest in landscape topics during the past ten years or so. The essays in this book discuss the reasons for this renewed interest and, more significantly, the subsequent possibilities that arise for landscape practices in the future. In particular, the book aims to suggest and clarify important directions for the fields of landscape architecture and urbanism, many of which are simply extensions or reformulations of some of these disciplines' most traditional and perennial concerns—issues such as site, geometry, representation, nature, and urbanization. The title *Recovering Landscape* is thus intended to invoke both tradition and invention, the latter transforming and renewing the former.

As a consequence of these ambitions, the reader may well find the term *landscape* used in a number of expansive—if not unusual—ways. Rarely is landscape used to refer solely to pastoral scenery or garden planting, for instance—images with which it is most conventionally associated. Instead, its usage is diverse and rich, embracing urbanism, infrastructure, strategic planning, and speculative ideas alongside the more familiar themes of nature and environment. This richness points to the reasons why the recovery of landscape is such a promising cultural enterprise, for it invokes less the recuperation and restoration of a passive artifact and more the extension and realization of landscape's hidden potential. Such insight and diversity rarely arises from a single point or locus, of course, and many of the essays that follow embrace an interesting range of sometimes conflicting issues and perspectives.

The essays carry the authority and voice of the individual authors and were collected from a number of sources. One of these was a symposium called "Constructing Landscape," held at the University of Pennsylvania in 1993, where a number of papers and discussions addressed the various conceptual and physical constructions that constitute the phenomenon we have come to call *landscape*. The participants attempted to clarify the inevitable constructedness of landscape (that is neither natural nor given) and how productive reciprocities among ideas, representations, and physical spaces may be better understood. In

Fig. 1. *Drainage washes.* Palo Verde, Arizona. 1993. Photograph by Alex S. MacLean.

this sense, the symposium reaffirmed and examined the fact that "landscape" is not equivalent to "land" or "environment"; landscape is less a quantifiable object than it is an *idea*, a cultural way of seeing, and as such it remains open to interpretation, design, and transformation. In constructing landscape, landscape architects provide some of the most revealing explorations of the interface between culture and nature, thus forging essential components of the construction of reality. Essays in this book by Denis Cosgrove, David Leatherbarrow, and Alex Wall are substantially revised versions of papers first presented at this symposium, which was organized with the kind support of Patricia Conway, then dean of the Graduate School of Fine Arts at the University of Pennsylvania.

A second source of this collection was a symposium held at the Architectural Association (AA) in London in 1994. This was organized by myself and Alan Balfour, then chairman of the AA school. We perceived a growing interest among not only architects and designers but also the general public and city administrators in landscape topics and, at the same time, we shared the concern that the formation of new landscapes was being suppressed by a general enthusiasm, obsession even, with pastoral and historical landscapes. Whereas many artists, architects, and urbanists have traditionally looked to the future when projecting new realities, dreams of new landscapes have been mostly overshadowed by concerns for conservation and preservation during the latter part of the twentieth century. In reaction to this, Alan Balfour and I invited a number of prominent landscape architects and theorists to discuss the formation of new landscapes—to project, if you will, an ambitious manifesto for landscape practice. We called the event "The Recovery of Landscape," and essays by Marc Treib, Georges Descombes, Christophe Girot, Denis Cosgrove, and Adrian Hemming originated here.

In assembling these essays into a collection, it became apparent that the book would be more forceful and coherent if other voices were invited to contribute, especially to expand its scope internationally. Consequently, I solicited contributions from Steen Høyer of Denmark, Sébastien Marot of France, Bart Lootsma of the Netherlands, Anuradha Mathur of India (now residing in the United States), Anita Berrizbeita of Venezuela (now residing in the United States), and Stanislaus Fung of China (now residing in Australia). In different ways, these essays each build upon the theme of landscape's recovery and transformation while complementing and enhancing other pieces in the book. In revising their essays, all of the authors were asked to discuss the ways in which landscape is being recovered today, and in what ways this recovery might be made more effective and relevant for contemporary situations.

The above account describes how and from where material was obtained, but in an important way the explanation has become obsolete; the work of editing and revision engendered a collection that left original purposes behind. Instead, a new entity evolved through the process of rewriting and negotiation among contributors. I think the reader thereby will enjoy a collection where the parts add up to more than the whole; each essay stands independent and complete and yet, taken together, the collection transcends any one part. Like a good landscape, the book is much less a record of past discussions and events than it is an enterprising *project*, searching and suggestive. In this regard, the collection possesses a slight manifesto-like quality, as essays provoke thought and redefine the terms around which new and reinvigorated forms of landscape architecture may be conceptualized and practiced. For landscape to be properly recovered it must be remade, designed, invented anew; it can not simply be restored, as an old painting.

Others should be identified as part of this enterprise. Laurie Olin, John Dixon Hunt, Martha Schwartz, Elizabeth Meyer, Rodney Beaumont, Alistair McIntosh, and Dan Rose all presented papers at the "Constructing Landscape" symposium, and some of their ideas and contributions are referred to in the book. Jeffrey Kipnis, Adriaan Geuze, Peter Latz, Enric Miralles, and William Curtis were speakers at the symposium on "The Recovery of Landscape," and many of their ideas are also invoked in the essays that follow. The symposium at the Architectural Association was complemented by a discussion organized by Michael Spens and the Academy Group at the Royal Academy of Arts in London; the abovementioned participants joined here with Dorothée Imbert, David Jacques, Ted Cullinen, and Peter Cook. This discussion, together with a number of essays, is published in *Transforming Landscape*, edited by Michael Spens (London: Academy Editions, 1996), and Spens's introduction to that book provides a particularly good account of much that transpired at the event. Since that time, this book has evolved alongside a number of insightful discussions with Peter Walker, George Hargreaves, Laurie Olin, Anne Spirn, and Stan Allen. And, of course, the innumerable discussions between Alan Balfour and myself over the past few years have proven stimulating and ultimately shaped the character of this collection.

Introduction

Recovering Landscape as a Critical Cultural Practice

James Corner

From a postmodern perspective, landscape seems less like a palimpsest whose "real" or "authentic" meanings can somehow be recovered with the correct techniques, theories or ideologies, than a flickering text displayed on the word-processor screen whose meaning can be created, extended, altered, elaborated and finally obliterated by the merest touch of a button.

Denis Cosgrove and Stephen Daniels
The Iconography of Landscape

This book gathers essays on topics in contemporary landscape architectural theory and practice. In particular, the collection is oriented around two aspects of landscape development: first, the apparent recovery of landscape, or its reappearance in the cultural sphere after years of relative neglect and indifference; and, second, the revisions of the very nature of landscape itself, rethinking what landscape actually is—or might yet become—as both idea and artifact. In the first case, recollection, in the second, invention. In both, landscape is understood as an ongoing project, an enterprising venture that enriches the cultural world through creative effort and imagination.

Through exploring various aspects of the landscape project, the essays aim to make provocative contributions to how our contemporary landscapes are designed, made, and culturally valued. It is less the passive pastoralism of previous landscape formations that inspires the content of this book and more the yet-to-be-disclosed potentials of landscape ideas and practices. Underlying this aim is the belief that landscape has the capacity to critically engage the metaphysical and political programs that operate in a given society, that landscape architecture is not simply a reflection of culture but more an active instrument in the shaping of modern culture.[1] Landscape reshapes the world not only because of its physical and experiential characteristics but also because of its eidetic content, its capacity to contain and express ideas and so engage the mind.

Fig. 1 Satellite photograph of part of Florida, with the city of Miami to the right meeting the Everglades to the left. The image captures the sense of landscape as a large environmental milieu that can no longer exclude or ignore the metropolis as part of its emergent and dynamic condition. Source: NASA.

Moreover, because of its bigness—in both scale and scope—landscape serves as a metaphor for inclusive multiplicity and pluralism, as in a kind of synthetic "overview" that enables differences to play themselves out. In these terms, landscape may still embrace naturalistic and phenomenological experience but its full efficacy is extended to that of a synthetic and strategic art form, one that aligns diverse and competing forces (social constituencies, political desires, ecological processes, program demands, etc.) into newly liberating and interactive alliances.

Understandably, the skeptical reader may find the above claims a little optimistic, too overreaching. Landscape probably appears to the general public too benign or passive ever to assume active and strategic roles in contemporary affairs. Certainly the attention being paid to landscape today assumes more the character of sentimental recollection—with attendant demands for either the re-creation or preservation of past landscapes—than of visionary or ambitious projects. A combination of nostalgia and consumerism drives this desire while suppressing ambitions to experiment and invent.

This image of inertia is intensified if one compares landscape to the innovative efficacy surrounding modern-day economics, information, media technologies, and corporate and political initiatives. In a globalized context of rapid and expedient production, landscape must appear an antiquated medium and its design a fringe activity sustained through the eccentric passions of a handful of romantics and gentle nature-lovers. Consequently, as an image that evokes a virtuous and benevolent nature, landscape is typically viewed as the soothing antithesis to the placeless frenzy of technological urban life; few would share the view that the contemporary metropolis can be construed as a landscape—as some in this book argue—or find it easy to imagine landscapes other than the pastoral and the gardenesque. In this sense, it is understandably difficult for many to imagine landscape as an innovative medium, one that might somehow dislocate the most conventional and regressive aspects of society while at the same time reorganizing these elements in the most liberating and life-enriching way. And yet this is precisely the position that this book seeks to recover for landscape architecture and its practitioners.

Such a position may not be so easy to advance, however. Owing to the aforementioned prevalence of conservative attitudes toward landscape, there is a concomitant loss of will or desire to forge new landscapes—a suspicion, perhaps, of past state regimes and modernist utopias, or simply a sign of a culture seeking escape from the difficulties of the present in the idealized images of the past. While Europe and the United States have developed superb national agencies and trusts for the preservation of landscapes, no equally strong institution is dedicated to cultivating the future. In those places where visionary and exciting work is taking place—the Netherlands, France, and Spain, for instance—there is an underlying public and political will to both nurture and support inventive urban and landscape design, and to see these activities as fundamental to both a healthy economy and a vibrant culture.

The difficulty of advancing landscape is not only an issue of sentimentality and conservatism; it is further hindered by a growing contingent that believes landscape concerns ought to be directed solely toward the stewardship of the natural world. The extreme proponents of this view protest that culturally ambitious landscape projects are largely irrelevant in the face of environmental problems—that is, of course, unless such projects are solely focused on biotic restoration and habitat diversification. A culturally ambitious landscape architecture that does not revolve around ecological concerns is often construed by environmentalists as belonging to the domain of elitist and intellectual art practices rather than to the more practical aspects of healing the earth. This view holds great sway at a sociopolitical level, of course, for in a world whose population continues to grow while its resources diminish, ecological expertise is especially timely and relevant. As with the rise of heritage groups, there is today no shortage of national and regional agencies dedicated to environmental improvement and research, and thankfully and rightly so. But here too, the culturally innovative aspects of landscape architecture are often overlooked or even suppressed as emphasis is placed on more technical procedures aimed at the restoration of an essentially cultureless natural world.

This last phrase is, of course, a telling contradiction in terms; while there may well be phenomena that escape culture, I doubt that the "ecology" and "nature" sought by environmental groups are as culture-free as they might argue. Owing to the inevitable imaging that enframes and represents nature to a given society, the possibilities of a cultureless nature necessarily remain absolutely unknown and unimaginable. Unfortunately, environmental advocates continue to attend to an objectifiable nature that they believe remains external to culture. In so doing, they fail to consider the profound consequences of the world's *constructedness*—its schematization as a cultural idea and, therefore, its subjugation. In mistakenly conceiving of the environment and its many effects and maladies as being outside and not within the cultural world, environmentalists tend only to repair and perhaps forestall damage while cultural ways of being and acting in the world (which lie at the very root of environmental problems in the first place) remain relatively unchanged. As with stitching up wounds to the skin that are only recurring symptoms of some larger failing, the continual patching over of problems is a well-intentioned and praiseworthy effort but one that fails to adequately address their source. While we ought to be thankful for the good work and increased visibility of both preservation and environmental groups, organized and funded at regional and national levels, the lack of any power or group aimed toward the cultivation of landscape as an innovative cultural agent is unfortunate; such forces are much needed.[2]

Landscape Agency

The essays in this book attempt to suggest ways in which landscape projects may serve as means to critically intervene in cultural habit and convention. The emphasis shifts from landscape as a product of culture to landscape as an agent producing and enriching culture. *Landscape* as noun (as object or scene) is quieted in order to emphasize *landscape* as verb, as process or activity. Here, it is less the formal characteristics of landscape that are described than it is the formative effects of landscape in time. The focus is upon the agency of landscape (how it works and what it does) rather than upon its simple appearance. Thus, the book's title is intended to emphasize the *activities* of design and the *effects* of constructed landscapes in time.

When the making of landscape is considered in terms of developmental process, the resulting project may assume any number of formal characteristics, depending on local circumstances and situations. Whether a particular project is naturalistic, rectilinear, curvilinear, formal, or informal is irrelevant; what matters is how the form and geometry of a project make sense with regard to the specific issues it is trying to address and the effects it is trying to precipitate. Thus, recovering landscape is less a matter of appearances and aesthetic categories than an issue of strategic instrumentality. Form is still important, but less as appearance and more as an efficacious disposition of parts. Many of the essays that follow elaborate on this principle. David Leatherbarrow's essay, "Leveling the Land," discusses issues of land form to invoke larger cultural themes and effects. Anita Berrizbeita's claims for the productivism of the Bos Park and Alex Wall's "Programming the Surface" both develop concepts of function, program, and instrumentality as primary considerations in design. Sébastien Marot outlines in his essay, "Reclaiming Sites," how many French landscape architects use landscaping strategies to extend the limitations of the client's goals and site

perimeters to implicate a larger field of forces and possibilities over time. Stanislaus Fung reminds us that Chinese landscapes ought not to be viewed in scenic
terms but rather as strategic fields, "setups" that exercise certain cultural effects
through "shuttling" among differences. Perhaps most directly, Bart Lootsma
describes how, in the Netherlands, landscape assumes a tactical role in the forging of new urban and regional projects whereby old habits are inverted and
turned to newly productive ends.

In various ways, then, all of the essays that follow are oriented around
themes of strategic efficacy; they return the instrumental function to design
while downplaying the strictly formal, the representational, and the contemplative.[3] They suggest how landscape architects and their projects may better shape
how a culture evolves and relates to the world. The concern is less for finding a
new aesthetic style than for increasing the scope of the landscape project in a
broader cultural milieu.

The Landscape Idea

An important distinction of this book with regard to advancing landscape as an
innovative practice is the significance it attributes to the imaginary in relation to
the built. Never is the power of the landscape *idea* underestimated or severed
from physical *space*.[4] In complementary ways, each author speaks of landscape
as both spatial milieu and cultural image. As such, the construction of landscape
space is inseparable from particular ways of seeing and acting. In this sense,
landscape is an ongoing medium of exchange, a medium that is embedded and
evolved within the imaginative and material practices of different societies at
different times. Over time, landscapes accrue layers with every new representation, and these inevitably thicken and enrich the range of interpretations and
possibilities.[5] Thus, both the idea and artifact of landscape are not at all static or
stable, a point memorably demonstrated by Alan Balfour in his story of the
Octagon in Berlin, and one echoed by Steen Høyer, Christophe Girot, and
Georges Descombes in their descriptions of sites in time.

Furthermore, the landscape idea is neither universally shared nor manifested in the same way across cultures and times; its meaning and value,
together with its physical and formal characteristics, are not fixed. To assume
that every society shares an American, English, or French view of landscape, or
even that other societies possess any version of landscape at all, is to wrongly
impose on other cultures one's own image. Indeed, there have been societies
and times wherein the notion of landscape simply did not exist. Even in Euro-

5

pean history, landscape is a relatively recent development. As Kenneth Clark observed:

> Until fairly recent times men looked at nature as an assemblage of iso-
> lated objects, without connecting [them] into a unified scene.... It was
> [not until] the early sixteenth century that the first 'pure' landscape was
> painted [and thus conceived].[6]

Moreover, it is clear that Oriental conceptions of landscape, which were historically related to a mystical reverence for the powers of nature, differ significantly from those of the West, which have traditionally been more scenic and
stylized. And, as Stanislaus Fung points out, there is an important aspect of
mutuality and inclusion to Oriental ideas of landscape as distinct from the
binary dualism characteristic of Western conceptions. But whatever the precise
origin, coding, and intensity of the lens, the landscape idea arises as an eidetic
filter through which different cultures view their woods, mountains, waters, and
fields, and gain a sense of social identity.

Consequently, whereas every society has historically been aware of an *environment*, that same physical setting has not always been elevated to the level of
landscape, which, as an explicit thematic genre, is intentionally set in the foreground in cultural imagery, art, and literature. Even the most modest of these
representations indicates a fairly mature development of the landscape idea
because they are products that arise subsequent to the act of conceiving a landscape. As Denis Cosgrove is right to remind us, "Landscape is already artifice in
the moment of its beholding, long before it becomes the subject of pictorial representation."[7] It is precisely because landscape is construed in an eidetic and
subjective way that it can not be equated with nature or environment. As
Augustin Berque wrote:

> Landscape is not the environment. The environment is the factual
> aspect of a milieu: that is, of the relationship that links a society with
> space and with nature. Landscape is the *sensible aspect* of that relation-
> ship. It thus relies on a collective form of subjectivity.... To suppose that
> every society possesses an awareness of landscape is simply to ascribe to
> other cultures our own sensibility.[8]

Thus, to John Stilgoe's oft-quoted definition that "the antithesis of wilderness is landscape, the land shaped by men," we might add that such shaping is as

much imaginary (encoded in language, myth, maps, paintings, film, and other representations) as it is physical (made and re-presented as material space).[9] Indeed, wilderness itself has today become so widely available (in images, legally protected preserves of land, and tourist sites) that this once forbidding and strictly "unknowable" territory is now entirely consumed as preconceived landscape, packaged as much in pictures and literature as in topographical fact. Wilderness is a socially constructed idea, a landscape, even though it appears wholly "natural." Thoreau recognized the profound existential aspects of this irony when he wrote, "It is in vain to dream of a wildness distant from ourselves. There is none such. It is the bog in our brain and bowels, the primitive vigor of Nature, that inspires our dreams."[10]

Changing ideas of nature, wilderness, and landscape continue to inform the physical practices of design and building, and these, in turn, further transform and enrich cultural ideas. "A landscape park may be more palpable but no more real, nor less imaginary, than a landscape painting or poem," write Daniels and Cosgrove,[11] and these various representations each affect and alter one another. The popular use of a polished copper mirror in eighteenth-century England, for instance, allowed a viewer to appreciate a particular scene as if it were painted by Claude Lorrain; the distance from it was doubled, in effect, as it was not the actual landscape scenery in front of the viewer that was the object of attention but its reflection in a tinted, beveled mirror and its subsequent allusion to a particular genre of painting. Indeed, an essential precondition for popular appreciation of picturesque landscape during the eighteenth century was prior knowledge of pictures—the landscape simply did not "appear" until it had been first presented through painting.[12] Similarly, the acquisition of "good taste" in landscape appreciation was not granted through education alone but through social background and occupation. Consequently, eighteenth-century developments in European landscape equated images of landscape with wealth, high culture, and power, an equation that was encoded not only in garden art but also in painting, literature, and poetry. Landscape, as in the French *paysage*, carries with it to this day a sense of nationhood and cultural identity, an image that is also reflected in the use of the English term "country" to indicate both *nation* and *that which is not the city*.

These instances point to landscape's inextricable bond with cultural ideas and images; it is thus a gross reduction to consider landscape simply as a scenic object, a subjugated resource, or a scientist ecosystem. To consider landscape in solely visual, formal, ecological, or economic terms fails to embrace the complex richness of association and social structures that are inherent to it. From a specifically landscape-architectural point of view, it is crucial to understand how cultural ideas condition construction and how construction, in turn, conditions the play of landscape ideas in a larger cultural imagination. The implications of reciprocity between ways of seeing and ways of acting are immense and point toward the means by which the landscape project may be critically revised and reformulated. With regard to design, how one maps, draws, conceptualizes, imagines, and projects inevitably conditions what is built and what effects that construction may exercise in time.

Techniques of representation are central to any critical act in design. If it is true that there can be no concept of landscape without prior imaging (and not just perspective but also maps, plans, and other modes of representation), then innovations in image projection are necessary for the virtual to be both conceived and actualized. Essays in this volume by Denis Cosgrove on liminal geometry, Charles Waldheim on aerial representation, Stanislaus Fung on cross-cultural shuttling, David Leatherbarrow on topography, Christophe Girot on site description, Bart Lootsma on mapping, and myself on eidetic imaging each address the topic of representation as the primary basis for innovative design.

Landscape in the Twentieth Century

It is perhaps inevitable that the landscape project will wax and wane with time. The degree to which the life of a particular view of landscape remains with a given society historically has been subject to periods of great cultural significance—as in eighteenth- and nineteenth-century Europe—and decline—as in much of the twentieth century, during which landscape has been largely neglected by progressive art movements and modernist culture in general, with the significant exception of the land-art experiments by artists such as Robert Smithson, Michael Heizer, and Richard Long.[13] Apart from these few works, the landscape idea throughout much of this century has come mostly in the form of picturesque, rural scenery, whether for nostalgic, consumerist purposes or in the service of environmentalist agendas.

As is widely prevalent in painting, film, communications media, and tourist marketing campaigns, contemporary representations of landscape typically invoke idealized images of countryside devoid of modern technology, urbanization, and change. Laura Ashley, Ralph Lauren, and various automobile corporations are obvious examples in this regard, but so too are the preservation and heritage groups that use pastoral, premodern images to promote their goals.

Landscape is presented as a place of escape from the ills of the present and anxieties about the future. This cycle of sentimental aestheticization compounds the difficulty of forging a critical and fresh landscape. Instead, the tendency today is to treat landscape as a giant commodity. The built result in much of Europe and the United States is typically not only of experientially deadening effect—your local corporate park, theme park, or the new housing development down "the lane" or along the "winding way," for instance—but also of a depressing cultural atrophy whereby all hope for the future is replaced by too high a regard for past accomplishments. The subsequent re-creations of previous worlds might not offend anyone were it not for their absolute absence of hope and invention; that they might also conceal and compensate for some of the more problematic aspects of modern life ought to be further cause for skeptical reflection. For all of their apparently innocent effect, landscapes without portent sound a death knell for any form of—and perhaps desire for—a truly modern and enterprising landscape.

Whether one has romantic or radical ends in mind, however, to hope for a recovery of landscape requires looking beyond the confines of strictly professional interests to see how pervasively (and persuasively) *cultural* the landscape phenomenon actually is. As earlier described, the practice of building landscapes will only become more marginal and irrelevant in the face of time if the culturally critical dimensions of the craft are forgotten or ignored. Making landscapes entails cultural vision that cannot be reduced to formal or ecological procedures. Thus, this book speaks as much to the rise in popular demand for and interest in landscape (in gardening, tourism, education, and outdoor recreation, for example) as it does to the resurgence of intellectual critiques and practices of landscape (particularly within the architectural arts, but also within geography, film, and literature).

Such a multidisciplinary perspective is crucial for any understanding of the contemporary landscape phenomenon, not least because the shifting of ideas across disciplines has traditionally affected design practice, modes of representation, and the way the built environment looks. Consider the effects of painting on the subsequent landscape architectural work of eighteenth-century Europe, especially England,[14] for instance, or the evolution of twentieth-century ecology and its impact on current planning and design practices.[15] The influence of contemporary film and communications media on landscape appreciation has yet to be fully studied, but I suspect it is immense, especially in American popular culture.

9

These effects go both ways, of course, for the building of new landscapes and their subsequent representation in art can also affect the evolution, value, and meaning of larger landscape ideas as well as other cultural practices. Central Park, for example, helped to solidify an urban community's view of itself and its relation to the natural world, just as the rectilinear surveying, delineation, and settlement of America's heartland, with its relentless, nonhierarchical grid pattern, helped to make manifest a collective ideal of equity, freedom, and accessibility.[16]

The reciprocal interactions between the built and the imaginary is what lies at the center of landscape architecture's creativity and contribution to culture. The field embraces significantly more than regressive, sentimental views of "nature" and "countryside" might lead one to believe, and its creative potential far outreaches that of the service professional offering ameliorative services after the land developers have done their damage. The largely domestic practices of modern-day "landscaping" simply fail to take the leap into the more interventionist ground of cultural and artistic production.[17] Just as it is simplistic to consider landscape lightly, as if it were merely a fashionable term or an expendable luxury, it is equally negligent to underestimate the transforming effect landscape practices exert on environmental, cultural, and ideological affairs.

The Dark Side of Landscape

The term *recovery* implies that something once lost, devalued, forgotten, or misplaced has been found again, retrieved, and brought forward with renewed vitality. Also implied are repossession, taking control, and the regaining of health and normalcy, as in a rightful return. Such meanings have been associated with land disputes and the marking of territory since antiquity. Recovery carries with it, therefore, an inevitable double connotation. On the one side, optimism and hope are attached to the reemergence of a precious cultural treasure—one looks toward new and exhilarating prospects. On the other side, recovery implies a degree of sentimentality (nostalgia) and power (possession), both of which are inextricably interrelated with regard to landscape and point toward a more insidious side of landscape formation. This condition was described by the geographer John Barrell as landscape's "dark side," a moral darkness that derives from landscape being used by power interests to veil and perpetuate their effects.[18] Such coercion of landscape's cultural sway points again to the distinction between environment and landscape, the latter assuming a subjective and rhetorical significance. As Raymond Williams remarked, "A working country is hardly ever a landscape,"[19] a claim echoed by Jean-François Lyotard: "To have a feeling for landscape, you have to lose your feeling of place."[20] Both these statements draw attention to the difference between working country as habituated place and landscape as objectified scene. In the former, the subjects are fully immersed within their milieu, active and distracted; in the latter, they are placed at a distance, passive and gazing. As a distancing device, landscape can be used (or deployed) by those in power to conceal, consolidate, and represent certain interests (whether of the aristocracy, the state, or corporate sector). Landscape is particularly effective in this regard because it so beautifully conceals its artifice, "naturalizing" or rendering invisible its construction and effects in time. This condition led Lyotard to conclude that "it is not estrangement that procures landscape. It is the other way around. And the estrangement that landscape procures...is absolute."[21]

Perhaps it is now possible to appreciate more fully Kenneth Clark's observation that "in those times when the human spirit seems to have burned most brightly the painting [and, thus, the concept] of landscape for its own sake did not exist and was unthinkable."[22] Clark is referring to landscape's estranged and estranging characteristic, the recovery of which marks a somewhat ominous and difficult time—a period where landscape is used more to mask or compensate for failings rather than to assume a newly emancipating and transformative role. As W.J.T. Mitchell has written:

> We have known since Ruskin that the appreciation of landscape as an aesthetic object can not be an occasion for complacency or untroubled contemplation; rather, it must be the focus of a historical, political, and (yes) aesthetic alertness to the violence and evil written on the land, projected there by the gazing eye. We have known since Turner—perhaps since Milton—that the violence of this evil eye is inextricably connected with imperialism and nationalism. What we know now is that landscape itself is the medium by which this evil is veiled and naturalized.[23]

This might be an excessive characterization, but it serves to remind the reader that landscape is not necessarily to the benefit of all in society, that its apparent innocence and idealism can often mask hidden agendas and conceal social inequities and ongoing ecological destruction. Inasmuch as landscape objectifies the world—in the form of "scenery," "resource," or "ecosystem," for example—it sets up hierarchical orders among social groups, and among humans and nature more generally. One is always an "outsider" as far as the beholding of manufactured landscape goes, for to be "inside" entails the evaporation of landscape into everyday place or milieu. It is in this deeper sense that landscape as place and milieu may provide a more substantial image than that of the distanced scenic veil, for the structures of place help a community to establish collective identity and meaning. This is the constructive aspect of landscape, its capacity to enrich the cultural imagination and provide a basis for rootedness and connection, for home and belonging.[24]

In many of the essays that follow, attention is paid to both insider and outsider perspectives, the inside view allowing for a deeper, socially informed, material sense of place and being, the outside view for a broader range of possibilities to be invoked beyond those of the known and the everyday. The former view grounds a project in the social practices and physical conditions of a locality while the latter brings a new and broader range of ideas to bear upon the site. Christophe Girot characterizes this distinction as the "intuitive" (the unalienated inside sense) and the "empirical" (the synoptic, factual analysis). This formulation echoes Augustin Berque's call for a new synthesis of environmental "facts" and landscape "sensibilities."[25] Similar threads are drawn by Denis Cosgrove (on geometry), Sébastien Marot (on site), Georges Descombes (on experience), and Steen Høyer (on place), all of whom address the importance of respecting the phenomenal specificity of sites while extending them beyond obvious formulations.[26] In working not only for the commissioning client or authority but also for a larger surrounding community and region, landscape architects can often exceed and escape the normal limitations of an easily consumed and hermetically packaged landscape.

Recovering Landscape

The essays are less occupied with describing or accounting for any recovery of landscape than they are with expanding the scope and efficacy of the landscape project. They look forward rather than describe past and current conditions. As already inferred, landscape is not given but made and remade; it is an inheritance that demands to be recovered, cultivated, and projected toward new ends.

A topic of particular importance to landscape architecture with regard to these theories of recovery is the specificity of site. Landscape architecture has traditionally sought to recover sites and places, employing site phenomena as generative devices for new forms and programs. In recent years, the recovery of sites has not only assumed mnemonic and temporal significance but also biological importance, as lost or impoverished ecologies are restored and diversified. Thus, the reclaiming of sites might be measured in three ways: first, in terms of the retrieval of memory and the cultural enrichment of place and time; second, in terms of social program and utility, as new uses and activities are developed; and, third, in terms of ecological diversification and succession. In this threefold way, the inventive traditions of landscape architecture actively renew the significance of those cultural and natural processes that undergird the richness of all life on earth.

Following the failures of universal and utopian trends in late modernist architectural and urban planning and design, the attention paid to landscape and site is gaining increased currency today. A significant reason for this relates to the abovementioned failing of planning and design approaches that ignored local characteristics and values. Landscape is instead seen as a means to resist the homogenization of the environment while also heightening local attributes and a collective sense of place. As David Lowenthal describes, the presence of the past offers a "sense of completion, of stability, of permanence" in resistance to the rapid pace of contemporary life.[27] As such, landscape has assumed increased popular value as a symbolic image, a picture laden with signs that lends cultural uniqueness, stability, and value to a particular place or region. Of course, as earlier noted, there are more creative reasons to reclaim sites and places than the merely nostalgic and compensatory—reasons that see invention as an essential ingredient of reclamation, engendering new kinds of landscape for public enjoyment and use.

A second aspect of recovering landscape concerns ecology and environment. Landscape is often equated with the expression of ecological phenomena. These expressions are found not only in preserved natural vistas but, more significantly, in the regional and global ecosystems depicted in aerial photography and satellite imaging—perspectives discussed by both Denis Cosgrove and Charles Waldheim in this collection. The remarkable images of Earth revealed through the windows of the first space flights allowed the idea of nature in landscape to escape the boundaries of the scenic frame. Suddenly, landscape became planetary, embracing and expressing the interrelational tenets of ecology. The effects of local events on regional, continental, and global ecologies was made emphatically clear, as the fluidity of water, air, and even movements of the earth's crust were revealed for all to see.

Increased satellite imaging, combined with massive media coverage of natural disasters and the rise of environmental activist groups, has increased public awareness of and concern for environmental issues. These range in scale from local problems of waste, pollution, and decreased diversity of habitat to global trends of ozone depletion, deforestation, extinction of species, nuclear waste, and resource depletion. In each case, landscape provides the idea around which such concerns are made visible and subsequently contested and engaged.

In the environmental sphere, the idea of landscape plays a double role, however. On the one side, landscape provides the most visible expression and measure of environmental atrophy—it is both victim and indicator—whereas, on the other side, it provides the ideal, arcadian image of a profoundly green, harmonious world, a world both lost and desired again. Consequently, as already described, landscape exists as a sign of the good and virtuous, a figure that is both victimized by technological evils and appropriated by competing interests. As a simulacrum of environment, landscape has been fought over in recent years by advocates of radically divergent and competing ecologies (from the resourcists and preservationists to the deep ecologists and ecofeminists).[28] Here, the equation of landscape with nature not only reveals the ideological and subjective essence of both terms but also their inevitable irreconcilability. As earlier described, those who continue to assert unreflective, sentimental ideas of nature and landscape simply suppress cultural experimentation and the development of alternative modes of landscape practice. Clearly, an ecology of human creativity—as exemplified in adaptive, cosmographic, and artistic practices—has yet to be developed in resistance to an increasingly uncritical, scientistic ecology that refers to an increasingly abstract "environment."[29]

A third phenomenon surrounding landscape's recovery is the massive process of deindustrialization that has accompanied the shift toward global communication and service economies. These changes have stressed both urban centers and rural areas, perhaps even collapsing their differences.[30] As a consequence, new demands have been placed on land use planning and the accommodation of multiple, often irreconcilable conflicts. Huge and complex postindustrial sectors of cities have presented new challenges for landscape architects and urban designers in the past few years.

Any innovative response to these developments will most likely come from a creative appreciation for how today's space and time are phenomena radically different from their historical antecedents. We are surrounded by a space-time landscape of electronic media, images, internets, information superhighways, transglobal commutes, and rapid exchange of materials both visible and invisible. It is a world of infinite communication.[31] Everything is now available and

14

immediate, without delay or distance. The geographical coordinates of one's place in the world are no longer simply spatial but deeply folded into the processes of speed and exchange. Authors as divergent as J.B. Jackson and Jean Baudrillard have shown how the modern landscape—at least in America—is no longer one of place, hierarchy, and center but one of transience, mobility, circulation, and exchange.[32] Essays by Bart Lootsma, Alex Wall, and Denis Cosgrove provide important clues for how landscape may assume newly formative roles in shaping emergent forces and trends. Sébastien Marot more subtly situates landscape as a "sub-urban" art, where the peripheral and in-between sites are those that ought to be of primary concern to contemporary landscape architects. And the nomadic blankness of the *maidans*, large tracts of open land in the center of Indian cities, as discussed by Anuradha Mathur, point to another form of indeterminate space and time, flexible and transient.

Associated with topics of site, environment, and new technologies, are a number of other factors that have promoted landscape in recent years. The unprecedented rise in recreation and tourism during the postwar years, for instance, precipitated not only a renewed interest in landscape but also—for capitalists, hedonists, and sentimentalists at least—a renewed value. At the level of both consumer (public demand) and producer (regional economic development interests), landscape is increasingly sought for its unique and intrinsic characteristics—its scenery, history, and ecology. Whether as theme park, wilderness area, or scenic drive, landscape has become a huge, exotic attraction unto itself, a place of entertainment, fantasy, escape, and refuge.[33]

Another factor in landscape's recovery is the emergence of land art since the 1970s. This continues to draw attention to landscape, this time as visceral and elemental art form. Here, landscape is both the venue (site) and material (medium) of artistic expression. Bound into the passage of time and natural process, the uniqueness of site and material circumstances makes landscape a more engaging and ephemeral phenomenon than that of distant scenery or pictures. In the hands of artists such as Robert Smithson, Michael Heizer, Walter deMaria, Christo, Robert Morris, Herbert Bayer, and James Turrell, landscape is less a scene for contemplation and more a shifting, material field of natural processes engaged through motion and time.[34]

Rosalind Krauss's essay, "Sculpture in the Expanded Field," provides a seminal moment in landscape architecture, revising traditional disciplinary distinctions among sculpture, architecture, and landscape.[35] Various intellectual activities have since further challenged the modernist negation of landscape and nature, criticizing the dominant forces of technology and expansionism over the voices of marginalized others (the feminist critique in particular, but also environmentalist and social critiques)[36]—themes picked up by Stanislaus Fung in his essay on the need to engender new mutualities among things once considered disparate. Together, these activities have precipitated an increase in intellectual and artistic reflection on landscape, even to the point of demanding new forms of landscape comprehension, design, and typology. As a consequence, the landscape recovered here is less that of the art historian, the descriptive analyst, or even the speculative hermeneutician, and more the physical ground itself. Here, both the site and materiality of landscape provides an experimental laboratory, a cultural testing ground to be directly engaged and experienced.

16

These physical and conceptual bases of landscape led to a resurgence of interest in landscape topics in leading architecture schools during the 1980s.[37] Since then, renewed interest in topography, site, ecology, and geography has emerged more generally in design schools. It was not long ago that architects drew the plans and elevations of their buildings without topographic features, trees, and larger horizons. Today, at least in the better schools of architecture, place and context permeate not only drawings and models but also the conceptual and material formation of the projects themselves. At their best, building projects are conceived less in terms of isolated objects and more as site-specific constructs that are intimately bound into larger contexts and processes.

The significance of the landscape context for the architectural and environmental arts lies not only in the deeply sensuous and experiential dimensions of the land but also its semiotic, ecological, and political content. Thus, as Marc Treib's essay, "Nature Recalled," argues, landscape can no longer be considered solely as decoration around the base of buildings; rather, it has come to assume deeper roles of contextualization, heightening experiences, and embedding time and nature in the built world. It is increasingly recognized that landscape harbors a profound environmental and existential promise for architecture and urbanism, provoking new forms of experience, meaning, and value. The still-emerging architectural conception of landscape, then, is less that of scenery, greenery, wilderness, and arcadia and more that of a pervasive milieu, a rich imbroglio of ecological, experiential, poetic, and expressively *living* dimensions.[38]

During the past few years, architects have produced a remarkable array of drawings and projects in which landscape figures prominently and in unusual forms: the remarkable graphic suprematism of Zaha Hadid's drawings and paintings, for example, with imploded fragments of building matter settling

uneasily into immense hillsides and regionally scaled infrastructures; the astonishing work of Rem Koolhaas and the Office for Metropolitan Architecture,
wherein new syntheses of building, landscape, and region are formed in every
project, big and small; the folded, single-surface ground planes of Peter Eisenman (many with Laurie Olin), which mark a similar recasting of territorial distinctions—both in disciplinary and geographical terms—to that of Koolhaas,
but differing by more textual references to site than to program.

Perhaps the single most significant project in terms of forging a new architecture of the landscape was Bernard Tschumi's Parc de la Villette in Paris,
1983–1990.[39] While still highly controversial, his park reversed the traditional
role of nature in the city, bringing the density, congestion, and richness of the city
to the park. Similar urban design projects in Paris, Barcelona, Stuttgart, and
Lille have also promoted landscape as a means of injecting social and institutional vibrancy into the city. For smaller-scale architects as diverse as Alvaro
Siza, Enric Miralles, Antoine Predock, Glenn Murcutt, and Georges Descombes, a formative attitude toward site and landscape deeply informs design
and construction, albeit in markedly different ways.

While architects have gathered renewed interest in landscape topics, professional landscape architects have not been without voice and effect. In the
United States, contemporary landscape architecture's contribution to the revitalization of landscape and urban public space has perhaps been most graphi-
cally demonstrated in the work of Peter Walker and Martha Schwartz, both of
whom continue to relentlessly promote the visual and formal aspects of modernist landscape design.[40] At the other end of the spectrum, recent advances in
creative habitat restoration and environmentally sensitive planning by practices
such as Andropogon and Jones and Jones have promoted renewed public consciousness about the land while constructing more ecologically adaptive modes
of settlement.

The tension between "artistic" and "ecological" approaches to landscape
formation has perhaps been most effectively bridged in the remarkably plastic
and complex work of George Hargreaves. Drawing inspiration from the great
earthwork artists while applying technical and scientific knowledge, Hargreaves has built a range of large and surreal environments atop landfills, old
dredgings, and along once polluted, flood-prone rivers.[41] The nearest equivalent
of Hargreaves in Europe is Peter Latz, who, with astonishing ingenuity and
restraint, has recently completed a new park amid the ruins of an enormous
smelting factory in Duisburg, Germany.[42] The park is designed to clean and

recycle the water, soil, and material of the site over time. Both Latz and Hargreaves demonstrate not only the effort to revitalize the derelict and polluted lands that surround the fringes of so many European and American cities but also to bridge the gap between artistic expression and ecological technique.

The remarkable landscapes of Adriaan Geuze and his Rotterdam-based practice, West 8, are discussed in this book by both Bart Lootsma and Alex Wall.[43] Here, striking visual geometries arrange vast new landscapes for the people of the Netherlands. Recovered in Geuze's work is the unequivocal constructedness of the Dutch landscape, its ecology, and its agency in advancing a modern society and affording new forms of public space. The ecological and programmatic ingenuity that Geuze brings to these projects elevates them to a level of significance beyond that of empty, graphic formalism. The cockle- and mussel-shell stripes in the Schelpen Project, for example, are both a source of food and a field of camouflage and sighting strips for coastal birds (Fig. 2); similarly, the huge planting strategy at Schippel Airport, with its incorporation of beehives, clover beds, and drainage ways, demonstrates a commitment to the formation of self-regulating ecosystems.

Examples abound; my point is to show how landscape has been seized by creative professionals in recent years as a critical and exciting medium of cultural expression and transformation. There is still much to be done, and a major motivation behind this book is that it might provide theoretical and eidetic frameworks to both provoke and guide even more adventurous future practices.

The Essays

The book is arranged in three parts. The first, "Reclaiming Place and Time," addresses landscape architecture as a practice of reclamation, recovering memories, places, sites, ecologies, and potential futures. The second, "Constructing and Representing Landscape," discusses the role of geometry, ideation, imaging, and technique in forging material landscapes. The third, "Urbanizing Landscape," reorients the landscape project toward issues of instrumentality, urbanism, infrastructure, and program.

Marc Treib begins the first section by outlining the development of landscape architecture in the United States throughout the twentieth century, lamenting the loss of opportunities due to a dominant view in modernist architecture of landscape as background or trim around the base of buildings. Consequently, Treib argues, many landscape architects shifted to more environmental and social disciplines at the expense of training in design, form, and space. He concludes that any recovery of landscape must derive from the artistry and poetics of the medium—the passages and rhythms of time, seasons, weather, and occupancy.

Sébastien Marot follows on from this by accounting for a general atrophy in landscape practices in France between the 1920s and 1980s. He then describes why and how landscape has come to gain new authority in France, emphasizing the role of the landscape architect in working creatively with sites. Marot posits

Fig. 2 Eastern Scheldt Storm Surge Barrier: coastal bird plateau. Zeeland, Netherlands. West 8, Landscape Architects, 1992. Photo: Hans Werlemann.

the "suburb" as the traditional laboratory and future ground for landscape architectural investment, describing how experiments in peripheral sites both precede and mediate new, larger urban forms.

Christophe Girot, a fellow Frenchman, picks up Marot's emphasis on mediated sites in "Four Trace Concepts in Landscape Architecture." These are identified as landing, grounding, finding, and founding, each a cumulative process of interpreting and reconstructing sites. Girot emphasizes the need for direct engagement with sites, experiencing places intuitively and privileging phenomena that are unique to that place.

In "Things Take Time and Time Takes Things," Steen Høyer describes a similar transition from synoptic modernization to more situated practices, this time in Denmark. Like Marot and Girot, Høyer identifies phenomenal characteristics of the Danish landscape and how these may be formative in designing future landscapes.

Georges Descombes follows with a description of his own approach to working with sites, elaborating his ideas with a project for a path in a glacial valley in Switzerland. Like the preceding authors, Descombes argues for more restrained and sensitive modifications of what is already given in a site than the single-minded determinism of modernist imposition. As Høyer does, Descombes identifies the subtleties of temporal and habitual experience as the basis for all significant design.

Alan Balfour's "Octagon" closes this section and describes the series of transformations the Leipzeger and Potsdamer Platz in Berlin have undergone over the past hundred years. This essay beautifully demonstrates the inevitable reciprocity between built form and collective desire, revealing also the radical differences and shifts a site can withstand while certain ideas persist through it all.

Denis Cosgrove's "Liminal Geometry and Elemental Landscape" begins the second section on constructing and representing landscape. Cosgrove distinguishes between the traditional origins of geometry and its uses today, describing, in particular, practices of cosmography, geography, and chorography. The aerial view is significant here, and Cosgrove discusses the effects of modern satellite imaging, suggesting that the unbounded geometries of contemporary space suggest a newly emancipated role for landscape networks.

Charles Waldheim focuses on one aspect of Cosgrove's discussion: the modern zenithal view and its effects on planning and design practices. He discusses the strategic and instrumental value of flatbed imaging in terms of designing new landscapes.

20

Issues of strategy are picked up by Stanislaus Fung, who suggests that multilateral exchange among the cultures that constitute landscape may provide a more propitious set of opportunities for landscape architecture than single-minded paradigms. The open-ended and playful forms of "shuttling" that Fung outlines echo remarks by Cosgrove on networks and Waldheim on planning. In each case, landscape becomes an affiliative and constructive agent, maximizing opportunity while itself remaining indeterminate and discreet.

My own essay, "Eidetic Operations," discusses the role of images—both graphic and cognitive—in transforming landscape. A distinction is drawn, however, between scenic images and images that are more fundamental to the (invisible) inhabitation and engagement of space.

21

David Leatherbarrow's essay demonstrates this kind of imaging as well as the erudite shuttling discussed by Fung, moving with ease among topics of topographic modification, masks, maps, gender, material, cultural practices, and social ethics. No longer will forming the land appear to be simply a matter of shape and form, for Leatherbarrow invokes the deeper range of cultural possibilities that are enacted through construction.

Fig. 3. Detail image from a design proposal for Toolonlahti Park, Helsinki. View across lake toward the city's horizon. James Corner, 1997.

Anita Berrizbeita's essay on the Amsterdam Bos Park begins the third section on "Urbanizing Landscape." Berrizbeita describes how the design and construction of the Bos Park developed a new and productive role for landscape within the city, constructing a working ground for contemporary collective experience. She shifts attention from the urban park as a place for contemplative retreat to the urban park as a productive and functioning entity integral to the modern metropolis.

Anuradha Mathur's essay on the Indian *maidan* echoes these themes to the extent that these fantastic empty fields in the center of congested Indian cities provide indeterminate and flexible territories for both nomadic and collective life. While significantly different, both the Bos and the *maidan* are landscapes that engage urbanism not through antithesis but through use and time. Thus, both Berrizbeita and Mathur discuss these sites less as scenes and objects (what they look like) and more as ongoing and evolving processes (how they work). Mathur touches on a particular poetic phenomenon, though, that of blank space, indeterminate and unrepresentable.

In "Airport/Landscape," Denis Cosgrove shows how Heathrow Airport may be viewed as a massive landscape, similar in some ways to past estates and parks, although less in appearance and more with regard to the synthesis of its parts. Buildings, infrastructure, fences, plantings, and borders are all reframed by Cosgrove into a picture of a new, mobile, transitory landscape. Paintings by Adrian Hemming complement the essay, heightening the fluid tension between airside and landside.

These synthetic and flexible concepts of landscape are developed by Alex Wall in "Programming the Urban Surface," which presents the view that the entire surface of roads, fields, blocks, buildings, and utilities might best be conceived as landscape—that landscape is no longer the pastoral scenery outside the city walls but is instead the continuous matrix that binds, relates, and structures individual parts. An emphasis on synthesizing the surface as a ground for future events is again to recover landscape as an essentially strategic practice, staging the conditions for uncertain futures to unfold.

Bart Lootsma further demonstrates these ideas in "Synthetic Regionalization: The Dutch Landscape toward a Second Modernity," in which he outlines the cultural and political conditions that have allowed recent developments in the Netherlands. He then presents examples that show how landscape can be tactically deployed to forge new cultural possibilities and newly synthetic urban conditions.

Conclusion

This book is meant to further stimulate the current resurgence of interest in landscape topics. At the same time, the essays reveal how much work remains to be done. While parts of this book might expose the stark inadequacy of many conventional methods in contemporary landscape architectural design and planning, a larger part indicates promising new directions while encouraging greater experimentation and daring in design. Indeed, the need to experiment, to devise more sophisticated modes of notation and representation, and to practice with greater critical foresight and cultural knowledge clearly must underlie any future revitalization of the field.[44]

As we enter the new millennium, dramatic changes in the world are putting forward challenges and possibilities for the landscape architectural arts. Ranging from the planning of new regions and infrastructures to the design of parks, gardens, maps, and journeys, the onus is on those who practice in topographical affairs to seize the opportunity and place landscape squarely in the foreground of cultural and political life. Designers and artists have a more actively engaging and interventionist role in the recovery of landscape than do those who are preoccupied with historical description, informational analysis, or consumerist development of land and, because of this, much of this book suggests that new ambitions, techniques, and desires must guide the education and practice of landscape architects.[45]

The creative potential and contribution of landscape to contemporary culture underlies the motivation of this book. In the pages that follow, landscape is neither fixed nor passive but changing and active, demanding extension and reinvention. The essays avoid being excessively theoretical at the risk of excluding practice while avoiding oversimplification of sometimes difficult and multifaceted ideas as well. Both the contents of this book and the larger landscape to which it is addressed are presented as engaging *projects*, vehicles of criticism, creativity, and social exchange. In this sense, what is being recovered is not the landscape of scenes and objects but the landscape of ideas, operations, and synthetic strategies. There is little mention of what landscape is or what it means; the focus is on what landscape *does*, as in its efficacy and scope of influence. This book is a speculative work, intentionally provocative. It aspires to nothing less than to promote and redirect the landscape project toward newly relevant and life-enriching ends. It is about the simple planting of seeds within the wilds of the landscape imagination, hopefully propagating a field more diverse and enabling than ever before.

23

Notes

1   See W.J.T. Mitchell, ed., *Landscape and Power* (Chicago: University of Chicago Press, 1994); and James Corner, "Critical Thinking and Landscape Architecture," *Landscape Journal* 10, no. 2 (fall 1991): 159–62.

2   See James Corner, "Ecology and Landscape as Agents of Creativity," in *Ecological Design and Planning*, eds. George Thompson and Frederick Steiner (New York: John Wiley & Sons, 1997), 80–108.

3   A useful reference with regard to landscape strategy is François Jullien, *The Propensity of Things: A History of Efficacy in China*, trans. Janet Lloyd (New York: Urzone, 1995). See also Michael Speaks, "Its Out There: The Formal Limits of the American Avant-Garde," in *Architectural Design Profile* 133: *Hypersurface Architecture* (1988): 26–31.

4   On the relationship between spatial formations of landscape and the cultural imagination, see Denis Cosgrove, *Social Formation and Symbolic Landscape* (1984; reprint, Madison: University of Wisconsin Press, 1998); and Denis Cosgrove and Stephen Daniels, eds., *The Iconography of Landscape* (Cambridge: Cambridge University Press, 1988). Also of interest is Simon Schama, *Landscape and Memory* (New Haven, Conn.: Yale University Press, 1995); Robert Pogue Harrison, *Forests* (Chicago: University of Chicago Press, 1992); and David Matless, *Landscape and Englishness* (London: Reaktion, 1998).

5   On "thickness" and interpretation, see Clifford Geertz, "Thick Description," in *The Interpretation of Cultures* (New York: Basic Books, 1973), 3–30. Also see James Corner, "Three Tyrannies of Contemporary Theory and the Alternative of Hermeneutics," *Landscape Journal* 10, no. 1 (fall 1991): 115–133.

6   Kenneth Clark, "Landscape Painting," in *The Oxford Companion to Art,* ed. Harold Osborne (Oxford: Oxford University Press). See also Kenneth Clark, *Landscape into Art* (1949; reprint, New York: Harper and Row, 1984).

7   Cosgrove, *Social Formation*, 16. See also D.W. Meinig, "The Beholding Eye," in *The Interpretation of Ordinary Landscapes*, ed. D.W. Meinig (Oxford: Oxford University Press, 1979), 33–48.

8   Augustin Berque, "Beyond the Modern Landscape," *AA FILES* 25 (summer 1993): 33.

9   John Stilgoe, *Common Landscape of America, 1580–1845* (New Haven, Conn.: Yale University Press, 1982), 12. On the complexity of landscape as representation, see Denis Cosgrove, *The Palladian Landscape* (State College: Pennsylvania State University Press, 1993); and James Duncan and David Ley, eds., *Place/Culture/Representation* (London: Routledge, 1993).

10   Henry David Thoreau, *Journal* (August 30, 1856), quoted in Schama, *Landscape and Memory*, 578.

11   Cosgrove and Daniels, *Iconography of Landscape*, 1.

12   See Norman Bryson, *Vision and Painting: The Logic of the Gaze* (New Haven, Conn.: Yale University Press, 1988), 42–44, for a discussion of painting in relation to the "true" landscape. See also James Corner, "Representation and Landscape," *Word and Image* 8, no. 3 (July–Sept., 1992): 258–60.

13   See John Beardsley, *Earthworks and Beyond: Contemporary Art in the Landscape*, 3rd ed. (New York: Abbeville Press, 1998); and Gilles Tiberghien, *Land Art* (New York: Princeton Architectural Press, 1995).

14   See Ann Bermingham, *Landscape as Ideology: The English Rustic Tradition, 1740–1860* (Berkeley: University of California Press, 1986); and Rosalind Krauss, "The Originality of the Avant-Garde," *The Originality of the Avant-Garde and Other Modernist Myths* (Cambridge, Mass.: MIT Press, 1985), 151–70.

15   See Ian McHarg, *Design with Nature* (1969; reprint, New York: John Wiley & Sons, 1992), and George Thompson and Frederick Steiner, eds., *Ecological Design and Planning* (New York: John Wiley & Sons, 1997).

16 See J.B. Jackson, "The Accessible Landscape," in *A Sense of Place, A Sense of Time* (New Haven, Conn.: Yale University Press, 1994), 3–10; and James Corner and Alex MacLean, *Taking Measures Across the American Landscape* (New Haven, Conn.: Yale University Press, 1996).

17 On the philosophical implications of this failure, see Peter Carl, "Natura-Morte," in *Modulus 20*, ed. Wendy Redfield Lathrop (Charlottesville: University of Virginia School of Architecture and Princeton Architectural Press, 1991), 27–70.

18 John Barrell, *The Dark Side of the Landscape: The Rural Poor in English Painting, 1730–1840* (Cambridge: Cambridge University Press, 1980). See also W.J.T. Mitchell, "Imperial Landscape," in *Landscape and Power*, 5–34.

19 Raymond Williams, *The City and the Country* (Oxford: Oxford University Press, 1973), 36.

20 Jean-François Lyotard, *The Inhuman*, trans. Geoffrey Bennington and Rachel Bowlby (Stanford, Calif.: Stanford University Press, 1991), 189.

21 Ibid., 190.

22 Clark, *Landscape into Art*, viii.

23 Mitchell, *Landscape and Power*, 29–30.

24 See Cosgrove, *Social Formation and Symbolic Landscape*.

25 See Berque, "Beyond the Modern Landscape." See also Augustin Berque, *Mediance: De Milieux en Paysages* (Montpellier-Paris: Reclus-Documentation Francoise, 1990).

26 The reworking of sites is demonstrated in a different way by David Leatherbarrow in *The Roots of Architectural Invention: Site, Enclosure, Materials* (Cambridge: Cambridge University Press, 1993), 9–64 and 215–224. See also Carol J. Burns, "On Site: Architectural Preoccupations," in *Drawing, Building, Text*, ed. Andrea Kahn (New York: Princeton Architectural Press, 1991), 147–167.

27 See David Lowenthal, *The Past Is a Foreign Country* (Cambridge: Cambridge University Press, 1985).

28 For a useful discussion of competing environmental viewpoints, see Max Oelschlaeger, *The Idea of Wilderness* (New Haven, Conn.: Yale University Press, 1991), 281–319; and Michael Zimmerman et al., eds., *Environmental Philosophy* (Englewood Cliffs, N.J.: Prentice-Hall, 1993).

29 See Corner, "Ecology and Landscape."

30 See Peter Rowe, *Making a Middle Landscape* (Cambridge, Mass.: MIT Press, 1991); Joel Garreau, *Edge Cities: Life on the New Frontier* (New York: Doubleday, 1991); Deyan Sudjik, *The 100 Mile City* (New York: Harcourt Brace, 1992); David Harvey, *The Condition of Postmodernity* (Cambridge, Mass.: Blackwell, 1989), and *Justice, Nature, and the Geography of Difference* (Cambridge, Mass.: Blackwell, 1996).

31 See Christine Boyer, *Cybercities* (New York: Princeton Architectural Press, 1996); and William J. Mitchell, *City of Bits* (Cambridge, Mass.: MIT Press, 1996). Further philosophical reflection on the consequences of modern time and speed can be found in Paul Virilio, *The Aesthetics of Disappearance* (New York: Semiotext, Columbia University, 1991); and Gianni Vattimo, *The Transparent Society* (Baltimore, Md.: Johns Hopkins University Press, 1992).

32 See Jackson, *Sense of Place*; Jean Baudrillard, *America*, trans. Chris Turner (London: Verso, 1988).

33 See Alexander Wilson, *The Culture of Nature: North American Landscape from Disney to the Exxon Valdez* (Cambridge, Mass.: Blackwell, 1992).

34 See note 13.

35 Rosalind Krauss, "Sculpture in the Expanded Field," in *The Anti-Aesthetic*, ed. Hal Foster (Port Townsend, Wash.: Bay Press, 1983), 31–42.

36 See Elizabeth K. Meyer, "Landscape Architecture as Modern Other and Postmodern Ground," in *Ecological Design and Planning*, eds. Thompson and Steiner. Also see E.A. Grosz, "Feminist Theory and the Challenge to Knowledge," *Women's Studies*

International Forum 10 (1987): 475–480; and Zimmerman et al., *Environmental Philosophy*.

37   This was particularly the case with the Architectural Association School of Architecture in London, where people such as Rem Koolhaas, Bernard Tschumi, and Zaha Hadid developed a distinct interest in large-scale projects that invoked landscape themes during the early 1980s. Later, Peter Salter, Peter Wilson, Jeanne Sillett, and Peter Beard developed other approaches to landscape, drawing more from geography and ecology.

38   Anne Whiston Spirn's *The Granite Garden* (New York: Basic Books, 1984) was one of the first books to argue for a synthesis of architecture, landscape, and city. Since then, others have described more animate and synthetic versions of the living city; see, for instance, Sanford Kwinter, "Landscapes of Change: Boccioni's Stati d'animo as a General Theory of Models," *Assemblage* 19 (1992): 50–65; and Lars Lerup, "Stim and Dross: Rethinking the Metropolis," *Assemblage* 25 (1994): 82–100. Significantly, both Kwinter and Lerup draw from Henri Bergson's much earlier *Creative Evolution*, trans. Arthur Mitchell (1911; reprint, Lanham, Md.: University Press of America, 1983).

39   See Bernard Tschumi, *Cinegramme Folie: le Parc de la Villette* (New York: Princeton Architectural Press, 1987); and, for an interesting discussion on this, see Bernard Tschumi, Christophe Girot, and Ernest Pascucci, "Looking Back at Parc de la Villette, *Documents* 4/5 (spring1994): 23–56.

40   See Peter Walker, *Peter Walker: Minimalist Gardens* (Washington, D.C.: Spacemaker Press, 1997); and Heidi Landecker, ed., *Martha Schwartz: Transfiguration of the Commonplace* (Washington, D.C.: Spacemaker Press, 1997).

41   See *Process Architecture* 128: *Hargreaves—Landscape Works* (January 1996).

42   See Peter Latz, "Emscher Park, Duisburg," *Transforming Landscape*, ed. Michael Spens (London: Academy Editions, 1996), 54–61; and Peter Beard, "Life in the Ruins," *Blueprint* (July 1996): 28–37.

43   See Adriaan Geuze, *Adriaan Geuze / West 8 Landscape Architecture* (Rotterdam: Uitgeverij 010 Publishers, 1995). See also Udo Weilacher, *Between Landscape Architecture and Landscape Art* (Basel: Birkhäuser Verlag, 1996).

44   See James Corner, "The Agency of Mapping," in *Mappings*, ed. Denis Cosgrove (London: Reaktion, 1999), 212–252.

45   On the search for the "new," see Jeffrey Kipnis, "Towards a New Architecture," in *Architectural Design Profile* 102: *Folding in Architecture*, ed. Greg Lynn (1993): 41–49.

Part One: Reclaiming Place and Time

Chapter 1

Nature Recalled

Marc Treib

The title of this book suggests that something previously lost now warrants restoration. While the very term *landscape* has come to include many varied meanings, I focus on the recovery of the *designed* landscape, the landscape shaped to convey human intention, providing accommodation and, perhaps, even beauty. If it is indeed the quality of the designed landscape that has been lost, we must also ask whether or not, or in what ways, it should be recalled. This essay addresses both aspects of the issue, the loss and regaining of quality in landscape, but alas, with no degree of finality.

The Modernist Landscape

One of the significant byproducts of the modern movement in architecture was the disappearance of the noticeably designed landscape beyond the small scale of the garden. From the late 1920s on, experimentation with garden design in France, England, and the United States consciously sought inspiration in the arts of the day, but this interest found few equivalents in the enlarged sphere of the private estate, the public park, and the region.[1] Certainly, economy was an important factor in the renewed consideration of style; formal landscapes require extensive maintenance and economic resources for such activities had dwindled. Public green spaces, particularly in the United States, came to rely almost exclusively on the vocabulary of naturalism. This model can be traced back to the eighteenth-century English landscape garden—if not nature itself—although more immediate American sources were the designs of Frederick Law Olmsted and Calvert Vaux for New York's Central Park (1858) and Brooklyn's Prospect Park, built about ten years later. With the exceptions of limited areas of formally planted flower beds and an occasional terrace, naturalism prevailed. So complete was its dominance that it remained unquestioned by architects and their landscape confrères for decades.[2]

By the end of the 1930s, the battle for architectural modernism in Western Europe and the United States had been more or less won, but efforts to formulate a modern landscape architecture had hardly started. Architects largely con-

Fig. 1. Rooftop running track and beyond, Miami, Florida, 1991. Photograph by Marc Treib.

trolled the dialog between the constructed object and its setting, and, for the most part, they proposed discrete objects set in undifferentiated green space. In the United States, coherent urban or suburban form derived from the models of Camillo Sitte, Eliel Saarinen, and Raymond Unwin, had almost completely evaporated.[3] Despite his early attempts to formulate a modern parterre, Le Corbusier also tended to regard landscape as a Virgilian park in which the building object rested or stood—much like an erect steak set amid garniture (Fig. 1).

This dissolution of formal contiguity had a twofold effect. It meant that neither architectonic elements nor the accompanying landscape joined structure to structure as a greater whole. Landscape no longer fulfilled its historical role as the extension of, or matrix for, architecture, but now served as the vegetal buffer between buildings. The norm of the building in a park implied that landscape superseded architecture—at least when seen from a distance—and that landscape comprised a passive and undifferentiated field of vegetation. Curiously, the modernist fascination for complexly interwoven spaces *within* buildings did not extend to the surroundings but instead seemed to expire on the doorstep. In retrospect, this appears to have been a curious turn. Why, despite their concern with modern science and technology, did architects rely on an almost classical landscape of architectural elements set in a green park?[4] Formally and kinetically, the landscape became an increasingly dull backdrop, and innovations addressed use rather than form or space. For its part, the landscape architecture profession did little to remedy the situation. During the Depression years, the profession's attention turned, quite rightly, to the pressing problems of soil management and social landscapes. Use, whether social or agricultural, directed most discussion and design, which remained attuned to a predominantly pastoral or rustic aesthetic. In effect, ideas of landscape design as spatial or formal design withered and retreated into the distance.

The war years directed professional attention to the greater project for victory. As the promise of a postwar era emerged, however, at least one group of landscape designers looked for a modern landscape based on a modern vocabulary. Particularly in California, where clement weather patterns allowed more months to be spent outdoors, landscape architects forged a new form of landscape design that wedded social patterns, spatial ideas, materials, and aesthetic vocabularies, creating new "landscapes for living."[5]

Some years later, however, another nail in the coffin of the designed landscape was drilled: the publication of Ian McHarg's *Design with Nature*, which cited the natural world as the only viable model for landscape architecture.[6] This text provided landscape architects with both an analytical method and sufficient moral grounds to avoid almost completely decisions of form and design—that is, if design is taken as the conscious shaping of landscape rather than its stewardship alone. McHarg emphasized the evolving study of natural ecology and remained within the bounds of natural processes and planning. A strong moral imperative underpinned the discourse; it mixed science with evangelism—a sort of ecofundamentalism. In his writings and lectures, McHarg took no prisoners and allowed no quarter.

The McHargian view was focused to the point of being exclusive, confusing and conflating two rather different arenas of landscape intervention. To be sure, it would be fatuous, if not dangerous, to manage a region without thorough analytical investigation; viable design begins with the study of the natural parameters. But the planning process rarely requires the active form-making and innovation that is central to landscape architecture. Reams of analytical overlays might establish the criteria for making a suburban garden, but they can hardly provide the actual design. McHarg's method insinuated that if the process were correct, the consequent form would be good, almost as if objective study automatically gave rise to an appropriate aesthetic. In response to his strong personality and ideas, landscape architects jumped aboard the ecological train, becoming analysts rather than creators, and the conscious making of form and space in the landscape subsequently came to a screeching halt.

Of course, one can hardly design *without* nature, but one should also be able to design viably *around* it. The Patio de los Naranjos in Seville, for example, testifies to the limits imposed by its environment, but it hardly replicates the proximate natural landscape. Instead, it elevates the pragmatic requirements for irrigation to the level of art. The genius of the patio derives precisely from its transcending of the local ecology to comfort and edify the visitor (Fig. 2). Most of all, the simple grid of ever-verdant orange trees embodies the poetic conjunction of nature and religion within a garden.

Fig. 2. Patio de los Naranjos, Seville, Spain, sixteenth century. Photograph by Marc Treib.

31

This bounded garden, now a part of Seville's cathedral, was originally the forecourt of an Islamic mosque. That the configuration of its greenery remains while its curatorship has changed raises its own questions of propriety. But behind any specific factors lies the idea of *intention*: the inspired and instigating reason for making this landscape here and at this time. Were we to design only with nature (if that is even possible), we would lack the human dimension that lies behind designing landscapes in the first place. It would seem that we need to consider a broader range of factors—cultural, imaginative, mythical, and intuitive—than the quantifiable ones alone.

The Designed Landscape

The ecological view of landscape architecture espoused by McHarg and others during the 1960s and into the 1980s was essentially atemporal, laying claim to a perpetual validity. However, landscape designers have always asked: What is an appropriate landscape architecture for our times and what makes it read as such? The varied answers have been far from clear, and landscape designers rarely distinguished the more broadly drawn cultural and technological issues from those that generated specific forms within the garden.[7] Trees tend to grow in a similar fashion, whether in a sixteenth-century villa garden or a twentieth-century corporate park. One can let trees assume their natural shape, or cut them into some prescribed form (Figs. 3, 4). These two practices mark out the extremes of the full range of horticultural options, and both have been so utilized throughout history that each remains free of associations with any particular era. Plants offer clues, but only to the expert horticulturalist will a certain specimen connote a specific time. For example, the magnificent wall of Lombardy poplars at André Le Nôtre's Parc de Sceaux could not have been achieved during the landscape architect's own lifetime. The poplar, a cultivar, was introduced to France only in the late eighteenth century, and the trees reflected in the canal today actually date from a 1930s refurbishing.[8] Few visitors would sense the anomaly, however.

Modernist theorists such as Christopher Tunnard argued for a "structural" approach to planting, choosing plants not so much for their horticultural beauty or rarity as for their formal contribution to the composition of the garden.[9] Tunnard thus suggested that modernity derived not from the selection of particular specimens but from the manner in which plants were employed. While tantalizing as an idea, the practical application of this proposition has been only vaguely applied in practice, and rarely does vegetation alone give us a sense of what is new and modern.

In many historical instances, it is the architectural frame rather than the planting that establishes the sense of "when." The stone balustrades of the Italian Renaissance garden signal the order and balance of their era; the follies of the landscape garden represent dispersed clues that anchor the landscape to its time—they constitute an architectural frame in fragments, so to speak. More recently, the zigzag or the biomorphic curve linked landscape design to contemporary movements in painting and sculpture.[10] Designs such as Thomas Church's Martin and Donnell gardens, both from 1948, draw on shapes first proposed in painting and sculpture by Jean Arp, Joan Miró, and Isamu Noguchi. But, as in the gardens of Roberto Burle-Marx in Brazil, the flowing lines of these Californian gardens only rarely echoed the actual contours of the landscape.[11] More often the biomorphic shape is a free-form gesture serving more to give a sense of contemporaneity than to underscore existing landform.

In the best work, however, these inherent differences are resolved. Other projects, while formally brilliant, lack any deep attachment to their sites— although they did appear quite provocative and current at the time of their conception. Formal landscape idioms drawn from painting and sculpture were as important for what they were *not* as for what they were; they were neither classical axis nor contrived naturalism. By sharing the styles of painting, building, furniture—and even drapery—they, too, attempted to engage the zeitgeist.

Fig. 3 (top). Pasture/forest edge, Scotland, 1988. Left to take their natural shape individually, the collective form of the woods has been managed. Photograph by Marc Treib.

Fig. 4 (bottom). Levens Hall, Cumbria, England. M. Beaumont, 1692. When trees are shaped. Photograph by Marc Treib.

To all but a few landscape architects still focused on the formal consequences of design, the 1970s and early 1980s were a time of third-hand versions
of Lawrence Halprin's mid-1960s fountains and tired reiterations of the down-
town plaza set before a high-rise and graced by modern sculpture.[12] This anemic
palette was filled out with a rehashing of picturesque fragments: minuscule last
gasps of the English estate, crammed with bumps and berms onto narrow parking strips and into microscopic backyards. The reasons for the perpetuation of
the naturalistic aesthetic extended beyond professional lethargy. For one,
reduced maintenance devoted to vegetation was less obvious when planting was
spaced irregularly and, for another, the residual symbolic connection of the residential garden or park to the noble estate retained its currency.

34

There were exceptions, of course, if only a few. Two key projects come to

mind. The first is Isamu Noguchi's 1984
California Scenario in Costa Mesa. I initially
found this plaza rather offensive because it
so neglects any notion of amenity, reflecting
the interests of the sculptor rather than the
landscape architect (Fig. 5). The harsh sunlight and the dazzling brilliance of the adjacent parking garage's white walls make it
difficult to traverse the space in the noonday
sun, both physically and psychologically. In
addition, I had the nagging feeling that
Noguchi had *furnished* the space with sculp-
tured objects rather than using forms to define the plaza. While to some degree
these remain valid criticisms, *California Scenario* as a whole is not so easily dis-
missed. In time I have come to appreciate not only the relationships among
Noguchi's forms but also their collective aesthetic power at a level beyond that
of physical comfort.[13] Noguchi rejected the idea of the corporate plaza as the
perceptual void between the building and the street. At the very least, he
engaged those at work in the adjacent towers by offering a subject to look upon.

The visual gradient of *California Scenario* is far more complex than, for
example, the forms of another landmark work of the 1980s, The SWA Group's
Mustang Square in Las Colinas, Texas. Despite the impressive overscale bronze

Fig. 5. *California Scenario*, Costa Mesa, California. Isamu Noguchi, 1984. Photograph by Marc
Treib.

horses slashing across the pool of the plaza, the drama is limited to a single point in space and is less effective in reality than in photos (where all the action has been stilled). In contrast, Noguchi's accomplishment is spatial and haptic, and his plaza is ultimately less a landscape with sculpture than a sculptured landscape.[14] In essence a Zen exegesis on California's varied ecosystems—hence the name *California Scenario*—the Noguchi plaza distills the features and scale of the natural landscape while magnifying their effect.

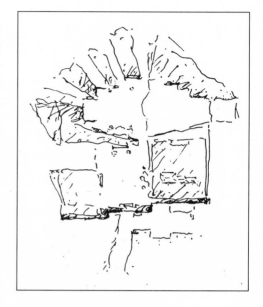

The second image that comes to mind is a sketch by Michael Graves for the garden to the Crooks House in Indiana dated 1975 (Fig. 6). The design itself is admittedly unspecific, but vegetation provides the basic stuff from which the spaces are cut, as if from some huge piece of green Styrofoam. This simple study signaled three aspects of the architect's, if not the landscape architect's, recovery of landscape. First, it said that outdoor spaces should *complement* internal ones, a much more classical idea than the continuous indoor-outdoor ideal of the modern California house and garden. Second, the sketch suggested that vegetation, like masonry, is a building material. Third, and perhaps most important, it intimated that regardless of stylistic predilection, architects should again consider and form the landscape. The time of the seemingly unformed landscape echoed by Le Corbusier was coming to an end.

If the Graves sketch suggested a return to a classical vision for landscape as vegetal mass and space, the work of sculptors such as Robert Smithson and Michael Heizer pointed landscape architects in a far different direction: toward primary forms as manner and myth as substantiation. Because so much of landscape practice in the 1960s and 1970s focused on ecological issues, sources within landscape architecture for a reinvigorated formal vocabulary were few. In reaction, younger designers looked beyond the limits of the profession, prima-

Fig. 6. Crooks House, landscape and *parti* sketch, Fort Wayne, Indiana. Michael Graves, 1975. Vegetation as space-making material. Courtesy of Michael Graves.

rily to the work of the so-called earthwork sculptors. Sufficient material has been published on both the artists and their influence on landscape design to eliminate the need to rehash the story.[15] However, one should not discount the importance of the earthworks—their scale, primary forms, and, in some instances, their neo-archaism—on landscape design recovered in the 1980s.

The Temporal Landscape

The recovery of landscape began almost two decades ago in the United States, as the emerging generation of designers turned once again to a concern for form, space, and a vocabulary reflective of their vision of contemporary life.[16] Since that time, much to the chagrin of their landscape architecture colleagues, architects have made numerous landscape proposals—many of them rather naive in terms of understanding ecology and natural process. Robert Riley, a professor of landscape architecture at the University of Illinois, once referred to the architectural predilection for Lombardy poplars and palm trees as the "fragrant I-beam" school of landscape design; trees are arranged essentially as "columns" with bits of greenery on top.[17] Despite their lack of technical expertise, however, I rather doubt that architects' interest in landscape will wane in the coming decade.

Why is the designed landscape enjoying a recovery in architecture? The plausible answers fall into two basic categories: cynical and optimistic. On the cynical side, architects have developed a new interest in landscape in order to work in a larger arena. Given the downturn of the economy in the later 1980s, even the more prestigious architectural firms undertook extensive development programs and hustled space planning and interior work they would not normally have accepted in the past. As layoffs were rampant and commissions few, it seemed attractive to take on landscape projects along with those for signage systems and interiors. All contributed to the notion of comprehensive services that was a euphemism for professional survival.

Related to these desires is the renewed and ever-growing desire of architects to control the entire project. In the 1980s the old idea of the *Gesamtkunstwerk* came to include not only the architecture and its interior furnishings but the surrounding exterior space as well. The inspiration for this renewed interest perhaps derived from the Renaissance past, and one of the first groups of architects to return to landscape was classically oriented. It is no mere coincidence that during the 1980s the price of used copies of Shepherd and Jellicoe's *Italian Gardens of the Renaissance* soared, ultimately instigating reprinting.[18] Thus, numerous models for contemporary landscape architecture are drawn not from the modernist designs of the 1920s and 1930s but from the gardens of the Italian Renaissance. However, this is slowly changing as a larger part of modernist history is being…I want to say recovered, but it is perhaps more accurate to say *formulated* for the very first time.[19]

That is the cynical explanation for the renewed interest in the designed landscape. But there is also an explanation far more positive and attractive, and it comes in reaction to the contemporary condition of the city and suburbia. The inert architectural debris that fills cities across the world is the devastating consequence of our detachment from place, other people, and history. Critics have returned our attention to considerations of regionalism or even a *critical* regionalism, if such a thing is possible.[20] The consensus is that the globalization of culture and the homogenization of building are not all for the betterment of culture, place, and individual well-being.

In addition to consuming inordinate amounts of resources, the hermetically sealed buildings around the world today rarely age gracefully. Instead, they deteriorate with time and need to be renovated or demolished. The majority of buildings are most impressive immediately after their construction, 1/125th of a second after they are completed, before they are furnished and certainly before they are inhabited. But life continues, and environmental forces continuously take their toll on the architectural fabrics. Louis Sullivan once cited a French proverb, asserting that time will never consecrate that in which it has been forgotten.[21] There is considerable difference between the modeled stonework of a building by H.H. Richardson and the sheer stone or impervious skins of recent high-rises; the former engages time as a collaborator, the latter denies active considerations of aging. One wonders how these thinly veneered buildings will appear in the future, when their initial luster has dulled and their joints have been recaulked for the thirtieth time.

Indeed, time is the crucial dimension of landscape, and time may ultimately be the single most important reason that architects are drawn outside their buildings. Landscape architecture is a pursuit quite distinct from that of building, requiring time for plants to become established, time for shrubs to flower, time for fruit trees to yield. Landscapes are usually better after ten or twenty years; after thirty years they are transformed into quite different entities. This is time taken linearly, rolling from today into the future.[22]

Change is the direct byproduct of time. It is necessary to understand that many an elaborate planting plan has materialized only as a few pitifully wispy trees propped up by massive staking (Fig. 7). In contrast, the contemporary

French landscape architect Alexandre Chemetoff made necessity a virtue in his motorway interchange near Toulouse. The diagonal tree-braces articulate the contour of the terrain that was itself modeled by the stripes of colored polyethylene that stabilize the soil and suppress the growth of weeds (Fig. 8). In time, all the supports will erode and disappear. In this project, Chemetoff recognizes the necessity for prosthetic devices during the early years of a landscape but elevates them above their normal supporting role. The landscape architect here acknowledges time as a critical dimension, and that landscapes must pass through stages from inception to maturity.

We may also reflect on how the small sapling planted in the rear yard when we were kids now dominates the entire neighborhood and how, conversely, the elms that once lined our streets are today all chopped and long gone. The change that accompanies time is not always positive, but the linear progression of time tends to be realistic rather than pessimistic. Its passing reminds us of change, which we hope will be for the best against all indications to the contrary (Figs. 9 and 10).

The second dimension of time in the landscape is cyclical. Successions of night and day are underscored by the passage of the sun, but the annual rhythms of branch and bloom are perhaps more noticeable than the diurnal, particularly in climates where the four seasons are distinct and the vegetation is deciduous. All landscapes have distinctive colors that reflect the unraveling of the year. The rusty golds of summer hillside grasses in California, the yellows of ginkgos and carmines and oranges of the maples in Japan,

Fig. 7 (top). Nascent planting, Benecia, California, 1980. Photograph by Marc Treib.

Fig. 8 (bottom). Interchange landscape, Toulouse, France, c. 1988. Alexandre Chemetoff, landscape architect. Photograph by Marc Treib.

38

the monochromatic wooded landscapes of Finland in winter—all denote characteristic times. Landscapes designed in conscience with the annual cycles resonate with their connection to the place and reflect the life within it.

Or even death.

Sigurd Lewerentz and Gunnar Asplund's celebrated Woodland Cemetery outside Stockholm (1915–1940) manifests the passage of the seasons as the green meadow beneath the streaked blue skies becomes articulated with fall color, only to be transformed into a series of skeletal frameworks and soft white contours in winter (Fig. 11). The seasons alter not only form and chroma but also the perceived limits of the space. The green line of the

horizontal elms in summer anchors the edge of the columbarium but leaps into yellow prominence in autumn, drastically affecting our reading of the central meadow. In winter, the leaves disappear, and the grass planes seem to address directly the edge of the pine forest behind the walled enclave.

The limits imposed by winter close the yearly cycle, while the promise of renewal in springtime marks its completion. Here, in Enskede, time passes and yet the landscape stands eternal. There is little in any element of the cemetery that smacks of contemporary idiom, yet the landscape and its architecture are without question modern. In its continued rebirth, the funerary landscape at Woodland provides a sense of hope for the future. Thus, even in a cemetery, landscape architecture can evince an optimism shared once by architecture but rarely discovered in today's cities.

While nature may be an inspiration to some, it is a burden to others, as our regard for nature is essentially a product of culture. I am a product of the city, trained as an architect, and I happen to prefer nature re-formed, that is to say, nature within a garden (Fig. 12). The garden represents the confluence of natu-

Fig. 9 (top). Vines, free and bounded, The Aventine, Rome, Italy, 1985. Photograph by Marc Treib.

Fig. 10 (bottom). Vegetal sheathing, La Jolla, California, 1987. Photograph by Marc Treib.

ral processes with human intelligence and sensibility. I like gardens because they change and evolve, even if pruned and restrained within an inch of their botanical lives. The planned and planted world of the garden gives us a different sense of our relation to time and place than does the essential stasis of architecture. Time reflected in change and change reflected in time may just be the keys to understanding the natural world and our place within it. To my mind, that is well worth recalling.

In this era of eroding boundaries between professions and even of eroding definitions of a profession, one could validly question the nature of contributions made by landscape architects today. There is no question that landscape architects have had an outstanding role in protecting the environment, providing a body of knowledge on which to base decisions concerning land and settlement. And there is no question that since the 1960s, landscape architects have played an important role in addressing social issues

Fig. 11 (top). Summer: the chapels, central meadow, and knoll at Woodland Cemetery, Enskede, Sweden. Gunnar Asplund and Sigurd Lewerentz, 1915–1940. Photograph by Marc Treib.

Fig. 12 (bottom). Daichi-ji, Shiga Prefecture, Japan, seventeenth century. When nature, religion and human intention meet in the garden. Photograph by Marc Treib.

Fig. 13. The Memorial Knoll, Woodland Cemetery, Enskede, Sweden. Gunnar Asplund and Sigurd Lewerentz, 1915–1940. A poetic meditation on existence. Photograph by Marc Treib.

regarding community planning, housing, and recreation. But is there not another, broader, and less easily identified dimension to landscape design that acknowledges its manifestation of cultural ideas and ideals?

In *The Art of the Novel*, the noted Czech writer Milan Kundera defined the novel as "a poetic meditation on existence."[23] We might do well to apply Kundera's aphorism to environmental design, treating the designed landscape, as well as architecture, as "poetic meditation[s] on existence." Existence involves change, and change demands time. Our time may now demand of architects a "recovery of landscape." But we should not invest this resurrection of interest in a landscape conceived as a banal buffer between the elements of the built environment, nor as a green balm for inept architectural planning. Instead, we might once again regard the landscape as an integral part of the designed world, reflecting in its own terms a poetic meditation on existence (Fig. 13).

41

Notes

1 For an informed survey of this trend in France, see Dorothée Imbert, *The Modernist Garden in France* (New Haven, Conn.: Yale University Press, 1993). The most important American developments in formulating a modern design landscape came over a decade later. For an outline of these design ideas, see Marc Treib and Dorothée Imbert, *Garrett Eckbo: Modern Landscapes for Living* (Berkeley: University of California Press, 1997); and Peter Walker and Melanie Simo, *Invisible Gardens* (Cambridge, Mass.: MIT Press, 1994).

2 Behind this seemingly tacit acceptance of the naturalistic aesthetic lay an idea of social improvement based on direct contact with nature. If workers could not leave the city to enjoy betterment in nature, nature must be brought to them. Ironically, perhaps, many of the people using Central Park today believe that it is a relic of the pre-urban landscape rather than a designed landscape that was created *de novo*.

3 A translation of Sitte's most important publication, *City Planning According to Artistic Principles* (1889), is included in George R. Collins and Christiane Crasemann Collins, *Camillo Sitte: The Birth of Modern City Planning* (New York: Rizzoli, 1986). Until the Charles Stewart translation, published in 1945, Americans knew of Sitte's ideas through the French edition of his work, or in the overview provided by Eliel Saarinen in *The City: Its Growth, Its Decay, Its Future* (New York: Reinhold Publishing Company, 1943). For a selection of Unwin's writings, see Walter Creese, ed., *The Legacy of Raymond Unwin: A Human Pattern for Planning* (Cambridge, Mass.: MIT Press, 1967).

4 Classical in the sense of paintings by Poussin and Claude, with architecture in their landscapes, rather than classical as in the stylized gardens of the Italian Renaissance. Imbert examines this question in relation to Le Corbusier in *Modernist Garden in France*, 147–183.

5 This phrase was used as the title of Garrett Eckbo's important book (New York: Duell, Sloan, and Pearce, 1950), whose purview extended far beyond the individual garden. More influential in the lay arena were publications of projects by Thomas Church, Douglas Baylis, and other California designers in the pages of *Sunset* magazine, and Church's own *Gardens Are for People* (New York: Reinhold Publishing, 1955).

6   Ian McHarg, *Design with Nature* (Garden City, N.Y.: Natural History Press, 1969).

7   I discussed this issue of *conceptual* versus *perceptual* aspects of landscape thinking in Treib and Imbert, *Garrett Eckbo*, 59–69.

8   See Marc Treib, "The Care and Feeding of the Noble Allée," *Arnoldia* (spring 1994): 12–23.

9   Christopher Tunnard, *Gardens in the Modern Landscape* (London: Architectural Press, 1938).

10 For an explication of this idea, see Henry-Russell Hitchcock, *Painting Toward Architecture* (New York: Duell, Sloan, and Pearce, 1948).

11 A rare instance of the congruence of topography and formal gesture is found at the Donnell garden in Sonoma County, north of San Francisco. Here, Church used a serpentine hedge to unify the pool garden and the house, which was built some years later. See Marc Treib, "Aspects of Regionality and the Modern California Garden," in *Regional Garden Design in the United States*, eds. Therese O'Malley and Marc Treib (Washington, D.C.: Dumbarton Oaks, 1996), 5–42.

12 James Wines once called this clichéd approach "the turd on the plaza"; the reason is obvious.

13 The amenities of seating and shade are provided by the caterer when needed for an event such as a wedding reception.

14 In this way *California Scenario* is certainly no worse and, in many ways, far more engaging, than recent exercises in visual landscape patterning seen around the world from Germany to Japan.

15 The principal source on these works is John Beardsley, *Earthworks and Beyond* (New York: Abbeville, 1984); see also Alan Sonfist, ed., *Art in the Land*, for an anthology of writings on art and nature. The construction of a formal manner, which considers the influence of sculpture, is treated in Marc Treib, "Must Landscapes Mean? Approaches to Significance in Recent landscape Architecture," *Landscape Journal* (spring 1995): 46–62.

16 Early leaders in the field were Lawrence Halprin, Dan Kiley, Hideo Sasaki, and Peter Walker. More recently, George Hargreaves and the firm Hargreaves and Associates, San Francisco and Cambridge, are exemplary with regard to the adaptation of land-art experiments to landscape architectural practice. Early projects relied almost directly on sculptural precedents; the later work, however, has actively attempted to use ecological dicta as the basis of a new aesthetic. This integration of content and form proposes a fruitful direction for future practice by effacing the boundary between analysis and synthesis. See *Process: Architecture* 128—*Hargreaves: Landscape Works* (January 1996).

17 Conversation, time and place lost to memory.

18 John C. Shepherd and Geoffrey A. Jellicoe, *Italian Gardens of the Renaissance* (London: Ernest Benn, 1925; reprint, New York: Princeton Architectural Press, 1986).

19 See Marc Treib, *Modern Landscape Architecture: A Critical Review* (Cambridge, Mass.: MIT Press, 1993). While an anthology of primarily new essays augmented by historical articles, this book constitutes the most detailed study of the subject available—by default, if for no other reason. Walker and Simo's *Invisible Gardens* appeared the following year. Since then, with the exception of Treib and Imbert's *Garrett Eckbo*, no studies of the modern period have appeared in English. Work is being done, however, in Denmark (the writings of Annemarie Lund, Lulu Salto Stephensen, Sven-Ingvar Andersson, and Steen Høyer are foremost among them), Sweden (primarily Thorbjörn Andersson and the editorship of the journal *Utblick Landskap*), Germany (much of it concerned with the war years—for example, the work of Joachim Wolschke-Buhlmann and Gert Gröening), and, more slowly, in other countries.

20 See Kenneth Frampton, "Towards a Critical Regionalism: Six Points for an Architecture of Resistance," in *The Anti-Aesthetic: Essays on Post-Modern Culture*, ed. Hal Foster (Port Townsend, Wash.: Bay Press, 1983); and Treib, "Aspects of Regionality," 5–42.

21 Louis Sullivan, *Kindergarten Chats* (1918; reprint, New York: George Wittenborn, 1947).

22 The temporal dimension is more crucial, and far more noticeable, in landscape than in most building. See Marc Treib, "On Paper and Plants," *Places* 3, no. 3 (1986): 56–59.

23 Milan Kundera, *The Art of the Novel* (New York: HarperCollins, 1987), 35.

Chapter 2

The Reclaiming of Sites

Sébastien Marot

The collection of essays in this book calls attention to a remarkable phenomenon that is gaining momentum today: the significance of landscape architecture's contribution to the discussions, the thinking, and the operations that
affect the management and transformation of sites and regions. Landscape
architecture is not, of course, a new profession. It is practiced in nearly all parts
of the world and holds a prominent position in the industrialized countries. In
some of these, most notably those of Western Europe, the field can boast of long-
cherished ideas and deep-rooted traditions.

Despite differences in culture from one country and time to another, the
profession of landscape architecture is more or less universally identifiable with
the creative design of outdoor and public spaces. Its history embraces not only
garden art and park design but also issues of agriculture, cartography, civil and
military engineering, and town planning. This history highlights certain vintage periods during which—in especially propitious political or technical circumstances—landscape architects seized the initiative, adapted to changing
conditions, and constructed new forms of space. The accomplishments of these
events vary significantly from place to place, lending a rich density to the corpus
of references that constitute the field of landscape architecture.

In what follows, I endeavor to clarify on a more modest scale the circumstances that account for the revival of landscape architectural ideas in our own
time. I address less the quality or aesthetic trends of contemporary design and
more the disciplinary traditions that underlie any significant recovery and reinvention of the landscape project. My focus is limited to developments in France,
but many of the points raised share characteristics with other places.[1]

The Situation in France Today

Since the early 1980s, a combination of circumstances has made France one of
the European nations most actively engaged in the recovery of landscape studies
within the larger architectural disciplines. At first glance, this situation may

Fig 1. *Parc du Sausset*, Villepinte. Claire and Michel Corajoud, landscape architects,
1982–1998. Photograph by Gérard Dufresne.

seem surprising, particularly when viewed in light of the relative indifference that has been shown in France for landscape generally—not to mention garden art—during the preceding five or six decades. If questioned about the period between the 1920s and the 1980s, it is unlikely that more than a handful of today's architecture students or designers would be able to name a single land-scape designer or to cite a single important built work. The most widely read might recall the gardens of Villa Noailles, and the most inquisitive might refer to Albert Kahn's microcosm, but the majority would have little to say. Yet this period was full of creativity, producing a range of places that we visit but fail to recognize.[2]

Rather than indifference, it might be better to characterize this condition as one of oblivion, almost as if a long parenthesis in history had been blocked out. The result has been forgetfulness of the power of design in making new land-scapes. People have generally lost the habit not of appreciating landscapes but of looking at gardens, public spaces, parks, and larger open areas as sites for active design. In the final analysis, it is as if the spaces around buildings and every other type of construction are viewed as little more than empty, leftover areas, void and forgotten. Such spaces may be considered necessary components of any city, but they are easily relegated to the functional status of generic green spaces.

This dismissal of gardens and landscaping took place during a period in which the ideals of the modern movement surged to predominance and then declined. This fact may seem odd, given that landscape specialists trained in the school of Alphand had been widely represented in France during the period immediately before this and enjoyed much success in relating landscape meth-ods and models to the city—as in garden cities, urban parks, and greenbelts, for instance.[3] Still, the landscape idea waned in France beginning in the 1920s.

Several factors related to economic and political trends offer a basic expla-nation for this prolonged era of decline and neglect; I cite just two of the more significant ones. First, government interests, spurred by postwar reconstruction throughout the so-called Glorious Thirty Years and lasting until the first oil cri-sis in the early 1970s, followed a policy of urban and regional planning that was based almost exclusively on the development of mass housing projects and infrastructural systems. The emphasis here was not on site or environment but on engineering, quantitative planning, and standardization. A second factor was a serious crisis of economy and culture in the rural world, with a correspon-ding breakdown of traditional landscape structures. This crisis occurred relatively later in France than in other European countries—first because a large proportion of the country is rural with many people owning and working the land, and second because the government prioritized cities and infrastructure at the expense of neglecting the rural world. This situation meant that the effects of globalization and new technology have been more brutally registered in the French countryside as change has had to occur quickly and with little time to adapt to new lifestyles.

The combined effects of these two factors—a national policy conducted with excessive determination to create new residences and infrastructures, together with a conscious neglect of the economic and cultural changes imping-ing upon the rural world—accounts, in large part, for the one-sided success that the mostly bureaucratic, modernist practices of regional management have enjoyed for almost fifty years.[4] This top-down style of planning and manage-ment, operating from the inside outward (or, as Le Corbusier described, *"du dedans vers le dehors"* or "from the inside to the outside"), has rarely taken into account local differences and history. The program, defined a priori, was given absolute priority over the consideration of the site. In representing localities and places solely in quantitative terms, the innate richness and history of sites were reduced into diagrammatic map-forms in which the image of the city was viewed and arranged as functional zones. Sites were seen as blank surfaces on which to organize urban functions in efficient and often standardized ways.

Reclaiming the Site

By now, the scenario painted above is an all-too-familiar history. We now recog-nize how public projects and their administrative authorities came to be organ-ized into specialized bureaucracies solely on the basis of a clear distinction between the elements and functions of the urban and regional sectors. More-over, we recognize how this situation is made all the more difficult as new economies of tourism, communications, recreation, and distribution and the rise of individual suburban homes extend their reach into the countryside, blur-ring traditional distinctions between town and country.

The later years of this scenario, however—the period of the *villes nouvelles*—were also the first years of a resurgence of interest and value in land-scape. This recovery of landscape began with the attempts of specialists to create that "filter of vegetation" envisaged in the sketches of Le Corbusier for the *cité contemporaine* and the *ville radieuse*, but never realized. Landscape was here promoted as a sort of palliative to modern urbanization. However, repressed by a development process that saw landscaping as an optional ingredient, the discipline of landscape design became more and more focused on the primary victim in this situation: the site itself. Landscape architects began to look more deeply and more creatively at the unique specificity of sites, especially at the borders and edges, the areas in between that were neglected by architects and planners. In so doing, landscape architects soon learned to take instant advantage of any opportunity to repair the damage done and to restore something of memory and a sense of place to these otherwise razed sites.

In a paradoxical way, then, the struggles that took place over the urbanization of peripheral areas and the *villes nouvelles* provided on-site training for a new generation of landscape architects. On the basis of that experience, they immersed themselves in teaching to further research and explore the possibilities of this newly recovered interest. Many others have since taken their place alongside Michel Corajoud at the new École Nationale Supérieure du Paysage in Versailles, which has been transformed in recent years into a think tank and laboratory of alternative approaches to landscape design. The vision being elaborated in Versailles today is not limited to merely changing priorities from building to landscape but instead takes as its starting point the "reading and writing" of the site itself. Such a view is less focused on the program of a proposed building project than on exploring the possibilities of site characteristics and hidden phenomena. As such, it outlines a critical and reflective approach to making new landscapes.

During the last years of the 1970s and into the early 1980s, the development of these new approaches to landscape architecture coincided with an important evolution in the political-economic realities outlined earlier. Although government policies concerning regional infrastructures lost little of their authority, the move toward decentralization led to a proliferation of new public commissions. Provinces, regions, and townships won back an impressive amount of influence in the fields of urban studies and land management and became promoters of design approaches that took into account an evaluation of sites and their local history. There was thus a sense in which landscape could be taken as a value in and of itself, presented as emblematic of what makes a given area special and unique.

Consequently, these new local markets, encouraged by national policies directing them to pay more attention to the environment, have begun to solicit alternative design approaches in which greater importance is given to interpreting the unique attributes of a site than to a priori building programs. Riding the wave of this general movement toward awareness of public space as landscape, landscape architects have begun to assume leadership roles in the design of public space. In the best examples, the work resembles stage design in that the landscape architect stages the conditions necessary for ensuring the participation and engagement of people in the new public spaces.

Since the mid-1980s, France has finally become aware of the true gravity of the crisis in the rural world and the agricultural economy. In an effort to prop up this economy, containment measures were taken that have since proven wholly unable to reverse the decline and abandonment of small land holdings and larger tracts of land. Moreover, the growth of other economies, such as tourism and recreation, has moved into these agrarian areas without evolving their own culture of place-making and settlement. Increasing awareness of this situation has led to the consensus that overall plans are necessary to help shape and direct the future of these areas. The preservation of the legacy of these agrarian communities, the care of their resources, and the adaptation to new, changing economies demands true invention in the form of innovative landscape projects. These issues are leading to an enormous amount of study at both national and local levels, the force of which reflects the emergence of an awareness of landscape as public space, with the consequence that landscape architects are increasingly assigned the important role of consultant or master planner.

This new context, based on the recognition of a dialectical relationship between the respective notions of landscape and public space, explains not only the rebirth of landscape studies in France but also the critical importance of the recovery. Placed by their culture at the crossroad of two heritages—that of the agrarian peasantry on the one hand and the artistry and high culture of the urban planning on the other—today's most interesting landscape architects take a radical approach to inverting the distinctions of their predecessors. The specific qualities of sites and their situations provide both the rationale and the raw material for making new projects. The form and character a subsequent design derives from the physical fabric as well as the inherited attributes (past conditions) of the site and its larger territory.

The key principle of this process involves careful survey, identification, criticism, and inventive analysis. The close coordination and complex representation of site and planning is worth emphasizing. It harks back to the origin and tradition of a discipline that has always been intimately linked to developments in surveying, painting, theater, and scenography. Just as the layout of the large classical gardens can be related to the progress and ambitions of cartography, so

49

the contemporary landscape architect becomes a special type of project manager, an exegete (or narrator) of the landscape.

A striking feature of this site reading and writing process involves a skeptical criticism of the abstract representations of sites found in maps, pictures, and conventional drawings (elevations as facades, etc.). The ambition to achieve a representation that is more sensitive (or "true") and more inclusive and complete than the images produced by regulatory planning techniques leads to an amalgamation of new imaging procedures: photomontage, composite views, references to analogous situations, texts, and so on. Collectively, these representations contribute to a fuller evaluation of the site and its planning measures. More precisely, there are four steps in the study and projection of site-based landscapes: anamnesis, or recollection of previous history; preparation for and the staging of new conditions; three-dimensional sequencing; and relational structuring.

Four Principles

Anamnesis. Without underestimating the importance of functional analysis or program performance standards, the landscape architectural reading of sites is not limited to quantities and capacities. Rather, it views the land and public space as an expression of ancient culture, or as a palimpsest that evidences all of the activities that contributed to the shaping of that particular landscape and no other.[5] Upon the tracks overlaid by the march of time, site interpretation detects potentialities to be nurtured and passed on. The reading is thus that of an inheritance and the eventual project a bequest.

Although this attitude of respect for the land and the continuity it demands is by no means a prerogative of landscape architects, it does have obvious roots in the traditions of landscape architecture—in the first place, because soil and ecology have their own special nature and one cannot simply impose any regimen on them without deleterious consequences, and, in the second place, because whatever is sown in the earth typically comes to fruition long after the original gardener has died. This is the meaning of the metaphor of continuity that Michel Corajoud uses to contrast his theories to the ideologies of domination and willful imposition: that of a conversation. One cannot participate in a conversation without first listening to what has been said before, listening to what others have to say, and speaking only to keep the discourse going.[6]

Preparation. A correlate of the anamnesis principle, this concept construes landscape as a process rather than a product. Consequently, any project must assume the role of an open-ended strategy, as in staging or setting up future conditions. Being itself in a process of becoming, a landscape is fully bound into the effects of nature and time: the cycle of seasons and the passage of time; processes of hydrology, weathering, and succession; and the alternation of day and night, sun and moon. Thus, in reading the site as a living and dynamic organism, the landscape architect is able to revitalize and incorporate once abandoned sites into present and larger fields of effect.

By bringing the effects of time back to life and appearance, the designer may both restore and prepare sites for often unforeseeable futures. Thus, there is also invoked an attitude of incompleteness; rather than building a final solution, seeds are sown, questions raised, and potential structured. In so doing, a designer may also highlight the stages of implementation and the measures required to sustain or develop it. Making these processes and stages visible not only facilitates execution but also invites the reading and interpretation of others who use and invest their time in such places.

Three-dimensional sequencing. This third principle involves a critical alternative to the limits of surface vision, especially plan and perspective views. The study of gardens has led to a qualitative perception of the layers comprised by public space. Rather than reading an open space as an emptiness defined by a series of surfaces and by light, in-depth vision sees the open space as a habitat in which the sky and what is underground engage in multiple relationships defined by the nature of each of them. This is a rich and complex vision, at once aesthetic and ecological, and it involves a project (even if minimally) with all the layers that compose the landscape: earthwork, topography, soil, drainage, utilities, planting, furnishing, and so on. Careful discernment of the qualities and elements of the three-dimensional landscape helps to facilitate the integration and linking of use and practices that the plan view tends to segregate, oversimplify, and suppress. As with the above two principles, issues of representation and techniques of design are central concerns to how one envisages and orchestrates relationships among all of the parts.

Relational structuring. This principle refers to the special attention that must be given to boundaries, adjacent areas, surroundings, and backgrounds. In general, it is about anticipating the next space. Because landscape designers are used to working on exterior spaces and spaces adjacent to buildings, and because they are trained to revive marginal and peripheral zones (roadsides, uncultivated

51

areas, "non-places"), they have developed to a fine art the activities of insertion, transition, and transplantation. These activities allow landscape architects to focus more on the relationships among objects than on the objects themselves. Thus, the quality of landscape and public space depends not so much on the perfection of its buildings or its services but rather on the quality of the relationships among them. Such relationships are constituted by transitions, sequences, visual connections, the "calculated capture of surroundings."[7] The complex combination of these articulations creates the overall sense of the site.

This kind of relational thinking may well be the best summary and expression of the teachings of landscape architecture as they apply to the management of cities and outlying areas today. This is a view that not only accords special attention to transitional and liminal spaces but also calls for the reading and designing of all landscape spaces as relative spaces. The criticism implied in this formulation is less targeted at the reifying trends of some architects than at the conditions of production in the public sphere. That landscape as a larger milieu is rarely subject to the control of a single authority means that the forms of relational structuring cannot be so much formal as they are vehicles for negotiation and mediation (among neighboring constituencies, management authorities, and so on). Here, relational thinking extends to the coordination of the various players and departments involved in public space maintenance (the streets, parks, utilities, and engineering departments, for instance). Thus, by its very nature, the relational thinking that is inherent to landscape architecture takes a dim view of the subdivision of land and the dispersal of authority and responsibilities, as these are the primary agents that have caused the disintegration of the landscape as a coherent fabric.

This situation has led some landscape architects to reconsider their role, prompting them to provide responses to client requests that consider aspects not usually considered germane and to call attention to issues far beyond their commission—in general, to transcend the limits usually assigned to such consultation in an effort to bring attention to broader objectives. These are landscaping strategies, if you will, evasive ploys that challenge the limits of bureaucratic authority while extending the scope of what is possible.

To encourage people to view public spaces as landscapes means getting them to reconsider their own habits and functions and, ultimately, to overcome the divisive thinking on which those functions are based. It means persuading clients to allow other aims to have weight, aims that can be shared among many people on the basis of reworking the way in which territory is directed and managed. The aim is to clear the way for new ambitions that can be shared by all the players involved in transforming and managing landscapes. This strategic and synthetic approach is what enables contemporary landscape architects to assume leadership roles in the design and coordination of large-scale projects. The contemporary designs and studies of the French landscape architect Alexandre Chemetoff are of particular relevance in this respect, as they are an example of a stance that dares to approach the provocative (Fig. 2).

The Suburban Frontier

Yet another aspect of the involvement of landscape designers in the French cultural debate merits mention, as it reveals a fascinating aspect of the aforementioned developments. This is the adroitness that many landscape designers have demonstrated in examining and reevaluating the history of their own discipline on the basis of the changes that they themselves have wrought. As we have seen, by a curious twist of fate, the contemporary context puts landscape designers at the convergence of the agricultural and urban traditions, which is to say they are at the center of an awareness that is directed, on the one hand, to consider public spaces (urban projects) as landscapes and, on the other, to see landscapes (rural expanses) as public spaces and therefore as possible objectives of projects.

There is, however, a third condition today, one that is increasingly prevalent and that blurs the traditional distinctions between town and country. This is suburbia, that third world, which is so vast and experiencing such profound changes that one forgets it possesses its own history, a history that leads back neither to the city nor the countryside. And yet, when one seeks the design tradition behind the art of gardens and landscaping, generally one is forced to turn to the study of suburban design. Almost all of the historical reference points in landscape architecture are derived from the suburban tradition, and it is these points that have, in large part, contributed to the invention and formation of such places as the gardens of suburban Paris: parks and picturesque areas, promenades outside city walls, city gardens, parkways, greenbelts, and park systems.

Fig 2. *Jardins d'Eau*, Nancy, Alexandre Chemetoff, landscape architect, 1991–1996. Photograph by A. Duboys Fresney.

All of these are outgrowths of efforts made to join the urban structure more smoothly to that of the countryside and to tighten the connection between the city and the larger region as necessitated by suburban expansion. Versailles, with its extensive radial geometry, is an outstanding example of the strategy to place both city and countryside into perspective, effectively mediating between *pars urbana* and *pars rustica*. The French *campagnes environnantes* provided the context for this mediation. Of course, it is well known how the model of Versailles presaged L'Enfant's plan for Washington, D.C., and Le Blond's plan for St. Petersburg.

Historically, gardens and landscapes have often provided the models for later urban creations. Each style and attitude has given rise to specific interpretations vis-à-vis town planning. Just as cities such as Washington and St. Petersburg—but also numerous urban *embellissements* and extension plans of the eighteenth century—drew from the radial and axial geometry of seventeenth-century French gardens, many nineteenth-century curvilinear residential suburbs derived their character from the eighteenth-century English landscape tradition. Thus, it is possible to show how landscape architecture—which, in the light of these examples, could easily be characterized as a kind of suburban design—was historically the developmental laboratory for new models for urban planning, well before urban planning decided—and not necessarily for the better—to turn itself into an autonomous discipline by abandoning the experimental laboratory of the garden.[8]

The most interesting aspect of the landscape experiments performed today in outlying areas is precisely this reintroduction of the long-neglected discipline of suburban studies derived from garden art. Here, certain landscape architects,

Fig 3 (top). *Le Socle de Bouleaux / Birch Trees Terrace,* project for the continuation of the grand axis of La Défense, Paris. Gilles Clement and Geoffroy Decheaume, 1992.

Fig 4 (bottom). *Serial Garden,* Parc Andrè Citroen, Paris. Gilles Clement, landscape architect, 1992. Photograph by Douglas Dard.

linked by their tradition and professional culture to the
middle suburban zone—the birthplace of their discipline—are among very few people today capable of
revealing the rich complexity of sites and situations
where other specialists see only chaos. To quote Michel
Desvigne and Christine Dalnoky:

> [These suburban areas] are not merely further
> expressions of "urban sprawl," but have their own
> history, which, while recent, is none the less rich and also diversified
> and fascinating. Urban sprawl is in no sense inevitable and, since there
> is no nostalgia here, since there is no earlier state to which we can
> make reference, we dream of cities rooted to their landscape, cities
> where one can feel the slope of a hill, sense the freshness of valleys,
> follow the flow of water and the cycle of the seasons, cities in which
> distances can be measured, in which night truly falls, in which time
> is inscribed on the earth, on the skin of the landscape. To get back its
> dignity, landscape architecture must learn to fight back, to hide out in
> the hills and struggle.[9]

55

Conclusion

The recovery that landscape is today enjoying in France derives in large measure from a critical reactivation of *suburbanism*. Here, "sub" points not only to the
land outside the city but also to the earth beneath it, as in the ground on which
the city is founded or the site that preexists and transcends the program. Landscape architecture traditionally is positioned at the interface of town and country as well as of site and program. Thus, landscape approaches differ from those
of architecture and planning in that they seek to *reclaim* rather than to conquer.
In this sense, *suburbanism* is a neologism (as was the term *urbanism* a hundred
years ago), and so, in ending, I propose the following lexicographic contribution
to the great dictionary of landscape for the twenty-first century:

Suburbanism: from *suburbia* and *urbanism*. (1) The body of management
experiments and structures in landscape architecture, town planning, civil engineering, and architecture that were developed for suburbia and through which

Fig 5. *Parc du Sausset*, Villepinte. Claire and Michel Corajoud, landscape architects,
1982–1998. Photograph by Gérard Dufresne.

suburban areas have shaped their own spaces and scenographies. (2) The discipline of design practice, first inspired by suburban situations (as contexts), where the hierarchy traditionally promoted in urbanism between program and site is reversed. Instead, the site itself becomes the matter and horizon of design. (3) The hypothesis (both theoretical and critical) that views the planning process as a movement from the outside (exterior) to the inside (interior), from the surrounding milieu to the city. This historiographic approach sees previous suburban experiments, including the landscape structures and particularly their gardens, as the true laboratories for urban design and regional planning. This perspective is not necessarily exclusive of its more traditionally accepted alternative.

56

In digging below the surface, in seaming, grafting, and reclaiming hidden and latent phenomena of places, landscape architects in France are today beginning to develop increasingly discriminating modes of interpreting and constructing sites and local situations. This is the promise of a profession concerned for the development and enrichment of built communities, and it is a promise that ought to provide a source of optimism for dealing with some of the most difficult, derelict, and seemingly inchoate sites that surround all cities today everywhere. To properly reclaim and improve these sites, the first and, perhaps, only thing we need to learn is how to look at them from a different point of view.

Notes

1   I developed similar arguments to those presented in this essay in "L'alternative du paysage," *Le Visiteur* (October 1995): 54–81, English version originally published in *Het Landschap / The Landscape*, ed. K. Vandermarliere (Antwerp: Centre deSingel, 1995), 9–36, and also in "The Return of Landscape," in *Desvignes / Dalnoky* (Milan: Federico Motta Editore SpA, 1996; English edition, New York: Whitney Library of Design, 1997), 6–9.

2   Besides the creations, often private, of architects and landscape architects related to the modern movement (see Dorothée Imbert, *The Modernist Garden in France* [New Haven, Conn.: Yale University Press, 1993]), I allude to some public places, parks and gardens created by landscape architects such as Jean-Claude-Nicolas Forestier and Edouard Redont (see Cardine Stefulesco, *L'Urbanisme Vegetal* [Paris: I.D.F., 1993]) and also to the major landscape studies and plans related to the creation of new infrastructures, such as in the works of Henri Prost for the "Plan d'aménagement de la Côte d'Azur Varoise" (in the 1920s, but unrealized) or for the "L'aménagement de la regien parisieure" (in the 1930s). After World War II, the decline and marginalization of these activities became more pronounced.

3   These skills and influences were even exported to other countries. The work of Jean-Claude-Nicolas Forestier in Buenos Aires and la Habana are examples of the success of French landscape architects abroad. No doubt this success owed much to the climate of colonialism at the time, but also to the international prestige of Alphand's school.

4   In using the term *modernist* here I am not referring to the architects of the modern movement (few of whom were actually given the opportunity to fully realize their

ideas at an urban level) but rather to the coarser and more technocratic modern *doxa* on urbanism that prevailed during this time and that affirmed the primacy of new *programs* at the expense of paying the most elementary respect to *places*.

5   On the term *palimpsest*, see André Corboz, "Le territoire comme palimpseste," in *Diogene* 121 (Jan.–Mar. 1987), 14–35. See also Eugenio Turri, "Il Teatro delle Memorie," in *Il Paesaggio comme Teatro: dal territorio vissuto al territorio rappresentato* (Venezia: Massilio, 1998).

6   See Michel Corajoud, "Le paysage comme synthèse," in *Composer le paysage*, ed. Catherine Bersani (Seyssel, France: Champ Vallon, 1989).

7   This expression is used by Michel Vernes concerning the public gardens designed by Alphand in Paris in "Du Jardin de Ville à la Ville Jardin," *Pages-Paysages* 2 (1994): 24.

8   See Gaston Bardet, *Paris: naissance et méconnaissance de l'urbanisme* (Paris: S.A.B.R.I., 1951); Lewis Mumford, "From the Suburbs to the City of Tomorrow," in *The City in History: Its Origins, Its Transformations, and Its Prospects* (New York: Harcourt, Brace, and World, 1961); and Peter Rowe, *Making a Middle Landscape* (Cambridge, Mass.: MIT Press, 1991).

9   Michel Desvignes and Christine Dalnoky, "Parcours dans le Paysage des Hauts-de-Seine," *Topos* 13 (May 1994): 36.

57

Chapter 3

Four Trace Concepts in Landscape Architecture

Christophe Girot

Might landscape architecture become the one and only environmental panacea of the next century? Looking at etymology, this is what the French would like to suggest. The word *paysage* means landscape (as in land and countryside) and much more, conveying qualities that are both visible and invisible. It refers not only to issues of environment and ecology but also to the mood of an entire nation, to its changing sense of identity and cultural belonging.[1] There is thus a deep sense of temporal continuity (both historical and inventive) that pervades the idea of landscape in France.

Yet most design interventions by contemporary French landscape architects focus on environmental conservation and restoration. The work is seen as a significant ameliorator of ecological damage and urbanization. It is, therefore, not surprising to find the notion of landscape recovery central to this field of action because it implies a focus on people's concern with the quality and image of their immediate environs. It is possible, however, to broaden this sense of recovering landscape, invoking cultural and imaginative horizons rather than limiting it to strictly environmental concerns. A recent spate of design competitions and projects in France has enabled such a broader practice of landscape to be developed.

Some of the more interesting French *paysagistes* have used these opportunities to demonstrate a critical and innovative range of ideas at both local and international scales.[2] As a practitioner and teacher based in France, I am interested in those methods and techniques that might expand the landscape project beyond the simple amelioration of sites toward practices that also reactivate the cultural dimensions of sites. In particular, I am interested in how one recognizes sites through design, especially in reaction to the general state of environmental and cultural amnesia that characterizes our time.

French landscape design theory is unfortunately not at the level of the questions that are asked of practitioners today.[3] It is precisely this void, this absence of

Fig. 1. Pierrelaye, Le Parc des Six Arpents, Christophe Girot, 1990–1996. Landing: In a wasteland where there is a decrepit old wall, a breach in it could become a key element in the design of the park. The breach operates as a hinge between the old village and a new housing district. Photograph by Christophe Girot, 1990.

a clear and demonstrable theory of landscape architecture, that explains why most French practitioners have chosen a rather intuitive and experiential approach to design. The age-old opposition of nature and culture, so central to French landscape design theory since the times of Descartes and Le Nôtre, has in fact become a much more complex tangle of interrelated phenomena. Despite Alain Roger's valiant attempt to oppose the two yet again in a superb Manichean treatise on contemporary French landscape philosophy, it appears that current landscape practice in France no longer sees the relevance of such clear distinctions.[4]

In the course of my own work I have unraveled four operating concepts that serve as tools for landscape investigation and design, especially with regard to recovering sites. These I call *trace concepts* because they cluster around issues of memory: marking, impressing, and founding. They also underline the fact that a designer seldom belongs to the place in which he or she is asked to intervene. How can outsider designers acquire the understanding of a place that will enable them to act wisely and knowledgeably? This is the question my four trace concepts address; landing, grounding, finding, and founding each focus on particular gradients of discovery, inquiry, and resolution. Each concept also designates a specific attitude and action that in turn nurtures a process of design and landscape transformation.

The demonstration of the role and efficacy of trace concepts can be verified directly only in the field of action. The specific site functions like a partition or container for a muse who may, through design, reveal hidden aspects of a given place. The partition requires that the order in which the four trace concepts are presented remains unalterable. Landing, grounding, finding, and founding must follow sequentially so as to enable the site to emerge in a comprehensible manner. The primary purpose of this highly intuitive and experiential approach to working with sites is to draw as much as possible from the potential of any given place and to assess which existing landscape elements might be of real significance for the design yet to come.

The notion of a landscape element escapes precise definition. On the one hand, a site element may be a physical entity that reveals certain characteristics of the place (stonework reveals geology, weathered surfaces reveal use and climate, ruins and foundations reveal past occupation, stains reveal floods or seepage lines, and so on). On the other hand, a site element may refer to something imperceptible but nonetheless significant (a past event, a local story, or chronology, for instance). This inclusive approach enables a designer to blend direct

physical experience and intuition with local
research. The important thing is that attention is
always focused on what already exists in situ. In
this way, the designer may carefully and knowledgeably assess what really needs to be recovered
(anew) from the relentless erosion of time (Fig. 2).

Landing

Landing is the first act of site acknowledgment,
and it marks the beginning of the odyssey of the
project. Landing usually invokes displacement and change of speed (as in
arrival), but it also conveys the idea of touching ground and reaching for the
confines of an unknown world. It describes the specific moment when a
designer still does not know anything about a place and yet is prepared to
embark on a lengthy process of discovery. Landing, therefore, invokes the passage from the unknown to the known, from the vastness of the outside world to
the more exact boundaries of a specific project.

Landing thus requires a particular state of mind, one where intuitions and
impressions prevail, where one feels before one thinks, where one moves across
and stalks around before seeking full disclosure and understanding. In this
sense, landing must induce a sense of complete displacement and outsideness to
be really effective. The idea of tapping the hidden energy of a place by playing
the innocent outsider is beautifully evoked by the author François Béguin: "The
exit from the humanized world, whether voluntary or involuntary, enables the
recovery of vital forces led astray or left dormant by society."[5]

Landing refers also to the moment when a designer reacts to the difference
between his or her preconceived idea of a place and the reality that appears during the first steps of a visit. Often, one comes to a site with a set of ready-made
impressions and opinions. It is precisely this juxtaposition of preconceptions
and the act of initial discovery that may generate a fertile tension in the initial
stages of design. During landing, nothing is allowed to remain obvious or neutral to the designer; rather everything is apprehended with wonderment and
curiosity, with subjective and interpretative eyes.

Fig. 2. Pierrelaye, Le Parc des Six Arpents, Christophe Girot, 1990–1996. Landing: What could
first be perceived as the collapse of an old abandoned structure becomes a precious relic for the
future. Photograph by Christophe Girot, 1990.

61

Landing also refutes the idea of a tabula-rasa approach to site design, where nothing can be learned or retained from a given site and where everything can be resolved by detached conceptual thinking. The moment of landing is, in fact, so important that every detail, no matter how slight, counts. Even the question of how one enters the site is of prime importance. It matters, for instance, whether landing occurs "properly" through a clear and determined sense of arrival, or "improperly" by stalking across brambles, wastelands, and broken fences. The state of just-landedness is precarious, but it plays a vital role in the genesis of design. Initial landing provokes impressions and insights that often last through the entire design process.

There is almost an idea of relativity in landing; one might argue that circumstances change at every moment and that the perception of a place can never really be twice the same. The sense of entry and landing is, therefore, personal. It escapes clear scientific methodology and is almost always the result of chance. Landing is an event open to the elements and to the seasons, to all the customs and risks at large. It is, in fact, a living manifestation of the experiential potential of a site and thus has potent spatial and psychological effects on the subsequent thinking-through of the design project.

The individual's sense of landing is what matters most in the beginning, and it is precisely this ontological trust in initial intuition that needs to be restored and nurtured. By analogy, this might be compared to a first encounter with another person. It is more meaningful to engage directly with that person, through conversation and eye contact, for instance, than to spy on him or her from afar and simply gather information from other sources. In this latter instance, the final encounter with that person will carry with it many preconceptions, whereas direct and immediate engagement remains open, empathetic, and sets the stage for future dialog.

Grounding

Grounding is the second step in landscape discovery and understanding. Grounding has to do with orientation and rootedness, both in the literal and figurative sense of the word. The difference between landing and grounding is essentially linked to time and moment. Landing only happens once, at the beginning, immediate and distinct, whereas grounding recurs indefinitely. Grounding is more about reading and understanding a site through repeated visits and studies. The site contains both a residue and a promise; its surrounding context, its soil, climate, water, ecology, and history are unique and special. Thus, grounding has less to do with the individual imagination than with careful research and analysis. It is like a probe into the successive histories of a place. I cannot think of a better example than the site of the Fontaine des Innocents in Paris to illustrate this point through antithesis. This is a place that has irreparably depreciated its ground to the point of no return: its only trace of memory can be found through excavating into what few layers still remain below the ground (Figs. 3 and 4).[6]

Grounding is a process implying successive layers, both visible and invisible. Sometimes the most important aspect of a given site is almost intangible. It is not necessarily what remains visible to the eye that matters most, but those forces and events that undergird the evolution of a place.

Finding

Finding entails the act and process of searching as well as the outcome, the thing discovered. It is both an activ-

ity and an insight. What is found can result from either a surprise discovery or some painstaking, methodical quest. Thus, it is rather difficult to speak of a method of finding because different activities yield different discoveries. Such discoveries may be tangible, like a relic or a significant tree or stone, or they may be more evanescent, like the death of a significant person. What is found is the *je ne sais quoi* ingredient that conveys a distinct quality to a place. As such, findings escape design invention and import; they are something unique (though hidden) that definitely belongs to a place and contributes durably to its identity.

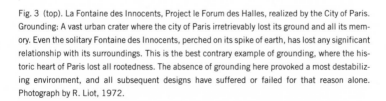

Fig. 3 (top). La Fontaine des Innocents, Project le Forum des Halles, realized by the City of Paris. Grounding: A vast urban crater where the city of Paris irretrievably lost its ground and all its memory. Even the solitary Fontaine des Innocents, perched on its spike of earth, has lost any significant relationship with its surroundings. This is the best contrary example of grounding, where the historic heart of Paris lost all rootedness. The absence of grounding here provoked a most destabilizing environment, and all subsequent designs have suffered or failed for that reason alone. Photograph by R. Liot, 1972.

Fig. 4 (bottom). La Fontaine des Innocents, Project le Forum des Halles, realized by the City of Paris. Grounding: During excavation, the ground reveals all the old layers of soil from the oldest cemetery in Paris. The old Renaissance fountain, raised on steel stilts, sits quietly inside a wooden box. Photograph by R. Liot, 1972.

The act of finding is also something that can be performed and experienced by everybody discovering a site for the first time. What people actually find can be an integral part of the landscape structure, like a breach in a forest, a fault on the side of a hill, a spring surging from the foot of a wall, a narrow street plunging down toward the sea. But finding is not limited to the discovery of objects; it also includes the experience of relating and associating ideas, places, and themes. Few projects can control and manipulate the process of finding because of the importance of chance and indeterminacy in discovery. Thus, what is found is an open question, an open possibility.

Finding is the alchemical component in the design process; it may be permanent or impermanent, the result of a fleeting vision or some resounding echo. Finding usually discloses the evidence to support one's initial intuitions about a place.

Founding

Founding is probably the most durable and significant of the four trace acts. It comes at the moment when the prior three acts are synthesized into a new and transformed construction of the site. Founding may be either conservative—referring to some past event or circumstance—or innovative—importing something new to a place. Whatever the case, the act of founding is always a reaction to something that was already there. The solution can be as ephemeral as a stage set, or it can take place gradually over an extended period of time.

Founding can be also understood as bringing something new to a place, something that may change and redirect a particular site. Examples range from the placement of a new object, to the framing of some new point of view, to simply changing the use of a particular place. Each

Fig. 5 (top). Invaliden Park, Berlin. Christophe Girot with Atelier Phusis, 1992–1997. Finding: Traces of an old military church in the trench axis of the wall. The military park of the Prussian Invalids in Berlin had several important traces to offer—unexploded bombs from the Blitz, old contorted trees from the time of Kaiser Wilhelm, huge slabs of concrete from defunct Vopos barracks, etc. But it was clearly the buried foundations of the bombed-out military church that conveyed the most fecund meaning about this site. Photograph by Christophe Girot, 1996.

Fig. 6 (bottom). Invaliden Park, Berlin. Christophe Girot with Atelier Phusis, 1992–1997. Finding: An inclined wall with a path joining the divided city glides above the ground. To find relics of the old Prussian church, one must run down the wall into the ground. The wall is an allegory of twentieth-century Berlin. Photograph by Christophe Girot, 1997.

act of founding corresponds, in archeological jargon, to an epoch—a given period in history when a cultural relationship to the landscape evolves and changes. Founding inevitably happens each time something new occurs, staking out the ground for future events. Still, it would be wrong and rather cynical to place all newly founded projects on the same level; a well-founded project remains clear in its approach and resolution, extending the legacy of a place toward a productive future.

Conclusion

Each time a landscape project begins there should follow an extended period in which one may simply discover what already exists, most of which will not be obvious or quickly ascertained. The introduction to a site project has all too often been reduced to systematic and quantitative formulas for analyzing the site from a distance. By contrast, trace concepts enable designers to come to grips

65

with their intuitions and experiences of place, allowing these impressions to direct the unfolding of the project. I am quite aware of the intrinsic limitations of this kind of approach, which might best be summed up by the statement of phenomenologist/geographer Yi-Fu Tuan that "So much emphasis can be put on the individual as maker and perceiver that the external world loses its objective standing; reality 'out there' seems to be only a human construct."[7]

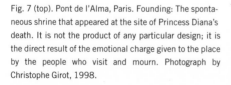
Fig. 7 (top). Pont de l'Alma, Paris. Founding: The spontaneous shrine that appeared at the site of Princess Diana's death. It is not the product of any particular design; it is the direct result of the emotional charge given to the place by the people who visit and mourn. Photograph by Christophe Girot, 1998.

Fig. 8 (bottom). Pont de l'Alma, Paris. Founding: New meaning on an old monument formerly dedicated to the Statue of Liberty. The flame monument was already there, but since the death of Princess Diana it has taken on a completely different meaning. The settling of meaning in a place sometimes completely escapes the control or intentions of a designer; sometimes it all comes down to a matter of fate. Photograph by Christophe Girot, 1998.

Augustin Berque, in his short essay on the origins of *paysage*, wrote of a similar thought:

> In this manner, European modernity looking at "nature" as an object, has torn it up into two incompatible modes: on the one hand there is what our senses reveal to us (*le paysage*), on the other there is what is to be learnt from science (*la vérité*). It is precisely this rift which still prevails today in the contradictory ambivalence of the word *paysage*.[8]

It is, therefore, most important to accept equally the two modes of thought that exist in our culture. The recovery of landscape will begin only when we are ready to reconcile our senses with our science.

Notes

1   In the introduction to his book, *Court traité du paysage*, Alain Roger underlines the articulation between the word *pays* and the word *paysage*, which is almost paralleled in English by the words *land* or *country* and the word *landscape*. I say almost, because the French words convey an aesthetic and experiential dimension that does not pertain in the English vocabulary. See Alain Roger, *Court traité du paysage* (Paris: Gallimard, 1997), 8. See also his earlier *Nus et paysages: Essai sur la fonction de l'art* (Paris: Aubier, 1978).

2   See Sébastien Marot's essay "The Reclaiming of Sites" in this collection. The most important consideration in this essay focuses on the notion of the primacy of site, which is central to the theoretical discourse most current in French landscape practice today.

3   In the introduction to their book titled *Le Jardin art et lieu de mémoire* (Besancon, France: Editions de l'Imprimeur, 1995), 17–18, Monique Mosser and Philippe Nys decry the absence of a strong body of theory in French landscape architecture and garden design today: "The prevailing absence of theory and clarity in the French world with respect to garden art today, together with the possibility that such a subject offers to the renewal of cultural meaning, is allied with a general pervasive condition of emptiness and malaise. This condition can precipitate and give rise to digressions where almost anything is allowed. Against such digression, landscape architects ought to reclaim a place they have long ago deserted: garden art. There is an urgent need to recover a distinct and renewed meaning for garden art, albeit not entirely separate from what is more generally understood as contemporary art; that is to say, the recovery of poetic meaning." (Translated by Christophe Girot.)

4   In a short treatise, Alain Roger relentlessly refutes the Germanic notion of deep ecology by means of the French notion of landscape aesthetic. See Alain Roger, "Maitres et protecteurs de la nature," in *Court traité du paysage*, 145–164.

5   Quote translated directly by Christophe Girot from the original text: "La sortie, volontaire ou involontaire, du monde humanisé conditionne la récupération de puissances vitales que la société avait détournées ou mises en sommeil." François Béguin, "Vagues, vides, verts," in *Le Visiteur N°3* (Paris: Société Française d'Architecture, 1997), 67.

6   See Christophe Girot, "La Fontaine des Innocents," in *Les Carnets du Paysage*, ed. Pierre Francoise Mourier (Arles: Actes Sud, 1998), 44–64.

7   Yi-Fu Tuan, *Segmented Worlds and Self* (Minneapolis: University of Minnesota Press, 1982), 151–152.

8   Translation directly in the text by Christophe Girot: "De ce fait, la modernité européene a déchiré 'la nature', dont elle faisait ainsi l'objet de son regard, en deux modes incompatibles: d'un côté ce que nous en révèlent nos sens (le paysage), de l'autre ce que nous en apprend la science (la vérité). C'est cette coupure qui se reflète encore aujourd'hui dans l'ambivalence contradictoire du mot 'paysage.'" Augustin Berque, "A l'origine du paysage," in *Les carnets du paysage*, ed. Pierre Francoise Mourier (Arles: Actes Sud, 1998), 137–138.

Chapter 4

Things Take Time and Time Takes Things: The Danish Landscape

Steen A.B. Høyer

The Danish cultural landscape is unique. For the most part, Denmark is a coherent and yet diverse fabric of fields, woodlands, small towns, and gentle, glacial topography bathed in changeably soft and luminous light. The character of the landscape derives not only from natural conditions but also, and perhaps in larger measure, from a collective and organized approach to its management. Since the time of the relocation of villages and the first regulations concerning forests in 1805 (Fredskovslovgivningen), subsequent legislation—Preservation Act of National Objects, 1805; Preservation Act of Natural and Historical Landscapes, 1917; and Town Development Acts, 1949 and 1969—has ensured a clear distinction between town and country. Consequently, Denmark continues to stand in a unique situation: The country enjoys a clarity of open order that expresses the Danish democratic and social tradition. Whereas many other European countries—France and Spain, for example—can boast of remarkable urban and architectural monuments, Denmark is characterized more by a synthetic and generous approach to the formation of a larger cultural landscape. In other words, space in Denmark is defined more by a collective approach to design than by authoritarian methods whereby objects are set within hierarchical and monumental urban structures.

Moreover, this uniquely Danish collective approach is profoundly influenced by a special regard for climate and weather. As Queen Margrethe II described in a recent speech, Denmark is characterized by "bicycles and buses in rain-soaked streets, woods and open fields with wind blowing from the sea." The monumental in Denmark lies in the landscape, in the meeting of light and weather with the ancient formation of the land. In describing the paintings of the Danish landscape artist Theodor Philipsen (1840–1920), Martin A. Hansen wrote, "Philipsen created a new atmospheric view; he painted cattle, for instance, as made by light and air in the humid berth of the earth."[1]

Fig. 1. East Jørlunde. Paths have crossed here since the Bronze Age. The spatial character of this landscape is, however, not only native but also global; various means define the space, from the first cultivated fields of Haydn to the F-16 fighter jet and the Tokyo stock market. A unique space, local and universal. Photograph by Steen Høyer.

As new pressures are placed on the landscape today, however, it is not at all clear how landscape architects should proceed with the design and planning of land. Since the 1960s, there has been enormous urban expansion in Denmark, with new extensive suburbs and associated infrastructure transforming the entire country. Transportation, energy, and communications infrastructures are perhaps the most significant landscape architectural features of this century. Furthermore, a shift to service economies has increased employment in urban areas, with a consequent demand for new recreational space in the countryside as traditional agriculture continues to decline. Today, the question is one of how to embrace these conditions and integrate them in a vision of the future Danish landscape.

Unfortunately, the prevalent view is that the traditional Danish landscape must be preserved rather than transformed. In this view, the landscape is a static, framed picture to be captured in the photograph, the car window, the television screen, the museum, and the tourist postcard. It is presumed that such scenic practices will ensure the continuity of Denmark's historic and national identity. In itself, this view might be thought sensible and reasonable, but a significant problem arises when contemporary, everyday modes of experiencing the land are reduced solely to the visual. The nostalgic and conservative attitude that continues to freeze the Danish landscape into scenic preserves misses a great opportunity to reshape the land as a democratic reflection of modern society and emerging conditions. Landscape ought to be treated as something to be worked with or "evolved," not held as an unchanging image.

The paradox inherent to scenic preservation is that the image to be preserved typically derives from a landscape that was once worked, productive, and transformed in practical ways. Moreover, the aforementioned planning regulations were themselves extremely forceful in changing the land, not in holding it

Fig. 2. Jammer Bay, south of Hirtshals. After a journey in glaciers of twenty thousand years across Scandinavia, granite blocks lie restfully in a weightless space. Clearly defined elements exist within a landscape that comprises many materials and processes. Each element reflects its history and, with absolute certainty, assumes a (temporary) position—a metaphoric image for landscape architecture. Photograph by Steen Høyer.

still. The scenic image stands only as a historical sign, a mere picture, while the experience of land moves from engagement and change to mere voyeurism. Today, it has become almost impossible to plan and design land for recreational or other new functions—including infrastructure—without setting these programs within a codified scene. There is little room for aesthetic invention, little room for *designing* the Danish landscape as an innovative and responsive expression of the new demands and activities placed on it.

And yet good design and planning has always properly derived from issues of practical and productive development, not from aesthetic or stylistic restrictions. We also know that as new and unusual (and sometimes shocking) landscape forms arise in response to changing needs and programs, they soon become valued as the norm. Such a process takes time, of course, and also requires visionary professionals who can look at situations in new and relevant ways and then show to others the range of possibilities. This is why designers draw so much, less for scenic representation and more for discovery and then conveyance of ideas.

The traditional Danish cultural landscape has lost much of its original symbolic value following the loss of an overall functioning structure. The question is, then, whether or not the Danish landscape, with its infinite history—from chalk to summer rain, from coast to coast—should (or can) be given a new role and identity.

The answer to this question is, on the one hand, pessimistic. The general fear of the effects that urbanization, infrastructure, recreation, and high technology might have on the traditional landscape is so pervasive that a conservative retreat into preservation is inevitable—the only prudent and safe way to go. Also, the increased priority given to urban areas results in limited public monies being spent more on the preservation of culturally historic monuments than on the everyday landscape. In effect, the landscape is increasingly neglected.

On the other hand, however, there is reason to believe in a more optimistic answer. For instance, the shift from local to global culture afforded by new economies and technologies means that people are becoming more interested in progressive approaches to the design of landscape. This is especially true when new approaches to design creatively reinterpret and extend past traditions. Moreover, new and changing forms of recreation—especially with the younger generation—place new demands on the design of landscape and hold open the possibility of real invention. Designers seem poised and ready for such a challenge, as new considerations of nonhierarchical, unified landscapes—where earth form, planting, and building are treated as mutually interactive parts of a whole experiential field—are suggestive of new theoretical and practical approaches to landscape formation. Of course, when a country can no longer afford to erect scenic pictures of long-lost landscapes, then perhaps their investment in the practical affairs of working the land in new ways might begin to assume a more important role.

Two things may have to be overcome before a new Danish landscape can be forged: One is the conservatism of administrators and land managers, and the other is the modern functionalist zoning approach to landscape planning. The first will take time and persuasion, but the second is something that many contemporary landscape architects are beginning to change. Moreover, they are doing this in ways in which the uniqueness of sites remains a central force or guide in the development of a design project. I want now to outline a number of principles around which a new approach to landscape formation in Denmark may begin to be practiced.

Specificity of Site

Traditionally, landscape architecture is the art of incorporating functional and aesthetic concerns within the peculiarities of a particular location, inherently marking the character and specificity of the time and place. The task is always the distillation of unique and individual expressions of a place and their subsequent transformation into new forms. This approach takes into consideration the dynamism of both the natural and cultural worlds as the logical evolution of time, materials, spaces, structure, light, and color.

Of course, every site is already unique. The topography, surface material, scale, and light peculiar to a particular place creates a special character. This character is built up in layers—from the bedrock, through chalk and clay sediments, to the Ice-Age deposits of stone and gravel that have been subject to the influences of climate and the actions of human settlement for centuries. These endless combinatorial possibilities provide the basis for the essential to be deduced. Local conditions of material, light, space, and structure ought to inspire and generate new forms of design as needs and desires change.

Fig. 3. Nordok. Landscape, building, and function literally meld as one ensemble, with a clarity one wishes were integral to every work. A simple set of demands realized beautifully as an architectonic space, where both simplicity and complexity are the norm. Photograph by Steen Høyer.

72

In Denmark, climate and local conditions vary significantly, even across relatively small distances. Wind direction and strength varies, as does the character and type of precipitation. Environmental and human factors can cause significant changes in vegetation and ecology, and it ought to be no surprise that many types of plant communities long considered traditionally Danish were actually imported. Even in Hans Christian Andersen's story "The Tinderbox," the poplar trees in the hollows where the witch hides were in fact imported from Canada. Similarly, the rose-hip bushes on summer beaches were introduced in the middle of the nineteenth century from temperate Japan to help stabilize the dunes. And, of course, the cooperative movement founded by the brewmaster Jacobsen (the founder of Carlsberg Beer) transformed the agricultural landscape into fields of barley. So, the character of a specific place is not necessarily native or unchanging but rather always subject to evolution and human agency.

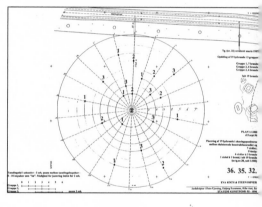

Perhaps the one ingredient of the Danish landscape that is uniquely native is its quality of light. The Danish light is special in its cool, Nordic character, even though it varies considerably from locality to locality. Surrounded by water and featuring a damp climate, this kingdom of islands is bathed not only in a soft light with many middle tones but also in a particularly intense light that is experienced most clearly on the coastal spits and peninsulas. Here, light

Fig. 4 (top). Plan, *Sculpture of Earth and Light*, Esbjerg Airport, Jutland, Denmark. Steen Høyer and Eva Koch, 1995–1998. Along a major road running to Esbjerg airport, this 30-hectare site is intended for both individual walks and large-scale events. The project comprises a 30-meter-high dome-shaped hill, covered with heather and speckled with circular lights in its surface; a 700-meter-long embankment, up to 6 meters high, with a horizontal crown; and serial rows of poplars that lend structure to a commercial development area. Legend: (1) Domed Hill, (2) Embankment, (3) Hedgerows, (4) Express Road, (5) Service, (6) Local Roads, (7) Airport.

Fig. 5. Plan of hill, *Sculpture of Earth and Light*. Steen Høyer and Eva Koch, 1995–1998.

reflected from two surfaces of water is refracted by the water particles in the atmosphere. This diffuse light acquires further complexion as rain-filled cloud formations move slowly across the horizon. The experience of such conditions can sometimes appear overwhelmingly monumental in the open, lightly overcast landscape, especially at places such as Vestamager and Asnaes.

Local phenomena such as light, weather, topography, horizon, and earth provide clues for how we might create new landscapes on the basis of what exists in a given location. One need not resort to stylized references from the past nor to wholesale renovation. Instead, the designer can draw from the specificity of what is given and what has past to project new futures based on the requirements of a brief or program.

Space as Strategy

A second attitude to invoke with regard to the development of new landscapes is the primacy accorded to space, and specifically to space as a strategic organization of new conditions, *not* space as a stylistic genre.[2] If one takes architectural experiences at their face value, as experiences and not as historical or textual references, then a vast wealth of architectural means are at one's disposal. From dense and closed to light and open, or from forests of columns, through massive

Fig. 6 (top). View of hill, *Sculpture of Earth and Light*. Steen Høyer and Eva Koch, 1995–1998. The focus of the project is not on the composition of forms but rather the interaction among the three horizons: (1) the lower penetration of the horizontal embankment, (2) the spherical horizon of the domed hill, and (3) the passing horizon of time from highway to town, agriculture, and the Northern Sea. Photograph by Steen Høyer.

Fig. 7 (bottom). View through embankment, *Sculpture of Earth and Light*. Steen Høyer and Eva Koch, 1995–1998. Photograph by Steen Høyer.

walls and squares, to tree-lined avenues, plantations, cuttings, and mirrors, the legacy of spatial design as experiential milieu is both rich and life-enriching.

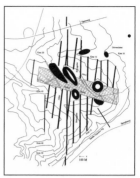

It is not a new design style that is needed today but rather a change in attitude and approach to building and to the integration of landscape into the city. Such integration can occur at many different scales, from garden to square to countryside. What is important is that this integration gives independence and presence to the experiential quality of landscape and architecture while allowing these constructions to change and adapt over time. In this scheme, a building is no longer simply sited to respect a particular view or to lean sculpturally on a slope but rather to establish a new and reciprocal mirroring of certain conditions. For instance, the summerhouse of Alvar Aalto, built in 1952 in the forest of Muuratsalo, is a formation born of local space and natural process; one must pass through a sequence of constructions to end at a fireplace built in the open courtyard. The house is never visible as an object but rather must be engaged in the cycles of nature. A similar example of mirroring local conditions is Sverre Fehn's Nordic Pavilion in Venice (1958–1962), which presented an open structure of space as a symbol of Nordic light and landscape.

Surface as Strategy

The surface as bearer of elements is the key strategic field on which landscapes may be organized and designed. It is on the surface that objects and spaces are crystallized in relationship to the surrounding forces of the place. Here, vegetation and building material, sky and earth, support one another and combine into a single, interactive entity. Albeit in different ways, such conditions can be seen in some traditional villages and in manor houses and their adjoining grounds. The scale is greater today, of course, and the systems of organization more complex, but inspiration still is drawn from the ground below the surface: from the geology, the light, the history, the depths of place and time. The weight of a building, the visibility across the horizon, the safe, cozy corner, and the June

Fig. 8. Plan, new housing project. Steen Høyer with Emma Hessner, 1998. A framework of allées is planted on the surface of 300 hectares of rolling chalk hills in the middle of Denmark. This structure provides a frame for housing and services without prescribing the specific form or layout of the housing. A large central area preserves a common of open space, with groves of forest shrouding dark, interior pools.

75

snowstorm of cherry-tree blossom—these conditions, and more, provide meaningful anchors in space and time.

Things Take Time

It is difficult to fully understand the present. One can never explain it properly, and it is difficult to see it all clearly. The present is experienced through all of the senses and interpreted primarily through instinct and intuition. Historically, it takes two or three generations before an idea (or a thing) is understood and accepted in society. New ideas and things often appear strange and different when they are first projected, but is this not exactly what is characteristic of a break with the past, the constancy that, paradoxically, comes before, during, and after canonization by the history of art?

76

Designers must, therefore, always anticipate varying degrees of *slowness* in both the practice and reception of their work. One trusts that things will change positively and that hopes and dreams provide wondrous shortcuts to new realities that the rational intellect denies. Inherent to the cultivation of hopes and dreams is an optimism, an openness, and a playful sense of possiblities.

The aforementioned themes are what I search for in my own projects, irrespective of whether they are new landscapes, land-art constructions, gallery installations, or drawings. The projects are created according to the place, the surroundings, and the circumstances, especially as these inform and interact with new content and materials. At the same time, I strive for the minimal definition of a formal order in the spatial expression as well as the greatest common denominator in the use of materials. Such economy determines the content of a work and, in part, deals with the question of making a mark in nature that is of our time.

Theories, projects, and interpretations are independent and unequal. In the best situations, however, they all come into play and interact in often fortu-

Fig. 9 . Ølst clay fields. Plastic, sea-bed sediments of clay with siliceous algae form Denmark's thickened surface. An advanced, ecological raw material, created over 50 million years ago, this muddy field provides a mirror of the past in the highly technological present day. In terms of breadth of scale in both time and dimension, we see here a landscape architectural *place*. Photograph by Steen Høyer.

itously productive ways. The making of a project, though, is a purely intuitive process, a kind of analogical creativity where words and reasons are often inadequate to the task, perhaps even to the point of distraction. And besides, regardless of the process of making, the built project always escapes intention—it comes to determine its own existence, with its own purpose and its own history. Things may indeed take time in the Danish landscape, but time inevitably also takes things.

Notes

1   Martin Hansen, *Dansk Vejr* (Copenhagen: Hasselbalch, 1953).
2   See Marlene Hauxner, "Parks Ideology in Denmark Today," in *Topos*, 19 (1997): 38–44; and Sven Ingvar Andersson, *Sven Ingvar Andersson: Anthology* (Copenhagen: Arkitektens Forlag, 1994).

Chapter 5

Shifting Sites: The Swiss Way, Geneva

Georges Descombes

My attitude toward intervening in the landscape circles around paying attention to that which one would like to be present where no one expects it any more. Thus, for me, to recover something—a site, a place, a history, or an idea—entails a shift in expectation and point of view (Fig. 1).

My work is essentially about achieving such shifts in complexity with minimum means.[1] I aim to discover all that is possible to accomplish when an occasion is offered or created—discovering, in the process, all that I did not know before. Thus, I aim for a precision of disposition, articulation, arrangement—*architecture*—so that a preexisting place can be found, disturbed, awakened, and brought to presence. I try to achieve an architecture of place, a construction that jolts its context, scrapes the ordinariness of a situation, and imposes a shift on what seems the most obvious. I hope that my work acts as a device for the revealing of forces that are (or have become) imperceptible, for generating a feeling of oddness, creating a source of different attention, a different vision, a different emotion. For me, the essential difficulty of landscape intervention is how to make certain forces conspicuous and, hence, how to make new forms, to create new feelings and associations.

In recent years I have become increasingly interested in movements and shifts of territory, specifically *landscape* experiences more than the apparent fixity of buildings and objects. I have therefore come to consider my work in provisional terms, as speculative constructions that are produced and transformed through continual reshaping processes: weather, seasons, light, growth, erosion, deposition.

If I spend time and energy investigating the traces that exist on a given site, it's certainly not for any archaeological purpose; I have never been particularly interested in reconstructing a historical lineage. Instead, I regard these remainders as manifestations of dynamics generated by different sources, forces, activities, events, and actors. This process never ends, and one ought to appreciate all the possible future developments that are already inscribed in the land, lying

79

Fig. 1. *Chanzeli*, a belvedere along the Swiss Way. Georges Descombes, 1991. Photograph by Georges Descombes.

latent, or fallow. The dynamic mapping of these routes and traces at different periods allows me to understand the shifts and modifications of sites-in-time.

My main interest, however, moves from the trace at one moment—as memorial—to the recognition of changes in time and future potential. Consequently, I believe that both buildings and designed landscapes must not only make the passing of time visible but also make this passage *effecting* of further potential.

The architecture that is necessary to mark and make possible such shifts must be more than visual. For me, a haptic, kinesthetic approach to design is essential for any deep form of site appreciation. Consequently, I try to mark the differentiations of a given situation through the use of changes in position, light, material, density, intensity, and geometry, embracing all of the geological, morphological, vegetal, animal, and human-made dimensions of a place. Certain elemental gestures seem to reflect relationships and concentrate them into their absolute essence. It is absurd that artists like Richard Serra have to remind architects that the human body should be the central point of reference in architecture, that a step is determined by the human stride, that tactility—touch—is important.

One has to remember, of course, that the routes and traces across a given site are as much mental constructions in their reality as they are material. Thus, my work is aimed at restructuring an imaginative sense of place as much as its physical experience. I believe that any environmental intervention is a creative cultural act that ought to be part of the history and future of the site and the lives of its occupants. It is not only terrain that changes with time but also the way people perceive it. This is why design is about *ideas* as much as it is concerned with material and space.

In the project for the Swiss Way, my aim was to make present and sensible an ever-changing net of paths, routes, traces, and possibilities—to make manifest the sheer complexity of the territory and to avoid the desperate reduction and negation of experience that plagues contemporary planning operations. I believe that we must vehemently resist any form of oversimplification of nature and landscape; our logic and imagining for future settlement cannot be allowed to be predetermined by the planners' formulaic equations and their neatly packaged prototype solutions. As a participant in such resistance, I like the idea of discrete, tactical operations over the clumsy "totality" of the master plan. I believe that the largest of territories can be irreducibly restructured through small, laconic interventions as opposed to the unbearable excess of everything—objects, forms, materials.

The Swiss Way

The Swiss Way is a creation comprising sections of pathway that link to form a continuous path around Lake Uri (Fig. 2). It is about 35 kilometers long and is characterized by altitude variations of about 400 meters. The path was conceived to mark the 700th year of the Confederation of Switzerland in 1991. The idea for the path was initiated by Peter Lanz and Stefan Rotzler, who saw the project as a kind of ecological counterpoint to the more grandiose projects that celebrated the same anniversary.

81

The path begins in the Rutli alpine meadow in canton Uri, where the Confederation is said to have been founded in 1291, and it ends in Brunnen, in canton Schwyz. Each of Switzerland's twenty-six *"state"* cantons is allocated a section of the path corresponding to its order of entry into the Confederation and proportional to its share of the Swiss population. The cumulative result is a simple footpath, newly laid out in parts, with a range of facilities and artistic features.

I was invited in 1987 by the canton of Geneva to design a 2-kilometer walking path for the section of the Swiss Way between Morschach and Brunnen. I collaborated with artists Richard Long, Carmen Perrin, and Max Neuhaus (Fig. 3). An earlier competition had solicited proposals for this path, but I found all of these pretentious and overwrought, somehow showcasing the wealth and prestige of Geneva rather than deriving sources of inspiration from the site itself. We therefore took a different approach. We saw the path as a way of researching the landscape, of experimenting with alternately big and little things with the often overlooked and neglected—blades of grass, flowers, stones, tree roots, small streams, and so on. I recognized early on that I could not carry out the practice of building that I was accustomed to; this place demanded a totally different attitude.

Landscape is never finished or completed, like a can of preserves; it is an accumulation of events and stories, a continuously unfolding inheritance.

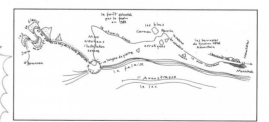

Fig. 2 (top). View of Lake Uri. Photograph by Georges Descombes.

Fig. 3 (bottom). Sketch plan of the Swiss Way, Geneva path section. Georges Descombes, 1991.

I wanted to amplify this aspect of landscape, to begin something that was already there. At the same time, I wanted to avoid pretentious references; I wanted to build a semantic void, allowing walkers to interpret their experiences however they saw fit.

I began thinking about the project by walking again and again around the site. I spent an enormous amount of time simply looking at things. I tried to look out for things that we normally do not see, such as flowers and mice, and anything else that moves around covertly, with the wish to remain undisturbed. At the same time, I wanted to leave a mark of our own time, to overlay an unequivocal trace of our activity. In other words, I wanted to respect the nature of the site and its history, but without nostalgia, without sentimentality.

Thus, we decided not to put anything on the path that was not already there. We wanted to emphasize its inherent qualities while revealing hidden ones. A typical architectural assumption is that one always adds something to a place. We chose to do exactly the opposite; we took things away. We took away all that was wrong—picturesque frames, bad kitsch constructions, and overgrown areas. Everything we needed was already there, and it was our job simply to find and re-present these features through a discreet architecture. Thus, we sought to clarify the landscape, to amplify its character through subtraction and modest—though highly calculated—intervention (Fig. 4).

In Godard's film *Lettre à Freddy Buache*, the director embarks on a long exploration into the people and places of Lausanne, looking into the details and small moments of everyday life. One can also dream up an architectural project that shows these characteristics and that, above all, gives this same emotion. On the other hand, however, the structuralists thought that in order to understand a system, it first had to be disturbed. From the way a system rearranges itself after disturbance, we can learn a lot about its nature. In landscape architectural terms, a precise and targeted intervention suffices. Thus, we did not wish to cover the field with research and analytical procedures but rather to partially disturb its organization so as to both discover and appreciate its essence. We also wanted to use this strategy to renew the emotions of the people who were going to walk on it—to draw their attention to

Fig. 4. Path in woods with steel drain detail. Georges Descombes, 1991. Photograph by Georges Descombes.

*leading the visitor through
their own adventure
imperceptibly*

the magic of the everyday. The issue is not nature education or environmental moralizing, however. I wanted walkers to be attracted by the things themselves and not by the instructions. I made every effort to replace explicit signs with some kind of imaginary thread, something that is picked up at regular intervals.

The contributions of my collaborators were immeasurable. First, the artists raised incredibly provocative and challenging questions. Whenever I decided something, I wondered what they might think of it. I enjoyed their responsiveness, their quickness of insight and unique perspective. The scientists were also of invaluable import. Some obvious particulars demanded the cooperation of a botanist, for instance (the forest—its herbs, flora, and ecology—are evidence of an extremely rich and diverse environment). Through the insights of ecologists, we learned a great deal about the interdependency of life-forms across the site, and how we might intensify the perception of these living entities through careful design strategies. Input from historians and geographers helped us to understand the thickness of the site's cultural legacy. We learned of the iconographic significance these glacial valleys have long held for the sense of Swiss nationhood. Maurice Pianzola, curator of the Museum of Art and History in Geneva, evoked the battles that were staged in this region. His words "so many footsteps" put the feeling of quiet and harmony provided by this peaceful nature spot today into a completely different perspective for me.

the value of an inter- disciplinary approach

83

All of these insights helped us to gain a better understanding of the place. They enabled us to determine the following principles: (1) Add nothing new to the existing confusion of the site. (2) Amplify certain potentials of the place, and (3) Respond economically to functional requirements—namely, guaranteed route, views, and safety. For instance, at the junction of the Neuchâtel section, in order to link the old railway track to the lower path, we constructed steps to bridge the differences in altitude (Fig. 5). Here we have three distinguishable elements: the railway, the route, and the steps. This connection is the link that permits interpretation. The railway climbs, the route climbs, and I chose to connect them by a straight, level line that is also a single step. The horizontal of this step-line measures the two slopes and their difference. Moreover, the steps are dimensioned so that they can be used as seats, to sit on and from which to look out across the landscape. The cows grazing like staggered figures on the slopes also form steps. The outcome—man-cow-terrain—is simply clarified and expressed by means of a playfully found geometrical coincidence.

guiding principles

an artistic approach

This procedure of clarification is echoed by Carmen Perrin's cleaning of glacial boulders—erratics—deposited during the last glaciation. Here, Perrin

removed the grass, lichen, and moss to reveal the stark white granite below, thus demonstrating the foreign and displaced nature of the boulders, their odd pattern of distribution, and their relative newness to the site (Fig. 6). *subtracting method*

My own interventions sought a similar clarity. I wanted to denaturalize any reading of the site. For instance, many well-meaning people wanted to have the metal drainage culverts that forest workmen had installed be quaint stone gullies of the domestic garden type. I wanted to avoid such rusticated ideas. I wanted to question attitudes such as "that's the way it's always been," to challenge "the normal way of doing things" by making changes and shifting the emotional accent. Hence, old stone borders were repaired where necessary with concrete slabs, old railing was extended with galvanized tubing, and old wooden treads were lengthened with metal steps. All modifications were thereby marked and the tectonic qualities of contemporary materials and assembly unequivocally expressed.

I am reminded of Aalto here, who knew how to give terrain and buildings a deep sense of place. Aalto often applied the simple techniques of gardeners: the system of osier revetment, for example. But he did so in the spirit of all his work—in search of a new, modern industrialized beauty rooted in place and circumstance.

At one extremity of the path, I constructed a circular, metallic structure, a belvedere, the *Chanzeli* (Fig. 7). This construction contrasts strongly with the natural context of the forest in which it rests. In an essay discussing the project, André Corboz says that the object *belvedere* is a place where you come and verify that the landscape really looks like a postcard.[2] The belvedere was integral to the nineteenth century's "invention of paradise," which was linked to new developments in tourism in the Alps. Our belvedere is situated on a vertiginous cliff, 150

Fig. 5 (top). Steps in hillside connecting path to railway tracks. Georges Descombes, 1991. Photograph by Georges Descombes.

Fig. 6 (bottom). Cleaned glacial boulder. Carmen Perrin, 1991. Photograph by Georges Descombes.

meters above the lake. I not only created a vantage point where one did not exist before but also amplified what already existed and highlighted its features. A circularity was already inscribed in this place, and I tried to concentrate this perception. In the direction of the lake, I cut an opening in the cylinder wall to make the postcard. By incurving this frame, the window is projected behind the viewer. The frontal postcard turns out to be a diorama.

The *Chanzeli* holds a great presence over the site; it is 16 meters in diameter and 9 meters high. But it is also light and transparent, soft in its embrace and playful in its interpretation. It thus summarizes our relationship with the path and its surroundings, and it does not deny a critical and inventive stance toward the Swiss landscape.

A further intervention was made not on the land but on the printed page. We published a small book on the path, with text, maps, and pictures.[3] I would love for this book to become a *mille-feuille* of emotions. Both the actual path and the book would function in the same way, using different materials. You can imagine that certain walkers would not consult it; others, who are not able to come to Morschach, will never see the path other than through the book; yet others will browse through the book during their walk. I find it completely satisfying that all of these attitudes are possible.

Through inscribing a project on the memory of a terrain, one gives to a site the opportunity to project into the future, to find a renewed place and value in the cultural imagination. To design for sites with this principle in mind is to perform an action that allows for reflection on totally ordinary matters—a shift in sensibility. Perhaps the matters that are not noticed are those that are essential.

Notes

I would like to thank James Corner for his helpful advice and comments.

1   See Giordana Tironi, ed., *Georges Descombes: Shifting Sites* (Roma: Gangemi Editore, 1988).

2   André Corboz, "Au fil de chemin," in Raymond Schaffert and Georges Descombes, eds., *Voie Suisse: l'itinéraire genevois—De Morschach à Brunnen* (Geneva: République et Canton de Genève, 1991), 121–157.

3   Ibid.

Fig. 7. Aerial view of *Chanzeli*. Georges Descombes, 1991. Photograph by Georges Descombes.

Chapter 6

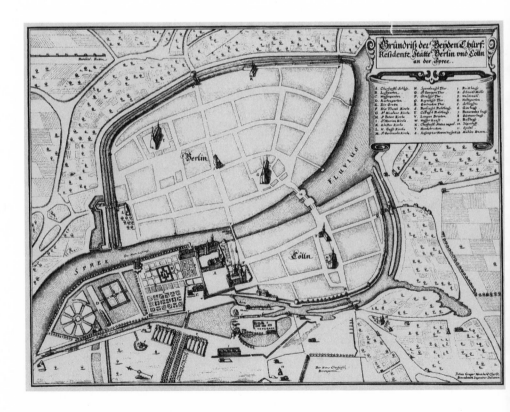

Octagon: The Persistence of the Ideal

Alan Balfour

What follows are images of one place but many realities—some intended, some created by catastrophe, some the byproducts of expediency. They are evidence of the shifting nature of the landscape of the city.[1] Layer upon layer, these images represent the succession of projects placed in a small area at the center of Berlin, land touched by the most significant events in the city's modern history. The site comprises two plazas: Leipziger Platz, formed out of eighteenth-century idealism (it was at first named to match its octagonal form), and Potsdamer Platz, out of the forces of mechanization. Taken together, these urban landscapes point to what ultimately persists in public space while everything else changes. They are living instances of the cycles of recovery, from periods of neglect to those of renewal.

The 1652 Johan Greger map of Berlin is a revealing document of a city in transition (Fig. 1). At the center, a river separates two cities. The more ancient on the left, Coln, was first named in documents in 1237, eight years before the first mention of the city on the right, Berlin. The river is the Spree. In medieval theocracy, all order radiated from God, reflected here in the concentric streets surrounding the great churches, all secure behind the defensive wall. Nowhere within the medieval imagination was it possible to idealize the profane and earthly realm. The medieval mind took great interest in plants but placed no sacred value on landscape. Introversion and introspection were demanded by a church whose deepest belief was that existence in the present was a mere shadow of the promised life in the City of God. Outside the city walls, land was made productive as needed, but beyond that lay the disordered and dangerous underworld of the wilderness, a place to be feared. Apart from the harmonic plantings in the kitchen gardens of the monasteries and in the country houses of the aristocracy, landscape as an ideal did not exist.

On the map, the great rectilinear masses of the ducal palace demonstrably mark a worldly consciousness. The Lustgarten, immediately north of the palace, is a sequence of regimented gardens laid out with carpets of carefully pruned plantings creating variety and incident along major axes. The gardens

Fig. 1. The City of Berlin in 1652, Johan Gregor Memhardt.

give the palace status within the city and a stage for courtly ritual. The combination of garden and palace on the map is so clearly an intrusion on the introverted order of the medieval city that it dramatizes the opposing views of reality held by the bishops of the church and the court of the Hohenzollerns.[2] Here, an earthly power that would change all reality is asserted. Its most visible expression is the imposition of enlightened order on the land: land ordered to enhance the power of the court, ordered to decorate courtly ritual and ceremonial performance. Here, nature is a component of deliberately constructed reality. Here is the first evidence of consciously formed city landscape.

West of the Palace lay another, quite different garden, one that would soon merge with the Lustgarten to form the idea of landscape in the city. These two gardens have separate but equally elemental and ancient qualities. Lustgarten—literally, "pleasure garden"—was the name given to the formal gardens of the palace, and Tiergarten—"garden of beasts"—was the deer and hunting park. The Tiergarten had for centuries been the game preserve for the royal hunt, a performance as much to do with the experience of landscape as with the chase. Such close proximity of closely managed lands of artificial wilderness exactly at the city's edge subsequently dramatized the benefits and pleasures at the conjunction of the natural and artificial. The first extension of courtly order beyond the walls of the city grew out of the desire to link the Tiergarten with the Lustgarten. This was achieved by planting linden trees in a regimented grove running obliquely from the main facade of the palace to the park (lower left on the map). The path was set by the glancing view of the hunting grounds from the great public rooms of the palace. Yet, this casually established axis set down the framework that was to govern the following hundred years in the expansion of the Enlightened City.

The second plan, engraved in 1737 (Fig. 2), is powerful evidence of centuries of violent change and transformation. (Its orientation is the reverse of the earlier map, south at the top and west on the right.) Depicted here is a number of large territories, each with distinct political, physical, and metaphysical attributes. These enlightened orders were first applied to the city toward the end of the seventeenth century, informed and inspired by intellectual advances in mathematics, reason, and instrumentality. The first phase, Dorotheenstadt (named after the queen), was developed on both sides of the linden trees, now Unter den Linden (clearly evident on the west side of the map). Unter den Linden evolved into a promenade framed by elegant houses and gardens built along the edge of the grove. Although still within the great fortifications, the area pro-

jected an almost rural character, distinct
from other parts of the city.

A significantly enlightened imagination led to the construction of the vast
fortifications that surrounded the old
city. Comprising thirteen wedged bas-
tions with concentric walls and moats,
these defenses were built in reaction to
acute insecurity felt throughout the
towns and cities of Europe following the
Thirty Years War. There was a sense of

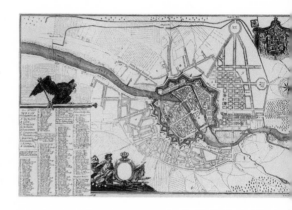

danger from all directions—in the west, militaristic and expansionist France;
the north, a surprisingly aggressive Sweden; and south and east, fear that the
army of the Ottoman Empire would return to claim Europe for Islam. Building
such ambitious fortifications allowed the advancement of skills in engineering
and large-scale construction. This, in turn, allowed the court to manifest its
absolute power and authority. Consider this map as an expression of a city under
stress, a peculiar mix of insecurity and idealism. The insecurity leads the city to
defend itself behind a spiked wall of defenses, which in the southwest are
quickly torn down to make way for a new order in building the Enlightened
City. From the map, one can almost sense the desire for a new order bursting out
of the medieval shell.

The second phase was laid out to the west of the walled city toward the end
of the seventeenth century. Planned, designed, and executed by the soldiers of
the prince under Dutch[3] engineers, an unrelieved grid was imposed on the new
city, named Sud Friedrichstadt. Here, the absolute authority of the court is
explicit. The city was laid out as a frame within which the landed nobility of
Prussia would live while serving the court. It was the mechanism by which the
duke maintained the allegiance and the support of his aristocracy. Visitors to the
city were critical of its lack of charm, however.

The Octagon was created in the last of the three phases of construction of
the Enlightened City. This last phase is visible on the west of the city map, and
its construction enlarges the idea of landscape in the city in distinct ways. The
octagonal plaza was laid out in 1736, again with the help of Dutch engineers. By
this time the German Enlightenment was anxious to rival the rest of Europe,

Fig. 2. The City of Berlin in 1737, G. Dusableau. Original: Deutsche Staatsbibliothek, Berlin.

particularly France, and these ambitions led to the creation of several new grand avenues and the provision of three new gates into the city, expanding the city south and west. The wall, which a hundred years before defended the city from attack in every direction, had become a device to regulate and tax trade between the county and the city.[4] Still, this expansion resulted in the creation of three imposing entries into the new districts of the city. From north to south, they were the square now called Pariserplatz, by the Brandenburg Gate, the Octagon of the Leipziger Platz, and the Rondel, at what is now Hallesch Tor.

These entry areas were shaped to be both militarily useful and symbolically impressive, rivals to the great spaces of Paris. Frederick the Great, on his way to and from his favorite palace of Sans Souci, could pass through his own version of Mansard's octagonal Place Louis le Grand (now known as Place Vendôme). The gateways were the result of provincial envy, but they represented the ambition to enlarge the idea of ordered reality from the merely enlightened to the cosmological. While these simple figures on the land have survived extremes of devastation, they have persisted in ordering various futures unrelated to any notion of metaphysics.

The last phase of the expansion not only made palpable the power and the formality of Enlightenment but also marked an increasing divide between the order of the city and the order of the countryside. As did other areas of Europe, Prussia's population was mainly rural and existed in a state of servitude to the landed aristocracy. Movement was restricted and landlords had the power of life and death over their peasantry. The conscious use of rational order, most obviously manifest in the design of urban layout and building, underlay all institutions and practices of the court. Where previously the Church had created common values and principles that made no extreme distinction between congregations, the enlightened order of the court increasingly emphasized the difference between burgher and peasant.

The Octagon was a first mark of modernism. Its presence framed the disturbances in the imagination of the culture between the end of the eighteenth and the beginning of the nineteenth century. In its space, the two most gifted court architects, Friedrich Gilly and Karl Friedrich Schinkel, teacher and pupil, conceived of monuments to inspire the idea of nationhood. Gilly, the most prescient modernist of his age, prepared a drawing for the same site in 1793 (Fig. 3). The plan for an elliptical forecourt and the Octagon can be seen on the right. At the center, a structure immortalizes Frederick the Great. For Gilly, the hero had to become a god and be housed in a temple to rival the ancients. Starkly white, the monument would have risen majestically over the walls of the Octagon. All such eighteenth-century desires were crushed, however, in the wake of Napoleon's aggression. Napoleon and his forces entered and occupied Berlin in 1807, mortifying German pride.

In 1817, aristocratic Europe united to crush Napoleon. Karl Friedrich Schinkel, the most favored architect of the court of the liberal Friedrich Wilhelm III, was asked to create a monument that would celebrate the victory and renew faith in the destiny of the German people. Schinkel conceived of a monstrous and disturbing cathedral of national unity, a vast series of assembly halls out of which would emerge a traced spire one thousand feet high. The concept was drawn from Goethe, who saw the cathedral of Strasbourg as the physical embodiment of the idea of the German people. For Schinkel, the tower was the race: one powerful, directed whole formed from myriad parts. By such an instrument, a

91

people would be united and a whole German nation formed. In the 1820s, Schinkel wrote that "no omissions must arise in the progress of an active state. As a result of such omission barbarism will again gain entry to the culture."[5] Omission for Schinkel was failure to build the monument and thereby failure to establish the idea.

This brief period of intense romanticism quickly passed and, in 1824, Schinkel created a modest entry to the city in the form of two small temples at the Potsdam Gates. The view from the gates suggests that nineteenth-century Berlin would have no great ambition beyond the petit bourgeois. In the center of the Octagon, his colleague, the landscape architect Peter Joseph Lenne, created a small *volkspark*, or "people's park." This was a simple landscape that reflected a changing political mood. Thus, a restrained park and gates stood in place of Schinkel's monolithic cathedral of national unity.

Barely fifteen years later, in 1838, a much more lasting revolution changed the order of Leipziger Platz. Along the trade wall and crossing in front of the Potsdam Gates came the first train. The city moved rapidly from the project of

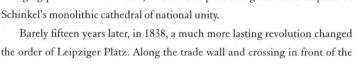

Fig. 3. Monument to Frederick the Great, Friedrich Gilly, 1793. From Friedrich Gilly, *Weidegeburt der Architectur* (Berlin: Hans von Hugo Verlag, 1940).

the Enlightenment to the project of industry and commerce. Immediately to the west of the Octagon, a new place emerged out of the needs of machines and industry: the city's first railway station. This was a pragmatic place, while the Octagon maintained the rational order of the eighteenth century.

In 1900, the gates that had sat at the fissure between the eighteenth and nineteenth centuries were poised to confront the twentieth century. Potsdamer Platz welcomed transformation (Fig. 4). It was the hub of a new city of trolley cars, apartment buildings, and the stores that carried the products from the factories to the people. The city had moved far from the clear, idealized landscapes of the Enlightenment to the disordered, expedient, and uncertain project of industry and modernity. The gates still stood between aristocratic rationalism and relative sprawl of industry, railways, canals, and factories. Within such division, of course, came increasing conflict between the urban peasants, brought in by the railroad to serve industry, and the new mercantile bourgeoisie.

In 1930, the city's most successful architect of the mercantile class, Eric Mendelsohn, contemplated the design for an office building on Potsdamer Platz. He created an extraordinary building, the most progressive in the city: Columbus Haus, in praise of America, complete with a five-and-dime store. In preparing the work, Mendelsohn made a drawing extending the form of Columbus Haus to the Octagon and to the adjoining roads to the west. The drawing appears to seek a cleansing of reality, stripping the building of the marks of history to prepare for a new beginning. Columbus Haus was completed within months of Adolf Hitler's rise to power, and immediately Mendelsohn left Germany with his family forever. Six years later, Hitler and his architect Albert Speer began to form a different idea of a city.

In 1940, a model was built depicting the grand north-south axis that would reorient the city of Berlin (Fig. 5). Even into the last year of the war, this project dominated Hitler's imagination and drove his belief in the justice of his cause. It is the landscape of a megalomaniac. In victory, Hitler planned to rebuild Berlin as the eternal city, the successor to Rome. He would take idealism out of the hands of the bourgeoisie and place it in the dreams of the people, the *volk*. In their name, the new Berlin would halt the decline of the West and provide a

thousand years of stability and world order. At the
model's center is Speer's translation of Hitler's
1924 drawing of the Grosshalle (the great hall), the
pantheon, as indestructible as an act of nature, one
thousand feet high. The oculus is the same diameter as the dome of Saint Peter's and the hall large
enough to contain more than a quarter of a million
people. Along the great axis is a triumphal arch.
Hitler anticipated the need for such a monument to
confirm victory and carry the names of the millions
who would have to die for the cause. Millions died,
and Berlin was decimated.

At the end of the World War II, Leipziger Platz
was gutted by bombing, although the shells of
buildings had sufficient volume to maintain the
form of the Octagon. The city was still active, and
business and marketing took place under
makeshift umbrellas and awnings. The old
volkspark in the middle was turned into what
Americans called *victory gardens*. Berlin was an
occupied city, divided between the four conquering
powers: to the west, the United States, Britain, and
France, and, to the east, Russia. Leipziger Platz lay
at the very edge of the Russian sector, the British
sector beginning just in front of the ruins of
Schinkel's gates.

Even in ruins, the Octagon held its ideal form. Unconscious landscapes
were formed out of these ruins. It was by both chance and convenience that the
dividing line between the eighteenth- and nineteenth-century city became the
border between the Russian and British sectors in the division of the occupied
city. East Berlin's discomfort with socialism flared in the riots of 1953 and Russian tanks showed their force in public spaces (Fig. 6).

Fig. 5 (top). Model of the New Berlin, Adolf Hitler and Albert Speer, 1943. Source: Lamdesbildstelle.

Fig. 6 (bottom). Russian tanks quell the worker revolt in the spring 1953, here seen at the limits of
their authority, at the border with the allied city by the gates to Leipziger Platz. Source: Lamdesbildstelle.

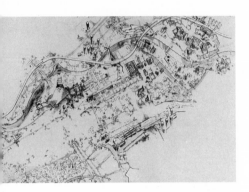

Ten years following the war's end, the swath of land between the Russians and the Allies simply withered. In 1957, a Western-sponsored design competition was held to draw world attention to Berlin and keep alive in the West a desire for the reunification of Germany. What form in landscape could give life to this dying place? One answer came from Hans Scharoun, who proposed strange and powerful visions for the rebuilding the city (Fig. 7). A complex but brilliant architect and planner, Scharoun called himself a bolshevist and was alone during the postwar period in being respected by both East and west Berliners. His proposal was for the city's reconstruction in terms of a "deconstruction" of all its past orders. His vision derived from the view that the only responsible reaction to such a dreadful and distorted history is to negate it and create a new order out of its inversion.

As years go by, Scharoun's drawing has emerged as the most compelling and disturbing vision for Berlin. The proposal was publicly condemned by the city *baumeister* while the competition for Potsdamer Platz was being prepared, and measures were taken to avoid such uncontrolled patterns of social order finding favor or support. And yet Scharoun's is a seductive and openly democratic landscape, one that few since have learned from. In the drawing, the city is fragmented into distinct parts—some villagelike, some intense and urbane, some returned to nature. Reinforcing the historic street plan, he creates powerful bridges, literally between the East and the West. The lower left of the drawing shows the restored Octagon and the forest of Tiergarten in through Schinkel's gates. Building a resilient and tolerant reality in the dislocation of historical order, Scharoun believed, would create the physical condition for lasting social change.[6]

On the evening of 13 August 1961, East Germany separated itself from the West by erecting temporary fencing around its borders. As a consequence, the half of Berlin occupied by the Allies (which lay 120 miles inside East Germany) was physically separated from the Russian half. Russia was acting to stop Western erosion of the East German economy.

Leipziger Platz was decimated, severed into sectors, the Octagon imprisoned between the two halves of the divided city (Fig. 8), as shown in this photo-

Fig. 7. Hauptstadt Berlin competition, 1957, Hans Scharoun. Source: Akademie der Kunst.

graph of the land dividing the cities. This elevated view contains a palimpsest of past orders. Still visible are the ellipse of grass that was the forecourt to the eighteenth-century city and the iron rails of the late nineteenth century. The foundations of Schinkel's gates are overbuilt by the second line of antitank defenses.

This became the most surveyed landscape of the Wall years. For Western tourists, mounting the platform whence this photograph was taken held immense fascination—postcards of the 1930s city in hand, people stared into the void, trying to derive meaning from the overlay of what this place had been and what it had become. Consider this field as it stood for almost thirty years—perfectly formed, well-attended lawns, the land seeded in stretches with antipersonnel mines, and guard dogs on chains. Despite the total destruction around it, the mark of the Octagon never disappeared.

A more distant view of the same place shows the bulk of Hans Scharoun's Philharmonic Hall in the foreground (Fig. 9). The great, unwieldy mass of the Hall was deliberately disconnected from the past. Clearly visible in the distance is the mark of an octagon. The Philharmonic Hall and the Prussian State Library are the only realized structures from the postwar master plan by Scharoun.

Slowly, year by year, the Wall became stronger and the deterrents to escape from the East more comprehensive. It became a focus for the anxieties of Western visitors, assuming a darkly metaphysical presence. An American family traveled to Berlin in 1986 and wrote on the Wall at Leipziger Platz, "SARAH PRYOR, wherever you are, we love you. Aged 9, missing Oct. 9, 85, Whalen, Mass. USA, GOD LOVES YOU."

Throughout the 1970s and 1980s, Berlin was a city divided. The map of the West presents a Berlin undivided (Fig 10). Just a soft red line marks a boundary.

Fig. 8 (top). The Wall at Leipziger Platz and Potsdamer Platz, late 1960s. Source: Lamdesbildstelle.

Fig. 9 (bottom). View of Leipziger Platz with the new Philharmonic hall in the foreground, 1947. Source: Lamdesbildstelle.

The map of the East denies the very existence of the West (Fig.11). They both take care to indicate the trees in the middle of Leipziger Platz and the S and U Bahn stations that once served it, marks on the surface of an evacuated space between the nations where nothing was allowed to exist. The most important information on the Western map is the outline of every property held at the outbreak of war in 1939, even though neither building nor road was necessarily still in existence. Though demolished at the end of the war, Hitler's Reich Chancellery survives as a trace one block north of the octagon.

On 4 November 1989, the East German government agreed to give its citizens free passage to West Germany, in effect breaching the Wall. On 12 November, the mayors of the two Berlins walked from east and west to meet in the middle of Leipziger Platz (Fig. 12). Crowds of people from both sides cautiously reentered this lost place. For twenty-eight years, the space had been an anti-reality, a field of death. The Wall was breached at a point that for many years had offered both residents and visitors to West Berlin the most dramatic view of the division of city and people.

With the collapse of the Berlin Wall, the task of recovering the reality lost in the divided city was carried out in three stages. First was a competition for a master plan that would reunite the city across the widest area of destruction, around Potsdamer and Leipziger Platz. The entries ranged from the fantastic and outrageous to the banal. Daniel Libeskind proposed reordering the city into a state of utter confusion beneath his "resonating plate," the *prytaneum* (Fig. 13). A vast floating plane would support the ultimate symbolic landscape: a field filled with the earth of every nation of the world where, he wrote, "in the plowed other earth/reality much would happen."[7]

Fig. 10 (top). Official map of the Senat of West Berlin, circa 1985.

Fig. 11 (bottom). Tourist map of East Berlin, circa 1985.

The custodians of the city, in deciding on the Hilmer and Sattler plan, chose to restore the order of the eighteenth and nineteenth centuries. The plan conformed to the major avenues of the pre-war city and featured varied grids of city block—smaller and squarer and, perhaps, more rational that those of the 1700s—all centered on the figure of the Octagon (Fig. 14). The committee passed over the many proposals that sought to make architecture and contemporary urban and land-scape design carry the vision for the city of the new millennium.

A further competition was held to fit architecture to the master plan. Success went to the project that resolved the relationship between the new master plan with the *Kultur Forum*—a collection of museums, concert halls, and the Prussian State Library—with the creation of a center at the edge of the Western city. The project also formed a rich connection with the massive, sprawling bulk of Scharoun's Prussian State Library. Italian archi-

tect Renzo Piano was the winner (Fig. 15). The building program is now under-way; it has been described as the largest construction project in Europe. It involves the work of several major European architects besides Piano: Rafael Moneo, Hans Kollhoff, Giorgio Grassi, and Richard Rogers.[8] It seeks to reestab-lish a city of streets and people engaged in many activities. The clients for this and adjoining sites are as powerful as any in the city's history. Dukes and Kaisers are replaced by multinational corporations, led by Mercedes-Benz and Sony, that are shaping the city to their own needs within the structure of civic order.

The Octagon is slowly being rebuilt. It has not had the same attention as some of the surrounding sites and the first building seems without distinction—appropriate, perhaps, given that the space is more important than the architec-

Fig. 12 (top). The mayors of East and West Berlin meet in the middle of Leipziger Platz, 12 November 1989. Photograph by Alan Balfour.

Fig. 13 (bottom). Potsdamer Platz master plan competition 1992, Daniel Libeskind.

98

ture. However, dominating the southern half of what was once the *volkspark* stands the *Infobox,* a temporary pavilion housing all the plans for the rebuilding.

Still undecided is the project to create a vast monument to the Holocaust north of Leipziger Platz. The design of architect Peter Eisenman and landscape architect Laurie Olin is favored to go forward, but the project is unlikely to be completed owing to politically opposing viewpoints. The design proposes the construction of a labyrinthine landscape out of a dense grid of concrete monoliths. It is opposed by many who view the creation of monuments as trivializing or masking the horror of the events; they say the concentration camps are monuments enough. To paraphrase Baudelaire, art veils mightily the terrors of the pit.

The extraordinary aspect of the continual evolution of Leipziger Platz is the survival of the figure of the Octagon. Throughout the forty years of division, many proposals were advanced for the rebuilding and reforming of the city, but, with reunification, the city around Leipziger Platz is returning to a weakened form of the order established between 1688 and 1737. This most potent example of landscape recovered gives cause for reflection on the idea of order in the present.

There are two clear reasons for this regression. First is the inherent strength of the historic plan and the authority with which it was established. Only two forces have threatened it in the postwar years. Scharoun's advocacy of multiple orders that would cancel the influence of the past is still evident in the ragged edge west of the Octagon formed by the Philharmonic Hall and the Prussian State Library. The other is the work of traffic engineers, both East and West, who believed for many years in the need to push highways through the city. Both of these influences have now

Fig. 14 (top). Potsdamer Platz master plan competition 1992, winning submission, Hilmer and Sattler Architects.

Fig. 15 (bottom). Model of the final program for the rebuilding of Leipziger and Potsdamer Platz, 1994. Masterplan by Renzo Piano.

faded. It seems that the idea of order in the present has neither the clarity nor conviction equal to the idealization in the eighteenth century. We no longer idealize physical order and seek instead validation in circumstance and expediency.

The second reason can be inferred from the results of the extensive program of design competitions the Berlin authorities held to generate visions for the future of the city. Although the results were seen as rewarding the more conservative proposals, the general impression from the many entries was that of a discipline unable to give form to the idea of public life, a discipline corrupted by subjectivity. Having tapped the dreams of the world, none gave as much confidence as a timid return to past orders. This case of landscape recovery gives cause for concern.

99

Notes

1   The essay draws material from two books by the author: *Berlin, The Politics of Order, 1736–1989* (New York: Rizzoli, 1990), and *Berlin, World City* (London: Academy Editions, 1995). The first, though ostensibly about Berlin, is, in essence, an examination of the changes in the character of the Western imagination as it moved through the ages of reason and enlightenment, and into modernism. Berlin is an ideal setting for such a study, as it combines a volatile political and social history with philosophical precision in the way in which each age defined itself. The second book brings this inquiry into the present with a critical review of the major architectural and planning projects of the last ten years.

2   The earliest extant map is from 1648, so there are no definitions of the first fortified castle built on the site between 1447 and 1450. A classically inspired earthly order framed the layout of the great Renaissance palace, built in provincial style between 1538 and 1540.

3   It is significant that mercantile cultures—particularly Holland, whose trade depended on accurate mapping—developed the most advanced techniques for measuring, ordering, and shaping land.

4   Beyond the Octagon, a landscape of interest is emerging to the north and east of the city, apparently outside of the court's influence. Here a new district is forming, still within the walls, whose pragmatic organization of roads and activities accommodates a new urban workforce. This pattern is responding to an industrial revolution that will, within a century, change the economy of the nation. This is a marginal landscape, expedient, circumstantial, and apparently without any interest in the symbolic or the natural, yet even in the mid-eighteenth century it anticipates the order that expanded the city in the nineteenth century.

5   Karl Friedrich Schinkel, *Karl Friedrich Schinkel Architectur Malerei Kunstgewerbe* (Berlin: Vertwaltung der Staadlichen Schlosse ung Garten und Nationalgalerie Berlin, 1981), 100.

6   In the margins, character is revealed. The Russians made it clear to the East German government that they should demolish the cathedral and save the imperial palace on Spree Island. Look closely at the right of both drawings. Scharoun removed all trace of the cathedral while restoring the many medieval churches—folk churches, he would have said. The East Germans, after many years, chose to restore the cathedral and demolish the palace. This struggle with history continues. One of the first mani-

festations of architectural politicking after the Wall came down was a so-called popular movement to restore the imperial palace; a subsequent competition formalized the intention to restore a building of equal mass on the site.

7   Daniel Libeskind, from the companion text to the Potsdamer Platz design competition submission.

8   See *Architectural Record* vol. ccv, no. 1223 (January 1999).

Part Two: Constructing and Representing Landscape

Chapter 7

Frontispiece of David Gregory's edition of Euclid's *Opera* (Oxford, 1703)
illustrating the shipwreck of Aristippus as related by Vitruvius
in the Preface to Book VI of his *De architectura*.

Liminal Geometry and Elemental Landscape: Construction and Representation

Denis Cosgrove

In this essay I examine parallels in the imaginative construction and representation of landscapes at global and local scales in the opening and closing years of the modern period—that is, in the late fifteenth and late twentieth centuries. Euclidean geometry, the language of absolute, three-dimensional space, was long regarded as the constructional principle of the created universe. Geometrically derived boundaries constructed cosmic order out of chaos, inscribed elemental surface patterns across the earth, and structured local space. Cosmography, geography and chorography respectively drew, in full or in part, on geometrical principles to represent the world to the viewing subject and assure the truth of their representations. Of these, chorography not only offered the greatest representational scope for human imagination and creativity but also was practiced at the scale at which humans, themselves deploying the creative principles of geometry, could engage directly with the elemental world through constructing culture in landscape. Sixteenth-century chorographic works by Italian and Flemish artists/engineers illustrate these constructional relations between the global and the local.

Such early modern constructions find echoes in contemporary representations of global and local landscapes. The widely reproduced Apollo space photographs stimulate metaphysical visions of landscape at global and local scales, simultaneously confirming and challenging geometrical order within elemental nature. They pose questions of landscape construction and meaning in a world where the conceptual grid of modernity, with its emphasis on boundary and separation, has dissolved, and where hybridity, polyvalency, and polyvocalism prevail.

It is a Platonic commonplace that abstract concepts, the products of mind, are more truthful, perfect, and ultimately real than empirical, material phenomena, which, existing in nature, are subject to change, corruption, and decay. For

Fig. 1. Frontispiece to David Gregory edition of Euclid's *Opera*, Oxford, 1703. Aristippus, shipwrecked on the shores of Rhodes, spies geometrical figures in the sand. Turning to his companions, he allays their fears; rather than wilderness, the haunt of wild beasts, this primary inscription of landscape reveals that the island is the home of "men"—that is, rational beings.

those who study metaphysics—and it is fundamental to the philosophy of the landscape tradition I shall be discussing—whatever consistent order might be found in the mutable and dynamic nature in which humans exist must be external to its material presence; it must be a product of a superordinate Mind. This belief provides the root meaning of *construction*. The world is a construction, a *fabric* or *machine*, to use the terms familiar to the discourse of natural philosophy during the Scientific Revolution at the birth of the modern world.[1]

Construction thus incorporates both the intellectual idea that will be given material form as well as the actual processes of giving form to that idea, of constructing it. Any *representation* of the world must, of necessity, employ the same constructional principles if it is to lay claim to truth and beauty. I take landscape to be a way of envisioning, contemplating, manipulating, and representing the natural world, always a construction and thus primarily ideational rather than inherent in nature. The principles of geometry thus connect landscape to nature and thus they must be reconsidered in any recovery of landscape that seeks to connect to landscape's own genealogy.

In what follows I pursue this Platonic line through the idea of geometry, paying specific attention to its constructional use of the line as boundary, marking difference and separation—initially of elemental nature, and subsequently of space at different scales. Within the bounding line of area, further lines and points of vision and vanishing differently construct and represent coherent geographical space, or landscape. Vertical and oblique perspectives construct different landscape relationships—for example, vertical perspectives provide a global view while the oblique offers a more local, conventional landscape vision. Their integration transgresses a boundary, raising questions about relationships between the global and the local. At the turn of the millennium, when boundaries have become porous and identities plural, and the aesthetic and utopian principles of modern landscape design and planning no longer command their former authority, geometry may be reconsidered—no longer a metaphysical truth but a discourse whose historical significance, at least in the West, offers a wealth of signifiers and references on which a more open, secular, and plural design culture may more freely draw.

Geometry

The sign above the entrance to Plato's academy provided that no one unskilled in geometry should enter its groves. The foundational elements of Euclidean geometry are three: point, line, and area. They are united, at their simplest, in the shapes of circle and triangle. Geometry is the pure spatial language of mind, the indicative capacity of the intellect to construct order out of chaos by establishing a bounding line between the two. Geometry's Egyptian origins, according to classical wisdom, lay in the requirement to redraw the boundaries of property after the annual Nile flood. Thus *geo-metry*—the measure of earth—is a primary act of constructing landscape out of the elemental confusion of water and earth, a fusion paralleled by human confusion: that be*wild*erment produced by *wild*erness, which reason seeks to tame in its acts of bounding and enclosure. Little wonder that Aristippus, engaged in the equally primary act of crossing an elemental boundary by stepping ashore from his shipwreck onto the island of Rhodes and spying geometrical shapes in the sands, puts aside his fears: "for here are signs of men" (Fig. 1).[2] Neither should we be surprised when, by contrast, Renaissance Europeans stepped on the shores of the New World, the absence of recognizably geometrical boundaries in what they took to be a trackless wilderness should confirm that they had landed among savages.[3]

For Pythagoreans, geometry is prior to human imagination and terrestrial needs; it is cosmic and divine. Geometry is regarded as the key constructional principle of the cosmos, bringing the unity of the One out of original, lightless chaos in the form of the circle. Observation of the phases of the moon and, even more dramatically, of solar and lunar eclipses, when the creative act—*fiat lux*—is repeated, offers empirical evidence of the first geometric theorems. Differentiating light and dark is the first of a series of cosmogonic or cosmos-making acts, which, in separating and bounding, define the elements that make up the fabric of the world, inscribe an order of lands, seas, and climates on its surface, and populate it with a distribution of inanimate and animate forms (Fig. 2). The primeval landscape of the world is thus created through acts of differentiation and bounding whose constructional language is geometry. It is the sign of humankind's unique place in the hierarchy of being, stretched between Creator and creature; the sign, too, that humans are able to imagine, represent, and ultimately deploy divine principles in their own creative acts, fulfilling a moral duty to make over nature into landscape in their striving toward civilization. The original landscape is thus nature, ordered in the mind of the Creator but barely distinguishable from wilderness and chaos at the scale of the creature. The cosmos is the first geometrical exercise, and the relations between this primary unity and the more spatially restricted landscapes over which humans may exercise their secondary creative influence are themselves governed by geometry.

Renaissance Europeans, at once midwives and witnesses to the birth of a new world and the construction of the modern world, were deeply immersed in this Platonic-Pythagorean faith in the constructional language of geometry.

The philosopher and cartographer Nicholas of Cusa; his student, the merchant and student of optics Paolo dal Pozzo Toscanelli, correspondent of Columbus; the architects Brunelleschi, Alberti, and Bramante, who transformed the landscape of the Renaissance city; the humanist scholars and translators Marsilio Ficino and Francesco Berlinghieri, all shared this faith in a discourse whose empirical expression had been codified by Claudius Ptolemy in the first century A.D. Both his *Almagest* and *Geography* were newly translated, printed, and studied during the fifteenth century as evidence of the constructional principles of a unitary world. The invention of the letterpress radically reinforced the *visualization* of discourse, including geometry, at the precise historical moment when a ten-thousand-year boundary separating the natural and human landscapes of Earth's two greatest continental land masses was about to be erased.[4]

106

Cosmography, Geography, Chorography

From the Ptolemaic texts came an influential three-part hierarchy of knowledge

and representation of the natural order: cosmography, geography, and chorography, dealing respectively with the whole created cosmos, the major divisions of the earth's surface, and the immediately visible local region. These distinctions were not arbitrary; they corresponded to different placings of the individual in relation to the world, different *perspectives* on that world within its governing geometrical structure, each of which allowed different representations of it.

Cosmography placed the individual at the stable center of the uni-

Fig. 2. *De Aetatibus Mundi Imagines*, f.3r., Francisco de Holanda, c. 1580. The first day of creation, according to Genesis 1:1–2: "In the beginning God created the heaven and the earth. And the earth was without form, and void; and darkness was on the face of the deep. And the spirit of God moved upon the face of the waters." This illustration, the first in a series created by the sixteenth-century Portuguese engineer, architect, and student of Michelangelo, draws on geometrical designs illustrating the solar eclipse taken from Sacrobosco's texts. Courtesy of Madrid National Library.

verse,[5] peering up through the revolving spheres to the zone of fixed stars and, imaginatively, beyond it to the choirs of angels and, ultimately, the Divine Presence. It thus linked time and origins to the unchanging structure of the cosmos.

Geography positioned the viewer high above the earth, beyond the elemental sphere, gazing vertically down on the pattern of continents, seas, and major land forms. Such a perspective is possible only from a stationary point outside the mutable Earth. A celebratory poem in Abraham Ortelius's atlas, the *Teatrum Orbis Terrarum* (1570), uses the conceit of the cartographer occupying the place of Apollo, able to circle the terraqueous sphere and trace its outlines (Fig. 3).

Chorography relocates us on the earth's surface, offering little more than the vantage point of a hill or a tower from which we may survey minutely the personality of a surface stretching away to the horizon. In chorography, both the viewpoint and the space viewed are relative and subjective. More than either cosmography or geography, chorography allows space for the imaginative and creative role of the individual. This is true in both the construction and representation of landscape. Chorography deals with the local, familiar scale of human interaction, the scale at which humans routinely intervene to cultivate wild nature: clearing, draining, and tending land, building on it, and in other ways constructing landscape. Representationally, chorography gives greater scope than either cosmography or geography for artistic

creativity, for *colore* as much as for *disegno*.[6] Renaissance chorographers, such as Peter Apian (1524) and Cristoforo Sorte (1590), were fond of quoting Ptolemy's claim that the skills of the chorographer included drawing and painting in addition to the mathematical acts of surveying and leveling.

Fig. 3. *Apollo and Diana*, Jacopo de' Barbari, 1502. This engraving, by an artist best remembered for his revolutionary woodcut bird's-eye map of Venice, places the sun god Apollo above the sphere of Earth defined by the geometry of great circles and the zodiac. His position and the arrows he shoots represent vision and rays of light. The lunar Diana, by contrast, represents a more rooted and sylvan relation to landscape, as her antlers indicate.

Chorography's relativities remind us that the constructional role of geometry varied among the three discourses. Cosmography was constructed by spherical geometry; the heavenly bodies were observably pure spheres and their movements described (in theory) perfect circles around the polar axis. Thus cosmographical knowledge could be simultaneously constructed and represented in the fixed and abstract geometry of the armillary sphere. The constructional scale of the cosmic landscape lay far beyond the capacity of human art (except, perhaps, occult arts) to intervene. Geography dealt with a less immediately apparent geometry and its scale allowed somewhat greater scope for human intervention. Mapping the earth's surface required the intellectual construction of an abstract graticule derived from astronomical observation. Its grid coordinates permitted European navigation across the trackless, elemental wastes of the Ocean Sea, revealing the outline of continents and islands to be conquered and claimed for religion and commerce. In the conquest of new geographic spaces, Europe's first constructional act was to cast the net of longitude and latitude, establishing the borderline between order and chaos and making landscape. The characteristic boundaries in European empire were lines drawn between astronomical coordinates.[7]

Finally, chorography too disclosed geometry as the constructional principle of local space. Visual survey—initially by traverse and offsets, later by triangulation—allowed the establishment of property boundaries for individuals, corporate bodies, and states. But, although capable of astronomical fixing, choice of the originating point for these geometrical surveys was arbitrary. Position was locally determined by a pattern of centers and boundaries authorized by local power and knowledge. Chorography is thus the spatial scale of geometric construction most closely tied to conventional meanings of the term *landscape*. Chorographic representation sets into dialog the distinctions between vertical and horizontal perspectives, mapping and painting, the global and the local, as sovereigns and their ministers and generals seek to piece together local representations into geopolitical patterns. The papacy, whose claims operated explicitly but rather differently at each one of the three spatial scales, offers an instructive example.

Papal Landscapes: Global and Local

The first and most enduring geometric act of construction in what was to become the New World was Pope Alexander VI's line of longitude drawn in 1493, one hundred leagues west of the Azores, to divide Portuguese from Spanish New World claims. Rome's authority for this act derived from its moral claim to Christendom, stretching the bounding lines of the ancient Roman Empire to embrace the globe redeemed by Christ's sacrifice. The Pope's mission was to bring One World into a single faith, spiritually erasing all terrestrial boundaries and human differences.

Time as well as space fell within the orbit of papal universalism. Ninety years after the Treaty of Tordesillas divided universal space, Pope Gregory XIII reconstructed universal time in his reform of the calendar. Part of the preparatory intellectual work for this global action was undertaken by the Dominican cosmographer Egnazio Danti (1536–1586). Danti's work for the Vatican offers an insight into constructions of landscape at the dawn of the modern world.

Egnazio Danti was among the most accomplished Italian cosmographers of the later sixteenth century. His lectures on Sacrobosco, the Italian translation of whose *De Sphera* he edited, on Ptolemy and planetary theory earned him chairs in mathematics at Florence and later Bologna. He erected the mathematical quadrant on the facade of Santa Maria Novella at Florence, the gnomon at San Petronio in Bologna, and the calendrical obelisk before Saint Peter's in Rome. In 1562 he was commissioned by Cosimo I to design a map gallery in the Palazzo Vecchio at Florence that would represent, "according to Ptolemy's rules, geographical paintings of all the regions of the world."[8] The scheme was part of Cosimo's Medicean universal vision, ultimately to be realized in capturing the papacy for his family. It is on Danti's work in the Vatican (1577–1583) that I concentrate here.

Danti was responsible for three geometric decorative schemes for Pope Gregory XIII. His great meridian, used to calculate equinox, solstice, and eclipse, was located at the Tower of the Winds, both representing and controlling cosmic geometry from the *axis mundi* of Christendom. In the Terza Loggia Danti designed an astrolabe, celestial and terrestrial globes, and geographical wall maps of the Earth. Cosmography and geography were thus secured in distinct, but geometrically related, representational spaces.

In a third, the Map Gallery of the Belvedere, Danti designed a scheme of painted maps devoted to Italy and the papal domains. The gallery ceiling illustrates the history of papal claims to this heartland territory of the ancient Empire, while individual panels are chorographies representing specific provinces within Italy. Each is constructed within a frame accurately identifying its latitude and longitude coordinates. Provinces are mapped to a measured scale; their topography, major rivers, boundaries, and settlements are indicated according to consistent conventions and a cartouche identifies major historical moments and characters. These are chorographies: landscape constructions in space and time

109

that simultaneously bound and frame the local from a specific perspective while binding it into a global and, indeed, universal construction. The Liguria map (Fig. 4) perfectly exemplifies the process.

Danti's *Liguria*

The geographical shape of Liguria, stretched along the coast of the Gulf of Genoa and the Ligurian Sea and narrowly confined by mountains, does not fit easily into the framing geometry of the rectangular panel, the window on the world that opens to us as we walk through the gallery. Its cartographic representation occupies no more than one fifth of the available space, leaving the rest as sea. Danti resolves this constructional problem by a dramatic geometric device. A great wind rose divides the sea into sixteen segments. The center lies offshore at the point where a marine cartographer of portolan charts might take his sightings and rhumb lines. The florid inscription naming the sea further divides maritime space latitudinally. Three designs—a cartouche, a ship, and a water chariot, to which I return below—provide a final triangular element to tie together the construction.

The province of Liguria is not viewed from within, as a local might picture it—from Genoa, for example. Indeed, Genoa, although celebrated in the cartouche as capital city, is not privileged representationally on the map. Liguria is constructed from beyond, from the God-like vertical position appropriate to a universal pontiff, and simultaneously from the perspective of an imperial sovereign entering a subject territory by land. We enter the map as the Pope himself might enter Liguria, from across the mountains, down a river valley. Two men-

Fig. 4. *Liguria*, Egnazio Danti, 1578–1581. In Danti's chorography, by a trick of perspective illusion the eye sweeps down from its privileged position over the coasts and mountains of the papal province into the landscapes of Liguria's valleys and seaports. Imaginatively, the landscape connects to a larger space as the coast of Corsica sails into view, the Barbary pilots mark the global contacts with Islam, and Columbus is carried in Neptune's chariot toward a new world. Courtesy of the Vatican: Galleria delle Carte Geografiche.

dicant travelers indicate our route; we gain a perspective over bosky hills and regular, cultivated fields that stretch away from the eye. The elision of vertical and oblique perspective is perfectly veiled and the global linked to the local via the trompe-l'oeil effects of cleverly constructed perspective.

Universal and local are joined at another scale in the decorative elements of the picture. Genoa's maritime glory is celebrated in the text of the cartouche and the city's struggle against the infidel across the Mediterranean boundary of Christendom recalled in the illustration of a Genoese challenge to Barbary pirates narrated in the galley portrait. The matching design on the right is of Poseidon's chariot being drawn by seahorses harnessed by the sea god, speeding west across the waves. Seated in the place normally reserved for the marine divinity is Christopher Columbus, Ligurian and *novi orbis repertor*—proclaimer of a new world.

Landscape Construction: Eye and Mind's Eye

Danti's chorographic landscape constructions combining the conceptual perspective from a vertical vantage point with local knowledge were not unique in late-sixteenth-century Italy. Others, such as the Veronese artist and engineer Cristoforo Sorte, designer of a similar map cycle for the Venetian Senate, also successfully combined vertical and oblique perspectives in their landscape representations. Indeed, Sorte claimed that chorographic painting, although constructed from a bird's-eye perspective, should reveal each valley, hill, and town such that those with intimate local knowledge may recognize their landmarks "without having to read their written names" (*senza leggere le lettere de'loro nome*).[9]

Both men's work went beyond simply representing landscape; as *periti*, or engineers, they were engaged in the practical transformation of nature into cultural landscape. Sorte was centrally involved in the great reclamation and drainage schemes that transformed the natural environment of Venetian mainland territories, separating and bounding the elemental mixing of land and water in the hydraulic regulation of the lagunar regions. Danti designed a canal scheme complete with locks to link the Tyrrhenian and Adriatic seas across the Apennines, along the line of the Arno valley. He also designed a geometric instrument, the *radius latinus,* to simplify large-scale territorial survey from horseback. He used such knowledge in his twenty-seven-day survey of the province of Perugia in 1578, recording, he claimed, everything "in ink, from nature."[10] The resulting chorography was used by the Bolognese state in defining its provincial boundaries and, later, by Abraham Ortelius in the 1601 edition of his *Teatrum Orbis Terrarum*, the first atlas or systematic representation of the whole earth.

The combination of abstract, universal geometry and direct observation through travel and local knowledge apparent in Danti's working method and his landscape chorographies characterizes the construction of *Teatrum Orbis Terrarum* and its companion volume devoted to cities, the *Civitates Orbis Terrarum* (from 1580). Ortelius's work opens cosmographically with the world spread out to the mastering gaze of the humanist Apollo and brings us down through the geographical scale of continental maps to the vast collection of local chorographies collected from his correspondents across Europe. The relationship between geographic and chorographic scales is not merely conceptual but

112

practiced in the extension of Europeans' lust to see the world, in what some have termed the "tourist gaze."[11] Abraham Ortelius himself, referred to in the *Teatrum* as Apollo, is differently represented in a series of landscape scenes from *Civitates,* the companion volume to his atlas designed by Georg Braun, Franz Hogenberg, and Simon Novellanus. Here Ortelius is shown journeying south through Italy to view the Virgilian landscapes of Campania Felix, the coast between Rome and the Bay of Naples (Fig. 5).[12] In classical times the region was the villa and garden playground of imperial Rome, and the framing devices of these landscapes in the text, complete with swags and curlicues, refer to a landscape of leisure. Ortelius and his fellow Flemish chorographer Georg Hoefnagel are pictured within each framed landscape as traveling companions, recalling the two monastic figures in Danti's Liguria. But their purpose is neither salvation nor territorial conquest and control; they are here to

Fig. 5. *Campania*, G. Hoefnagel; *Civitates Orbis Terrarum*, Book 3, Georg Braun, Franz Hogenberg, Simon Novellanus, 1578. The Flemish humanist and atlas maker Abraham Ortelius and his companion, Hoefnagel, follow the routes of the Grand Tour through the classical landscapes and natural wonders of Campania toward the Straits of Messina in an illustration from the multivolume collection of city views.

see, to construct pleasing or sublime prospects and imaginatively to reconstruct landscapes from the past. They are Northern humanists, dedicated as much to the recovery of an image of the ancient world as to the discovery of the new. Their interests construct a mythical landscape out of natural wonders (the sulfur springs at Pozzuoli or the Straits of Messina), recovered classical literary reference (the cave of the Sybil or the bottomless lake of Averno), archaeological exploration (temple of Apollo), and designed nature (Tivoli). The *bel paesaggio* (the term given to the embroidered landscape of fruiting trees and vines) of these and similar *veduti* (staged views) would become the stock in trade of the modern tourist gaze, connected in the geometrical construction of framed drawing and paintings to the vertical perspective of the topographic map.

This structural connection between survey and landscape remained even when the former was deployed for military defense or conquest and thus abandoned the oblique perspective of the chorographer for the precision of hachures and contours to indicate relief more precisely for the artillery soldier. In such mapping, the eye, if you will, was subordinated to the mind's eye, the local to the global, although the tourist gaze was never totally subordinated.

Twentieth-Century Constructions

At the end of the 1960s, for the first time in history, a human eye was able to achieve the vertical perspective that geometry had imaginatively constructed for the mind's eye and that had structured the European imperative of universal global *imperium*. Astronauts on the Apollo 8 mission, the first to leave Earth's orbit, gained sufficient distance to see the whole planet.[13] Such a view had, of course, been anticipated by aerial photography and has been succeeded by satellite photographs and remote sensed images of the earth's surface at all scales. So powerful are the combined claims of photographic mimesis and cartographic representation that it is easy neglect the geometrical constructions that determine also the design and semiosis of these images.

Despite the vast numbers of existing satellite earth images, a mere handful record a human presence—*eyewitness* views in the manner of Ortelius and Hoefnagel. Indeed, as far as popular recognition goes, there are only two. These date precisely from the beginning and end of that brief, four-year period during which humans were able to see their earth from outer space. The first image was taken by the Apollo 8 crew in December 1968, the second by members of Apollo 17 in December 1972. Intriguingly, they represent the two perspective geometries we are discussing: the oblique and the vertical. Their use and the meanings

113

attributed to them suggest that these two perspectives remain distinct but intimately related to discourses on the global and the local in our relations with nature.

NASA photograph *AS17-22727* (Fig. 6) must be one of the most widely reproduced, but rarely examined, images of our times. It has illustrated countless texts, among them Ian McHarg's *Design with Nature*, the thesis of which clearly reflects the dominant ecological and environmentalist assumptions with which this image has been quite arbitrarily associated. The photograph shows the unshadowed earth as a perfect disk, wreathed in veils of silvery cloud, dominantly oceanic blue, but with the recognizable continental outlines of parts of Africa, Arabia, and Antarctica visible. It is an elemental picture—yet, unlike medieval and Renaissance cosmographic images, this earth is not securely enclosed within those vital spheres of the celestial and supercelestial realms that provide a reassuring cosmological coherence. The earth appears bereft, isolated in an empty, black void.

Another difference is that the image dissolves boundaries. Atmosphere softens the circular outline of the globe; cloud cover hides the borders of land and sea; desert shades into savannah and again into rain forest. The elements are merged rather than distinct. Above all, the geometry of straight line, point, and angle is absent; only the unitary figure of the sphere has presence. There is no graticule of latitude and longitude, certainly no human boundaries, nor indeed any visible human presence whatsoever. It is as if, when finally seen from the Apollonian perspective previously only imagined, the earth as construction dissolves into something closer to the pregeometric flux of *prima materia*.

The other, and earlier, space photograph of earth, *Earthrise* (Fig. 7), taken in 1968, presents a different perspective, at first sight more apparently constructed. In the foreground is the lunar

Fig. 6. *AS17-22727*, 1972. The first and, effectively, only photograph of the unshadowed sphere of Earth taken by a human eyewitness from Apollo 17 and subsequently reproduced as the image that contributed, more than any other, to the vision of earth as a single landscape. Source: NASA.

surface, seen in oblique perspective—a gray, inorganic topography sharply edged against the eternal black void. The eye is drawn across this dead landscape, moving upward in an inversion of the convention of nocturnal landscape scenes, to the image of a silvery, partly shadowed earth. If *22727* is geographic, *Earthrise* is both cosmographic and chorographic. The eclipse of the earthly planet recalls that

elementary geometry of circles inscribed in astronomical texts and the emergence of the primary sphere from black chaos, while the perspective across the lunar surface localizes the view of an uncannily familiar topography. But here, too, the dominant impression of the watery earth itself, the geographic scale, is of a labile and mobile organism, scarcely a construction of either mind or geometry.

The meanings attributed to these images and their subsequent use in popular culture have been dominated by two related but apparently opposing discourses. One of these—the one implicit in McHarg's use—emphasizes the vulnerability of the earth, its ecological delicacy, and the idea that this is the sole home of life in an otherwise dead universe. The moral imperative therefore is to protect Planet Earth against a human hubris that threatens to pollute and destroy the only home we have. This sense of domesticity, expressed in such phrases as "the home planet," connects strongly, if somewhat ambiguously, with an approach to design that seeks to minimize signs of human occupation by following ecological principles supposedly inherent to life on the surface of earth rather than metaphysical ones discovered at the scales of the cosmos and conceptualized in the human mind.

The associated imperative to think globally and act locally is a contempo-

Fig. 7. *Earthrise*, 1968. Taken by astronauts in Apollo 8, this now familiar image inverts a classic trope of romantic landscape: the view of the cold nocturnal moon rising over a sleeping landscape. But here the landscape is, in the words of the astronauts, "dead and cold," while the Earth appears a "home" of warmth and life. Source: NASA.

rary restatement of the chorographic vision articulated in Danti's *Liguria*. Danti and his peers, however, were secure in the constructional and moral or social relationships between the local and the global. The former were geometrical; the latter were provided by Christendom's appropriation of the imperial mission. They were both ultimately legitimated at the cosmographic scale. The ecological construction lacks such security. The moral and social relations it constructs between local and global rest on an imagined unity of all life *on Earth*. It claims no legitimacy beyond the planetary prison, for the geometrical assurance of the cosmographic scale has disappeared; human consciousness is alone on a floating earth. Life, in this discourse, does not extend in a bounded hierarchy from the Creator but spreads sui generis and without boundaries, horizontally across the evolutionary spaces of Earth's surface. What characterizes, above all, the differences between early modern and postmodern landscape visions is the disappearance of lines, the dissolution of boundaries, both conceptual and visible. Not only have Earth's framing spheres and the boundaries of the geographic map dissolved in these satellite photographs, but the categorical grids with which the modern world was conceptually constructed have also been erased. Life is life, a unitary phenomenon, human, animal, and vegetable, that privileges no particular form or species.

The alternative discourse related to these images emphasizes even more explicitly the erasure of boundaries, although it is rather more precisely geometrical in its constructions and representations. This might be called the One World perspective, as opposed to the Whole Earth perspective, and it tends, if anything, to use *22727* rather than *Earthrise*, occasionally making a collage of the two images. This is the vision of the global communications corporation. Transnational airline, telephone, dispatch, and media companies have all used the globe image, stretching a network of lines across its surface to emphasize their global reach and the interconnection of localities, the latter conceived as mere points scattered across a spherical surface. This is a connecting geometry rather than a separating one of borders and boundaries. It may focus on one or more hubs from which control over global space may be projected, but the network, with its complex geometry of interconnections, lays claim to both a democracy of location and perfect mobility, an erasure of the friction of distance, effectively rendering all points equal across the surface and that surface itself equivalent to a single point. Armand Mattelart demonstrated how the communications network (*reseau*) is associated with visions of global social and political utopia since the early eighteenth century.[14] Such universalist proclamations have become insistent in writings about the Internet, the decentered, boundaryless, and rhizomelike pattern of virtual connections that map invisibly across the earth's surface, bouncing through inner space to and from communications satellites. The networks illustrated against the Apollo image are actually invisible to the eye; they construct virtual geometries whose simultaneities warp space-time at the speed of light. If the discourse associated with a Whole Earth forecloses the possibilities for landscape as an improvement on nature, that associated with One World erases landscape's ocular and scenic connections.

Conclusion: Landscape Construction without Boundaries

The Apollo photographs appeared at the historical moment of global decolonization, the end of empire, when the world system originated by the West, constructed and represented by its version of modernity, was being deconstructed practically and intellectually, cartographically and politically. A claimed feature of the postmodernity that has accompanied the postcolonial world is multiperspectivism. There is no longer a single vantage point from which a Western, white, male Apollo may construct or represent one world but rather an infinity of local perspectives that are spatial, social, and personal. These are not so much constructions as individualized, culturally self-conscious, knowing takes on the world that, like the act of filming from which the metaphor derives, simultaneously construct and deconstruct, destroying any faith in stable or permanent spatial structures. Yet, simultaneously, the relentless technological and economic compression of space and time, equally characteristic of postmodernity, destroys the local, erasing boundaries, bringing the exotic to our doorstep while rendering the distant familiar and mundane. Nowhere is this more apparent than in the global reach of tourism and Net surfing that now frames all the world into fantasy landscapes, imaginatively constructed, like Ortelius's and Hoefnagel's *Campania*, out of adventitious elements of history, aesthetics, and nature.[15]

In the Platonic vision, the authorizing center and the bounding line constructed order out of elemental chaos and distinguished the local from the global and the cosmic. Those distinctions are bound to collapse without a constructional language of order and scale. Conventionally, the language was Euclidean geometry and metaphysics. Contemporary physics tells us that space-time itself is warped and that geometries are no longer a simple matter of grids and graticules, of vertical and oblique, but of inconceivable multidimensionality. In this they correspond to the practicalities of existence for an ever-increasing proportion of life on Earth, not only humans moving across its surface, physically in passenger jets or virtually through their modems, but also other forms of life—animals, plants, bacteria, individual organs—all increasingly migrant, circulating and connecting in patterns beyond the scope of graphic representation.

Today, in landscape, as in every other field, intellectual and practical, the most intriguing questions lie precisely *at the boundary*—which is, of course, no longer a boundary—at the very point where such interactions and transitions occur: in nature at the ecotone, in society along the transgressive lines where identities merge and hybridity rules. Landscapes designed and represented today cannot avoid engagement with the geometries illustrated and implied by global images and the emerging forms of locality implied by networks. Premodern cosmography provided the geometrical language through which landscape was initially constructed; the unbounded geometries of a postmodern cosmography may already be playing a similar role in the recovery of landscape.

Notes

1. See my discussion of this term in Denis Cosgrove, *The Palladian Landscape* (State College: Pennsylvania State University Press, 1993), 201–203.

2. Aristippus was a pupil of Aristotle; the event at Rhodes is narrated by Vitruvius. Clarence Glacken, *Traces on the Rhodian Shore: Nature and Culture in Western Thought from Ancient Times to the End of the Eighteenth Century* (Berkeley and Los Angeles: University of California Press, 1967).

3. See the discussion in William Boelhower, *Through a Glass Darkly: Ethnic Semiosis in American Literature* (Venice: Helvetia, 1984), 46ff.

4. William Crosby, *Ecological Imperialism: The Biological Expansion of Europe 900–1900* (Cambridge: Cambridge University Press, 1986).

5. The reference, of course, is to a pre-Copernican model of the cosmos. The Ptolemaic model remained dominant into the early years of the seventeenth century.

6. In Renaissance Italian art theory, *colore* referred to artistic virtuosity in such technical matters as line, color, and brushwork, while *disegno* referred to intellectual conception: narrative, composition, and perspective of a work. In Florentine art, particularly, the latter was privileged over the former because it demonstrated the creative mental powers of the artist rather than merely technical skill. Venetians took a more tolerant position in praising *colore*.

7. Jerry Brotton, *Trading Territories: Mapping the Early Modern World* (London: Reaktion, 1997).

8. Alberto Maria Ghisalberti, ed., *Dizionario biografico delgi Italiani*, Vol. 32, entry on "Egnazio Danti" (Rome: Istituto della Enciclopedia Italiana, 1961), 659.

9. See my discussion of Sorte's chorography in Cosgrove, *Palladian Landscape*, 167–187.

10. Francesca Fiorani, "Post-tridentine 'geographia sacra': the Galleria delle Carte Geografiche in the Vatican palace," in *Imago Mundi* 48 (1996): 124–148.

11. Dean MacCannell, *Empty Meeting Grounds: The Tourist Papers* (New York and London: Routledge, 1992).

12   See the discussion by Lucia Nuti, "Alle origini del *Grand Tour*: immangini e cultura della citta italiana negli atlanti e nelle cosmografie del secolo XVI," in *Cultura del Viaggio: ricostruzione storico-geografica del territorio*, ed. Giorgio Botta (Milan: Unicopli, 1989), 209–252.

13   See my detailed discussion of this in Denis Cosgrove, "Contested Global Visions: *One World, Whole Earth*, and the Apollo Space Photographs," *Annals, Association of American Geographers* 84, no. 2 (1994): 270–294.

14   Armand Mattelart, "Mapping Modernity: Utopia and Communications," in *Mappings*, ed. Denis Cosgrove (London: Reaktion, 1999), 169–192.

15   See Jennifer S. Light, "The Changing Nature of Nature," *Ecumene* 4, no. 2 (1997): 181–215.

Chapter 8

Aerial Representation and the Recovery of Landscape

Charles Waldheim

The society of spectacle has been replaced by the society of surveillance.[1] At the close of the twentieth century, people around the world occupy vast surfaces traversed and consumed by untold numbers of surrogate eyes. For the state, if not yet for all of its subjects, the power-knowledge principle of panoptic vision is fully mobilized as actions within the landscape are conditioned by their susceptibility to surveillance, if not manipulation, by unseen aerial lenses.[2] Correspondingly, the idea of landscape has shifted from scenic and pictorial imagery to a highly managed surface best viewed, arranged, and coordinated from above.

This global landscape is everywhere and for all to see. If landscape architecture once represented a self-conscious act of place-making set against an unknowable and untamable wilderness beyond, it has now become a practice of reworking an indexed terrestrial surface about which all is known and managed through the lenses of remote aerial representation. Maps and plans are key here, but so are aerial photographs.

Since the mid-nineteenth century, photographic representations of landscape have implicitly referred to the vast extent of wilderness beyond the camera lens as a kind of other against which the foregrounded landscape might be read.[3] This relationship between landscape and wilderness is comparable to that of caged animals in the zoo and their counterparts in the wild. Contemporary photographs of the landscape now refer to the exhaustive imaging of the earth's surface to the point of representational domestication. In the same sense that certain species now exist only in captivity, the relentless imaging of the earth's surface from above has changed the meaning and status of landscape irrevocably.[4]

A Brief Account

Beginning with the development of the camera in the late eighteenth and nineteenth centuries, the making of photographs from a height above the ground has been a minor genre within landscape photography as well as a major obsession for a handful of individuals.[5] If, following Roland Barthes, one accepts Niepce's

Fig. 1. *Untitled*, or *The Murderous Aeroplane*. Max Ernst, 1920 © 1999, Artists Rights Society (ARS), New York.

photograph (circa 1823) of a dinner table bathed in natural light as the first photograph, then one can also take that image as the first photograph of a landscape.[6] Without question, the first recorded photographic representation made from the air is credited to another Frenchman, Gaspard Félix Tournachon (Nadar). Nadar first succeeded in taking a photograph from the air in 1858 while standing behind a dark curtain in his Goddard balloon (Fig. 2). Nadar's photographs of the Champs de Mars in Paris were followed by a decade of technical improvements that culminated in his aerial documentation of Haussmann's renovations to the city in 1868. These balloon's-eye views of the Haussmannization of Paris are the first aerial photographs to reveal the urban order at work in the cutting of boulevards, sewers, parks, and other civil constructions through the fabric of the city.[7]

122

In the United States, George Lawrence's kite photographs documented the devastation of San Francisco as early as the 1906 earthquake, while the cities of the eastern seaboard, their civic parks and natural features, had already been photographed from the air well before the Wright brothers' flight.[8] While most early examples of aerial photography focus on the city as an object, technical advances in photography taken from airplanes moved early experiments in aerial representation toward the collective potential of looking down on a landscape. Ultimately, this new form of mass spectatorship was experienced by populations of air travelers and occasioned new audiences for the reception of landscape.

Among the earliest landscape projects to incorporate this new form of aerial subjectivity was the International Columbus Lighthouse Competition in Santo Domingo, Dominican Republic. Between 1929 and 1931, an unknown British architect, twenty-four-year-old Joseph Lea Gleave, won both stages of an international competition for the design of a lighthouse to commemorate Columbus's "discovery" of the Americas.[9] Selected from hun-

Fig. 2. *First Result.* Nadar, 1858. First aerial photograph, taken from a balloon over the Champs de Mars, Paris. Courtesy of Bibliothèque Nationale, Paris.

dreds of entries by a jury that included Raymond Hood and Eliel Saarinen, Gleave's project, finally completed in 1992 for the five hundredth anniversary of Columbus's first American landing, was unique among the competition entries as the only scheme that was intended to be viewed primarily from the air.

Gleave proposed the construction of a massive cruciform earthwork from which vertical shafts of light would illuminate the sky over the city of Santo Domingo (Figs. 3, 4). As a representational marker of the colonization of the Americas, Gleave's "lighthouse" was intended to be viewed in two distinct ways by two distinct populations: those flying into or out of Santo Domingo would see the monument as a vast landscape sculpture cut into the ground of the New World, while those on the ground would see it as a light installation cutting through the night sky above the island. Interestingly, Gleave's scheme for the project and both phases of the competition predate Le Corbusier's writings on urbanism and aircraft, and come early in the development of passenger air travel.[10]

The modernity of Gleave's concept was remarkable in three ways: political (having negotiated the two-stage competition process and captured the jury's imagination), representational (conceiving of a new aerial viewing subject), and technical (proposing a new and, at the time, nonexistent lighting technology). Also significant were the sixty years required to finally complete the built work over several political regimes and fiscal difficulties. The project is remarkable less for the execution of the monument as a building, however, than for the

Fig. 3 (top). Columbus Lighthouse foundations under construction. J.L. Gleave, c. 1956. Courtesy of Patronato Faro á Colon, Santo Domingo.

Fig. 4 (bottom). Aerial view of the Columbus Lighthouse. J.L. Gleave, c. 1970. Courtesy of Patronato Faro á Colon, Santo Domingo.

clarity and power of thinking of the landscape itself as a monumental construction. As the Statue of Liberty gained part of its power from the countless immigrants who viewed it for the first time from the rail of a ship, Gleave's landscape monument gains part of its power from the potential of countless numbers of future air travelers flying into and out of the Western Hemisphere via Santo Domingo.

The story of Gleave and the Columbus Lighthouse Competition is significant for featuring one of the first architectural projects to postulate an aerial viewing subject. This conception of architectural subjectivity was unique because it suggested, a priori, that the primary understanding of the work would derive less through the bodily experience of its spaces than through a detached and remote viewing position. Viewers experience the project in very different ways as they perceive the two subjects of Gleave's monument—one terrestrial and nocturnal, the other aerial and bathed in sunlight—visually and from a distance.

Together with aerial photography, the mass availability of air travel has today produced a distinctly modern perceptual mode for the airborne subject. This is distinct from previous modes of perception based on a sequence of ground-level views. This form of collective subjectivity has influenced a number of cultural practices, each founded on the notion of an aerial viewing subject as spectator-consumer.

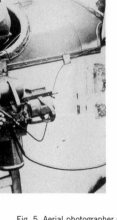

As a technique perfected during the first world war for representing the continually changing face of battle, aerial photography became a metaphor for the surveillance, control, and projection of military power across the landscape (Fig. 5). The capacity for landscape viewed from the air to produce a particular kind of human subjectivity for the terrestrial spectator is especially evidenced in the writing of the futurists as well as by its use in Soviet and Fascist propaganda (Fig. 6).[11] The triple perception-representation-projection mechanism of the aerial view was manifest in the use of aerial photographs as a primary tool of Fascist propaganda during the 1930s. The power of the state was displayed in the disseminated aerial photographs of mass audi-

Fig. 5. Aerial photographer sighting camera from the open cockpit of a Curtiss Jenny aircraft, c. 1917. U.S. Defense Audiovisual Agency. Source: Priscilla Strain and Frederick Engel, *Looking at Earth* (Atlanta: Turner Publishing, 1992).

124

ences assembled to simultaneously project and perceive a new form of collective subjectivity.

Among the first theoretical appreciations of this
new form of subjectivity was Le Corbusier's book *Aircraft*. Densely illustrated with images proclaiming the
eroticism of aeronautical objects, this book speculates
on the utility of aerial observation in revealing the failure of cities as well as the potential of new, synoptic
planning practices. The unsentimental image of the
city as photographed from above offered Le Corbusier
the most telling evidence of the moribund failure of
traditional cities. On the utility of aerial representation
in revealing the conditions of twentieth-century
urbanism, he writes, "[T]he airplane indicts!"[12] Interestingly, as Le Corbusier implies elsewhere, the lack of
a picturesque sentimentality to the aerial image of the
city is precisely what recommended it as a urban planning tool.[13]

The development of aerial photography during
this century has been largely dependent on the funding, practical experience, and theoretical principles
developed as a result of military applications of the
technology. Among these, military techniques of surveillance, countersurveillance, and camouflage offer
directly applied research on the impact of aerial repre-

sentation on the built and natural environments (Fig. 7).[14] As developed by the
military, with generous funding, technical expertise, and popular political support, the practice of renovating the landscape so as to avoid aerial observation
can be seen to mirror developments in aerial imaging itself. Whereas most military camouflagers in the first half of the century came from the ranks of visual
artists, set designers, and architects, postwar techniques of countersurveillance
increasingly are in the purview of technicians and specialists in military surveil-

Fig. 6 (top). *To the Fallow Ground.* Vladimir and Georgii Stenberg, 1928.

Fig. 7 (bottom). Aerial view of aircraft production plant (camouflaged to resemble surrounding
suburban landscape), southern California, c. 1942. Source: Seymour Reit, *Masquerade: The
Amazing Camouflage Deceptions of World War II* (New York: Hawthorn Books, 1978).

lance. With the development of supersonic spy planes, intercontinental missiles, and aerial reconnaissance satellites, the Cold War became a pretext for global surveillance of the earth's surface.[15] This synoptic conception of continual satellite surveillance continues to this day as a pervasive cultural condition.

In an article titled "Cities and Defense," Ludwig Hilberseimer called for the post–World War II dissolution of cities and their dispersal across the landscape as a strategy of civil defense (Fig. 8).[16] Recalling Wright's Broadacre City project, Hilberseimer proposed an American urbanism dispersed across the landscape with infrastructure and environment comingling so as to make the demarcation of city and countryside virtually impossible. The scattering of population across the landscape in a thin exurban settlement pattern would be useful not only in reducing the casualties of a nuclear attack but also, just as importantly, in preventing the attack in the first place by frustrating attempts at target acquisition by aerial observation.

126

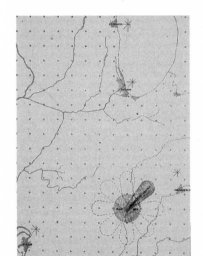

This example of an urbanism of dispersal and reduced density finds its corollary in the construction of the U.S. interstate highway system as a part of the nation's civil defense infrastructure. Based on similar arguments, the highway transportation system as an engine of dispersal across the landscape had an incalculable effect on postwar settlement patterns. With parallels in contemporary debates surrounding the natural environment and its relation to urban development, the impact of systematic aerial surveillance on contemporary understanding of the landscape cannot be overestimated.

One illustration of the importance of airborne spectatorship to the cultural construction of landscape can be found in the increasing attention paid to the landscape of the airport itself as a site of inevitable aerial observation. This is an expansion of the practice of landscape onto sites not historically considered landscapes.[17] This shift in the understanding of what actually constitutes landscape says as much about contemporary landscape practice as it does about contemporary cultural conditions. Among these cultural conditions is the predominance of the purely

Fig. 8. Plan for decentralization of cities based on the threat of the atomic bomb. Ludwig Hilberseimer. Source: Hilberseimer's *The Nature of Cities* (Chicago: Paul Theobald and Co., 1955). Courtesy of the Art Institute of Chicago.

visual dimension of landscape (the airport landscape is among the least physically accessible) in lieu of its bodily occupation, phenomenal experience, or material quality.[18]

Picturing Landscape

Much has been made recently of the limits of the purely pictorial and the importance of alternatives to the visual basis of much contemporary landscape practice. While a number of authors advocate a renewed interest in the material, phenomenal, and temporal aspects of landscape, fewer question the historical construction and effects of visual representation within the discipline. The representation of landscape—its *picturing*—is not simply the recording of a visual perception as inscribed on a two-dimensional surface but also operates as a mechanism for the construction of space. The world is visually prefabricated through its potential for being seen. Perhaps even more than in any other field of cultural endeavor, the picturing of the landscape has become synonymous with the discipline itself, *as if landscape only existed through its picturing.* This is remarkably close to the truth insofar as our knowledge and experience of the category landscape have (at least in part) been conditioned by visual representations and pictures.[19]

127

While the questioning of this tradition is a necessary (and belated) portion of the critical recuperation of landscape, imagining the complete overthrow of this representation-projection mechanism in favor of solely ecological, material, and metrical concerns is tempting. More profitable, however, might be the critical investigation of the picture-making economy itself and, in particular, a close reading of contemporary developments in the production and consumption of visual representation in other fields. Among these, at least two recommend themselves as capable of shedding light on the present debates.

First is the relation of the pictorial tradition to the modernist category of *space*. Most historical accounts suggest that the development of modernist understandings of space are directly at odds with the cultural tradition of nineteenth-century landscape. Recent scholarship in this area takes an apologetic tone and tends to suggest that either the extant continuity between modernism and the landscape has been overlooked or that a failure of modernism was its inability to translate its themes into landscape practice. In both cases, a profound gap is postulated between the nineteenth-century pictorial inheritance of landscape and the modernist interest in space and spatial experience as a fundamental category of phenomenal experience. Yet it is possible to show the codependency of spatial issues with those of picturing, framing, and composition. In fact, a more recent argument is that the modern formulation of space can be seen to have developed directly out of the nineteenth-century use of serially sequenced pictorial frames, a fundamental component of landscape perception and representation.[20]

A second avenue of critical investigation might be a reevaluation of the picture-making process itself, together with contemporary understandings of vision and their relationship to perception in the making of visual representations. Over the past decade or so, a number of art historians have been engaged in the critical reevaluation of the picture-making tradition within painting along the lines of semiological, structuralist, and materialist critiques.[21] Among these, Norman Bryson's *Vision and Painting* offers a fully matured account of the picture-making and reading process that represents a profound and fundamental critique of the "perceptualist" or "gestalt" accounts of vision and its relationship to the making of pictures.[22] Bryson's account questions the humanist assumptions of much of the pictorial tradition within landscape and provides a powerful critique capable of transforming the reading of aerial representations of the landscape. In his account of visual representation as a semiological activity, images are read in much the same way as texts—that is, depending on the viewer's facility to interpret a given system of representation. This account of picturing the landscape suggests that the potential of "seeing" a landscape and being able to "read" a photograph of the landscape come from two sides of the same culturally produced literacy.

Bryson's theory replaces the humanist accounts of Gombrich, Arnheim, and others that depend on (and even postulate) a verisimilitude between the perceptual field of a viewing subject looking at a given landscape and the visual representation of that landscape in painting or photography.[23] The humanist account depends on something Bryson terms the "essential copy" and an essentialist understanding of human visual perception as the retinal record of a given material condition. In its place, he offers a semiological account by which the reading of a visual representation is essentially akin to the reading marks on a page of text based on fluency. This has the effect of shifting picture-making/reading from an essentially optical operation to one that is primarily concerned with the codes of visual literacy within a particular discursive system. As such, the visual representation has a different relationship to the material conditions that it represents than to the perception and production of a given landscape.

It is important to distinguish between these contemporary approaches to the reading of visual representations of the landscape and the humanist practice of reading landscapes as a means of iconographic analysis.[24] The former—a semiological approach—creates a problem of the making of visual representations as they relate to the visual perceptions of a viewing subject. By contrast, the latter presupposes a naturalized and timeless economy of image-making as a retinal reproduction of visual perception. As far as aerial representations of landscape are concerned, the semiological account of picture-making allows for a renewal of speculation into the fundamental effects of photography. This begins with questioning the generally accepted assumption that photography is an objective, mechanical copy of a given optical condition. In fact, the status of photography as an objective record of material reality has solidified only recently. In the nineteenth century, several competing explanations of the conditions of photography were developed with different assumptions from those commonly held today.

Among these was the notion of photography as a kind of drawing.[25] This approach suggests that the photography of landscape and its parallels in landscape painting share familial origins in drawing. The notion of a drawing as a kind of index (or trace) recommends itself to the conflation of painting and photography as symmetrical representations.[26] Rather than opposing the supposedly objective recording of a photograph with the subjective interpretation of a painting, an indexical understanding of visual representation reconciles the paradox of simultaneous optical and metrical veracity found in the aerial photograph.

At the intersection of the photograph as index and the aerial viewing subject as audience, the work of Robert Smithson offers a case study in landscape informed by airborne spectatorship. In 1966, Smithson was retained by Tippetts, Abbett, McCarthy & Stratton Engineers and Architects to serve as an "artist-consultant" for the design of the new Dallas–Fort Worth Airport. In this role, Smithson consulted on the design of an aerial gallery and landscape that was intended to be experienced from the air as well as from the ground. The introduction of a gallery or museum as part of the terminal complex was meant to serve as a kind of curatorial or representational lens through which the aerial experience of the landscape could be read. Two articles by Smithson, "Towards the Development of an Air Terminal Site" and "Aerial Art" explore the theoretical potential of these new forms of cultural production and reception. Smithson's interest in the dialectical relationship between the representation of a site within the gallery and the subsequent aerial experience of that site culminated in his development of the "non-site" as a representational and projective practice. His conception of aerial art and his formulation of the non-site as a representational mechanism warrant further investigation, as they postulate an aerial viewing subject for contemporary landscape practice.[27]

Recovering the Metrics of Landscape Vision

To invoke a recovery of landscape is to simultaneously acknowledge a loss and profess a hope for renewed vitality. As a cultural project, recovering landscape suggests the need for a period of convalescence, a period of restoration to an original health and vigor.[28] One of the more important debates with respect to the cultural renewal of landscape concerns the historical tension between the scenic and the metric. The term *landscape* itself circumscribes that tension with its simultaneous reference to a measurable plot of land as well as to that property's view and appearance. The intersection of these two (seemingly irreconcilable) categories recommends itself as a site for prolonged questioning.[29] This is especially the case given the general polarization of scenic approaches to the landscape medium from its metric, instrumental, and programmatic conditions. The subsequent privileging of the pictorial in contemporary landscape architecture has been one of the more significant points of recent discussion and criticism within the field and, as such, is already engaged in a process of recovery (Fig. 9).[30]

However, whereas much of this discourse has revealed a renewed interest in the material, phenomenal, and ecological dimensions of landscape in lieu of the purely pictorial, the danger of a relapse into a polarization that privileges one aspect (such as the ecological, the his-

Fig. 9. *North Carolina Museum of Art Amphitheater and Outdoor Cinema: The Textualized Landscape,* aerial photograph. Smith-Miller + Hawkinson Architects with Barbara Kruger and Quennell/Rothschild Landscape Architects, 1996. Courtesy of Smith-Miller + Hawkinson Architects. Photograph by Bill Gage/North Carolina Museum of Art.

torical, or the technical) over all else remains. More important to the renewed vigor and vitality of the discipline is the development of critical lenses that are capable of accommodating the "both-and" condition of landscape and its various representations. Aerial photography might be construed as a representational and projective mechanism capable of reconciling the pictorial with the metric. Since its inception, the idea of landscape has been robust enough to simultaneously encompass both the pictorial representation and the metric description of a view. While the visual representation of landscape has been historically bound up with the making of landscapes, the past century has seen a growing disparity between the pictorial and its metric counterpart in landscape practice.[31]

Increasingly, in modernist practice, the objective, factual, and legal veracity of the plan or map holds greater sway over the more imaginative and culturally engendered dimensions of landscape. Thus, the visual aspects of landscape are severed from their metric utility.[32] This split between the beautiful and the true did not arise first or solely within landscape but is evidence of a broader cultural rift between competing representational modes. Daniel Bell has referred to this "disjunction of realms" as one aspect of a cultural malaise that continues to spread in capitalist cultures.[33] Landscape, more than any other form of cultural production, has depended historically on the conflation of the metric with the scenic. As a result, the modern severing of those categories (and the increasing distance between them as ways of representing the world) has caused greater confusion within the practice of landscape than in other fields.

One manifestation of this split is the increasing distance among divergent forms of practice within landscape itself, and especially between the two landscape practices of design and planning. The first is increasingly concerned with the scenographic and "artistic" redemption of otherwise visually irredeemable sites, while the second is concerned with technical aspects of large-scale management and arrangement of land. While these practices occasionally intersect profitably, they more often sit uncomfortably next to one another, both in the office and in the ground. They also tend to utilize significantly divergent forms of landscape representation.

Mirroring this divided condition in contemporary practice, aerial photography produces richly evocative as well as flatly banal representations of the landscape. This duality is evident in the parallel mechanisms for the production and dissemination of these images. On the one hand, high-end coffee-table books of artistic aerial photographs have become an identifiable genre in art book pub-

131

lishing while, on the other, the aerial photograph is ubiquitously available as a utilitarian, metrically scaled print useful for purposes of land ownership, description, and sale.[34]

These two conditions—one beautiful, expensive, and exclusive, and the other available to all, inexpensive, and neutral—can be seen to apply to the split personality of contemporary landscape practice. As expressed in the disparate terms *image* and *instrument*, the aerial representation of landscape has diverged over the past century, with equally deleterious consequences on the making of environments. In this sense, the recovery of aerial photography as a meaningful and synthetic representational practice might be a useful step in the larger cultural project of recovering landscape.

Aerial photography provides a modern rupture with previous modes of representation and allows an implicit critique of the objectification of land. This reading suggests the aerial photograph's complicity with the map as a modern tool of instrumentality, surveillance, and control, useful for exposing hidden relationships between cultural and environmental processes while establishing new frames for future projects.[35] Aerial imaging over the course of the twentieth century has effectively shifted the definition of landscape from a premodern, measurable view to a modern measure that can be viewed. This shift is from a purely visual representation toward an indexical trace.[36] In this sense, the aerial photograph can be understood to function as a kind of map.

One account of the origins of aerial photography, like other genres of landscape photography, can be found in the history of landscape painting. As has been argued elsewhere, the visual representation of landscape in painting played a major role not only in the development of landscape as a distinct cultural practice but also as a distinct mode of perception or spectatorship.[37] Landscape painting, as developed in the eighteenth and nineteenth centuries, can be read as the production of a simultaneous representation and projection mechanism. Visual representation is here not simply the passive recording of a previously extant perception but is also fundamentally engaged in the production of new landscapes. To the extent that aerial photographs are now available for mass consumption, aerial photography operates as a projection mechanism similar to painting. At the very least, this form of collective imaging has the effect of shifting the definition of landscape away from the self-conscious construction of measured views and toward the re-viewing of measured constructions. As such, the entirety of visually surveyed ground is now available as landscape. This understanding of the entire earth's surface as landscape is clearly a modern construction, first enabled by the Apollo photographs of a lonely and yet exquisitely beautiful planet.[38]

In his seminal *Design with Nature*, Ian McHarg codified a methodology for envisioning a new definition of this globally scaled landscape. This method made extensive use of aerial photography and maps as tools of environmental analysis and planning.[39] The historical fact of having imaged the earth from such a great vertical distance has had a profound impact on collective representations of landscape and environment, with the two terms becoming increasingly synonymous.

Whether for purposes of military surveillance, property description, or environmental analysis, aerial imaging has become a preeminent scientific tool for a variety of purposes. While these representations may sometimes be quite beautiful to look at, their primary utility is to visually collate quantifiable data in a global economy of information. Such data allow for the analysis of weather patterns, land use, military maneuvers, natural disasters, population estimates, and limitless other forms of social self-objectification.[40]

133

While certain of these instrumental aerial representations are useful analytical tools for revealing a given condition, the use of aerial imaging has increasingly conflated the analysis of the given with its renovation toward possible futures. The projective potential in the seemingly neutral and objective information of quantification is evident in the speed with which census becomes population control, military surveillance becomes intervention, land-use analysis becomes planning, and weather prediction becomes emergency management.[41] In this sense, the ultimate coincidence of aerial photography with the instrumental control of landscape is found in the bombsight-photograph mechanism of military aircraft, or in its contemporary equivalent: the video feed from a missile's camera in real time. This representation-projection mechanism allows for the simultaneous recording and renovation (or destruction) of the landscape as an instantaneous and seamless set of practices.[42]

The tendency for a (seemingly distanced) representation of a given condition to collapse into a (seemingly benign) reordering of that condition can be found in other genres of landscape representation, such as maps, paintings, and texts. To picture landscape is to infer its renovation. Thus, one strategy for recovering landscape today might derive from a practice that develops both the imaginary aspects of the instrumental and the quantifiable dimensions of the pictorial. Such "mis-taking" of instrument as image and image as instrument proposes the development of new techniques of landscape representation that

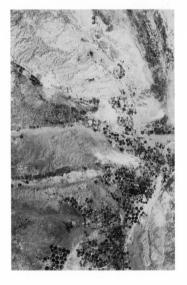

134

conflate the quantifiable with the visible and vice versa.[43]

One compelling intersection of the imaginary and instrumental in contemporary culture may be found in the notion of the flatbed as a simultaneous representation and projection mechanism. In the context of the aerial landscape representation, a working definition of the flatbed can be found in the fortuitous coincidence of Leo Steinberg's notion of flatbed painting as well as the flatbed light table on which aerial reconnaissance photos are analyzed. Steinberg coined the term *flatbed* to describe the painter Robert Rauschenberg's transformation of the picture plane from a vertical surface replicating bodily perception to a horizontal surface of cultural signification (Fig. 10).[44] Steinberg likens the flatbed to a printing press as a horizontal surface capable of accumulating diverse cultural contents. As the daily newspaper accumulates an absolutely irreconcilable collection of diverse contents, Steinberg's flatbed is a surface of visual representation that rejects the humanistic assumptions of upright posture and visual verisimilitude in favor of a problematic heterogeneity of semiological signification.[45]

Fig. 10 (top). *Third Time Painting.* Robert Rauschenberg, 1961. Courtesy of the Henry N. Abrams Family Collection.

Fig. 11 (bottom). Landsat satellite photograph of Najd Plateau, near Riyadh, Saudi Arabia, 1992. Source: Priscilla Strain and Frederick Engel, *Looking at Earth* (Atlanta: Turner Publishing, 1992); NASA.

Also significant is the shift from the handcrafting of a picture's surface as an original artifact to the mechanical reproduction of a plate (either photographic or textual) with the attendant loss of aura and problems of authorship.[46] This reading of visual representations as signifying semiologically rather than optically shifts the site of reception from the retinal field to that of culturally accrued language. It also infers that indexical traces of light on an emulsion become imbued with meaning through a system of reading and writing cultural contents.

In contemporary practice, the interpretation of remote satellite imagery for purposes of military surveillance operates under similar assumptions. Across flatbed light tables, specially trained analysts pore daily over endless reels of footage of the earth's surface (Fig. 11).[47] Rather than reproducing some fictive picture plane of an aerial viewing subject, these filmic swaths of landscape are read semiologically for the indexical clues they hold with regard to movement patterns, human construction, and changes in environmental processes. As horizontal surfaces for the collection of diverse cultural contents, these swaths allow the incongruous juxtaposition of missile launch site with soybean field, nuclear plant accident with seasonal crop burn, and secret airfield with regional farm road. The flatly banal and the politically charged, the mundane and the mistaken, accumulate on the daily strip-sampling of the planet from unseen aerial eyes. The flatbed light table of aerial interpretation (presently being replaced by vertical computer monitors) recommends itself as a point of fortuitous conflation of the recording of the earth's surface and its reading as cultural content.

Conclusion

Whether as discursive system or indexical trace, the contemporary practice of aerial photography offers several opportunities for the recovery of landscape. Among these is the critical recuperation of the picture-making/picture-taking economies of the discipline. Without question, landscape has been constructed through visual representations (plans, maps, views). Beyond that simple assertion, landscape comes prefabricated in two senses. On the one hand, our capacity for visual recognition (to see a landscape as a landscape) has been constructed by our experience with, and fluency in, visual representations known as landscapes. On the other hand, landscape has been constructed so as to be seen as a landscape. This accounts for the privileged status of views, vistas, and choreographed sequences, or frames, in much humanist landscape dis-

135

course. It also suggests, through the modern category of space and postmodern semiological or materialist critiques of vision, a rich and diverse range of contemporary possibilities for rethinking the representation of landscape.

In critically recovering aerial representation as a distinct mode of picturing, perceiving, and projecting, countless possibilities for the critical and contemporary recovery of the practice of landscape might be disclosed. First among these are the opportunities afforded by new audiences for the reception of landscape. New audiences imply new sites for work, not the least of which are the vector spaces into, out of, and around well-traveled urban transportation corridors and infrastructural easements. Especially along the flight patterns of urban airports, trajectories of mass aerial spectatorship suggest the possibility of twenty-first century flyways in much the same way that mass automobile ownership suggested urban drives and parkways in this century.

New audiences and sites for work also offer the possibility of new formulations of landscape, recasting its image from green scenery beheld vertically to a flatbed infrastructure that includes both natural and urban environments. A critical reevaluation of the relation between urbanism and the natural environment could solidify landscape's role as a disciplinary heir to the bureaucratic and uninspired failings of the planning profession. In this way, landscape might be recovered as a primary ordering mechanism for a genuinely diverse, transparent, and contemporary urbanism.

Notes

1   See Jean Baudrillard's description of the replacement of the spectacle and scene with surveillance and simulation in Jean Baudrillard, *Simulations* (New York: Semiotext(e), 1983). Also see his account of the "disappearance of landscape" and references to Guy Debord's "society of the spectacle" in Jean Baudrillard, "The Ecstasy of Communication," trans. John Johnston, in *The Anti-Aesthetic: Essays on Postmodern Culture*, ed. Hal Foster (Seattle: Bay Press, 1983), 129–130.

2   See Michel Foucault, "Panopticism," in *Discipline and Punish*, trans. Alan Sheridan (New York: Vintage Books, 1979), 195–228.

3   For an account of the development of landscape photography, see Joel Snyder, "Territorial Photography," in *Landscape and Power*, ed. W.J.T. Mitchell (Chicago: University of Chicago Press, 1994), 175–201.

4   For a description of the self-consciousness induced by photographic objectification, see Roland Barthes, "He Who Is Photographed," in *Camera Lucida*, trans. Richard Howard (New York: Hill and Wang, 1981), 10–15.

5   See Naomi Rosenblum, "Photography from the Air," *A World History of Photography* (New York: Abbeville Press, 1984), 245–247.

6   Barthes, "Authentication," *Camera Lucida*, 85–89.

7   See Shelley Rice, "Souvenirs: Nadar's Photographs of Paris Document the Haussmannization of the City," *Art in America* 76 (Sept. 1988): 156–171.

8   See Simon Baker, "San Francisco in Ruins: The 1906 Aerial Photographs of George
    R. Lawrence" *Landscape* 30, no. 2 (1989): 9–14. Also see Alan Fielding, "A Kodak in
    the Clouds," *History of Photography* 14, no. 3 (July–September 1990): 217–230.

9   See Eugenio Perez-Montas and Manuel Valverde-Podesta, "El Concurso Más
    Importante en la Historia Universal de la Arquitectura: El Faro a Colón," in *La
    Española 92* (Santo Domingo: La Comision Dominicana Permanente Para la Cele-
    bracion Del Quinto Centenario Del Descubrimiento y Evangelizacion de America,
    1988), 27–37. This research depends on the invaluable contributions of Marili San-
    tos-Munné and access to the archives of the Patronato Faro á Colon, Santo Domingo,
    Dominican Republic.

10 See Le Corbusier, *Aircraft* (London and New York: The Studio, 1935).

11 See Karen Frome, "A Forced Perspective: Aerial Photography and Fascist Propa-
    ganda," *Aperture* 132 (summer 1993): 76–77.

12 Le Corbusier, *Aircraft*, 5.

13 For a description of Le Corbusier's relation to the picturesque, see Sylvia Lavin, "Sac-
    rifice and the Garden: Watelet's *Essai sur les jardins* and the Space of the Picturesque,"
    Assemblage 28 (1996): 16–33.

14 See Roy Behrens, *Art and Camouflage: Concealment and Deception in Nature, Art and
    War* (Cedar Falls, Iowa: North American Review, 1981).

15 See Jeffrey Richelson, *America's Secret Eyes in Space* (New York: Harper and Row,
    1990).

16 Ludwig Hilberseimer, "Cities and Defense," in *In the Shadow of Mies: Ludwig
    Hilberseimer* (New York and Chicago: Rizzoli/Art Institute of Chicago, 1988), 89–93.

17 See Denis Cosgrove's and Adrian Hemming's essay, "Airport / Landscape," in this
    collection.

18 See James Corner, "The Landscape Project," in *Designed Landscape Forum I*, eds.
    Gina Crandell and Heidi Landecker (Washington, D.C.: Spacemaker Press, 1998),
    32–35.

19 For a history of the "view" in landscape, see Gina Crandell, *Pictorializing Nature*
    (Baltimore, Md.: Johns Hopkins University Press, 1993). See also James Corner's
    essay, "Eidetic Operations," in this collection.

20 Sylvia Lavin presents a thoughtful and convincing account of the historical develop-
    ment of the modernist category of space directly out of the protomodern sequence of
    pictorial "frames" evident in late-nineteenth-century landscape. See "Sacrifice and
    the Garden."

21 Among these are Norman Bryson, *Vision and Painting* (New Haven, Conn.: Yale
    University Press, 1983), and Jonathan Crary, *Techniques of the Observer: On Vision and
    Modernity in the Nineteenth Century* (Cambridge, Mass.: MIT Press, 1990).

22 Bryson, "Perceptualism," *Vision and Painting*, 37–66.

23 See Bryson, "The Essential Copy," *Vision and Painting*, 13–35.

24 See John Dixon Hunt, "Reading and Writing the Site," in *Gardens and the Picturesque*
    (Cambridge, Mass.: MIT Press, 1992), 3–16.

25 See Charles Hagen, "The Encompassing Eye: Photography as Drawing," *Aperture*
    125 (fall 1991): 56–77.

26 Rosalind Krauss, "Notes on the Index Part I" and "Notes on the Index Part II," in *The
    Originality of the Avant-Garde and Other Modernist Myths* (Cambridge, Mass.: MIT
    Press, 1986), 196–219.

27 Robert Smithson, "Towards the Development of an Air Terminal Site," *Artforum* 6
    (June 1967): 36–40; and "Aerial Art," *Studio International* 177 (April 1969): 180–181.
    This understanding of Smithson's interest in aerial representation is illuminated by
    the research of Mark Linder, whose unpublished manuscript, *Fictive Space: Robert
    Smithson and Architectural Criticism*, clarifies the relation between Smithson's work

137

as an "artist-consultant" to the Dallas–Fort Worth Airport and his subsequent development of the "non-site."

28 The project of recovery must acknowledge at least three countervailing tendencies resisting a critical renewal within landscape. One is a general intellectual inertia in the practice of landscape architecture that appears indifferent to the larger social and cultural transformations surrounding it. A second is the historical construction of landscape as a culturally conservative profession concerned primarily with maintaining a suitable scenography for the propertied classes. Third is the invocation of "nature" as a category preceding human construction, leading many landscape architects to evidence a nearly metaphysical faith in the natural world as it might have existed apart from human intervention. Each of these work against significant renewal of landscape as a significant cultural practice.

29 For this definition and the etymological relationship between *landscape* and *survey*, see Carol Burns, "On Site," in *Drawing Building Text,* ed. Andrea Kahn (New York: Princeton Architectural Press, 1991), 147–166.

30 Contemporary landscape architectural theorists in the United States, including James Corner, Elizabeth Meyer, and Julia Czerniak, are formulating critical positions and strategies for rethinking the landscape as a vital and contemporary cultural concern. In some ways this work can be seen to share a cultural lineage with the critical renewal of the architectural discipline over the past two decades.

31 See James Corner and Alex MacLean, *Taking Measures Across the American Landscape* (New Haven, Conn.: Yale University Press, 1995).

32 Ibid. See also Rem Koolhaas, "Bigness, or the Problem of Large" and "Whatever Happened to Urbanism," *S,M,L,XL* (New York: Monacelli Press, 1995), 494–516, 959–971.

33 Daniel Bell, *The Cultural Contradictions of Capitalism* (New York: Basic Books, 1976), 1–30.

34 Aerial photography books come in two types: the work of Georg Gerster, William Garnett, Alex MacLean, and others are essentially posed as artsy coffee-table books of aerial photographs, dependent on careful cropping, highly edited abstraction, and a selectively stylized lack of orientation and scale for their evocative effects. On the other hand, more anonymous anthologies such as *Above New York* and *Above Chicago* depend on the urban, geographical, and architectural legibility of their subjects rather than the name recognition or aesthetic stylization of the photographers for their visual currency.

35 See James Corner, "The Agency of Mapping: Speculation, Critique and Invention," in *Mappings*, ed. Denis Cosgrove (London: Reaktion, 1999), 212–252.

36 See Krauss, "Notes on the Index."

37 See Crandell, *Nature Pictorialized*.

38 See Denis Cosgrove's essay "Liminal Geometry and Elemental Landscape" in this collection, and his "Contested Global Visions: *One World, Whole Earth* and the Apollo Space Photographs," *Annals, Association of American Geographers* 84, no. 2 (1994): 270–294.

39 Ian McHarg, *Design with Nature* (Garden City, N.Y.: Natural History Press, 1969).

40 See Priscilla Strain, and Frederick Engle, *Looking at Earth* (Atlanta: Turner Publishing, 1992).

41 The sentiment that representation already implies a renovation is evident in Foucault's histories of the social sciences. See Michel Foucault, "The Human Sciences" in *The Order of Things*, ed. R.D. Laing (New York: Vintage Books, 1970), 344–387. A more direct political critique of this effect can be found in James C. Scott, "State Projects of Legibility and Simplification," in *Seeing Like a State* (New Haven, Conn.: Yale University Press, 1998), 9–84.

42   The photographs made of the atomic blast over Hiroshima from the bombsight mechanism of the Enola Gay were the first examples of an aerial representation-projection that used the same energy (blast of heat and light) to simultaneously represent and renovate (destroy) the landscape. For detailed analyses of the photographic conditions of the atomic bomb, see Jeremy Millar, "Fatal Trajectories," *Creative Camera* 334 (June–July 1995): 30–33, and Rachel Fermi, *Picturing the Bomb: Photographs from the Secret World of the Manhattan Project* (New York: Abrams, 1995).

43   See Corner, "Eidetic Operations"; and *Taking Measures*, 15–19, 25–37.

44   Leo Steinberg, "Other Criteria," in *Other Criteria: Confrontations with Twentieth-Century Art* (New York: Oxford University Press, 1972), 55–91.

45   See Douglas Crimp, "On the Museum's Ruins," in *The Anti-Aesthetic: Essays on Postmodern Culture*, ed. Hal Foster (Seattle: Bay Press, 1983), 43–56.

46   See Walter Benjamin, "The Work of Art in the Age of Mechanical Reproduction," in *Illuminations,* trans. Harry Zohn (New York: Schocken Books, 1969), 217–251.

47   See Richelson, *America's Secret Eyes*.

Chapter 9

Mutuality and the Cultures of Landscape Architecture

Stanislaus Fung

For most of this century, landscape architecture has been propagated as a form of institutionalized knowledge from centers of activity in a few Western countries. Over a number of decades and in quite diverse circumstances, there emerged different and overlapping milieux of landscape architecture, sometimes identified by national boundaries, sometimes by linguistic communities, and sometimes by cultural horizons. Distinct circuits of reputation both for professional practitioners and for academics are tied to patterns of national, international, and cross-cultural exchange.

For most of this century, because of political and other factors, China and countries in which Chinese is a principal language were caught up in a milieu quite separate from Western centers of landscape architecture. As contact between Chinese students and professionals and Western institutions increased in recent years, two issues emerged. First, it became evident that while the Chinese have imported ideas and practices from the West, it remains very much a puzzle what a genuinely significant cross-cultural exchange might entail. There is usually much shaking of hands, smiles all around, but the cultural import and substance of such encounters are often beclouded by platitudes. As the twentieth century comes to an end and China and the Asia-Pacific region becomes a focus of intense development, how can we begin to imagine a new scenario of productive cross-cultural encounter? Second, educators, universities, and their specific practices have played major roles in establishing subtle but powerful horizons of expectation for cross-cultural contact. How can these agents of landscape architecture work to develop our sense of possibility for moving from one-way cultural trafficking to real multilateral exchange?

In this essay, I attempt to address these questions of cross-cultural exchange and the agency of educational reform in a now global world. My thinking is exploratory rather than prescriptive; it tries to speculate and evoke a sense of cultural possibilities, of shifts in expectation and viewpoint. To extend James

Fig 1. *Tactile Index:* detail from the Älsvjö project, Stockholm. James Corner, 1999.

Corner's introduction to this volume, recovering landscape as a critical cultural practice is here understood in three ways: (1) being critical of attitudes toward cultural horizons that naturalize and legitimize certain forms of parochialism while displaying the colors of cosmopolitanism, (2) recovering some forms of landscape and culture (viz., Chinese ones) from neglect or marginalization, or reenlivening them, by discovering their pertinence to contemporary predicaments, and (3) explaining why recovering landscape might also involve recovering theory, which for all sorts of bad reasons has been maligned by busy practitioners and mystified students alike.

My premise is that recent developments in landscape architectural theory have, more than at any other time in this century, opened possibilities for fruitful engagement with Chinese cultural interests. My method is ostensive and selective: I point to specific moments in recent writings well known to Western readers in landscape architecture and show how this work might harbor new possibilities for cross-cultural exchange. I cite authors without necessarily affirming or criticizing their views. My main interest is the sense of possibility that emerges from cross-cultural shuttling and, in order to shuttle, I cannot be too much detained by in-depth critiques. Nevertheless, insofar as the shuttling might open up a sense of possibility, I hope that it also evokes a sense of the limitation of individual views.

Before I begin, I would like to set aside three inappropriate assumptions. First, I am not interested in culture as static content but rather as a series of trajectories or processes of becoming. Thus, the context of cross-cultural exchange involves people in landscape architecture trying to respond to specific predicaments and getting caught up in larger processes of change and influence. In the midst of such change are possibilities for genuine cross-cultural exchange.

Second, the occasion for cross-cultural exchange is not to be limited to situations where one can localize "Chinese" or "non-Western" concerns. The possibilities of cross-cultural dialog extend beyond those moments when one is discussing a Chinese garden, a Chinese community center or embassy, or Chinatowns. Even on those occasions when writers are ostensibly *not* dealing with Chinese concerns, they might nevertheless be raising issues germane to cross-cultural ideas and exchange.

Finally, difference is no reason for assuming irrelevance. On the contrary, it is where differences in situation, predicament, cultural trajectory, and preoccupation make it difficult for us to envisage relevance and mutual illumination that provocative discoveries might be made.

Landscape Process, Tactility, and (Poetic) Language

Understanding landscape in purely visual terms has attracted a lot of criticism in recent years. In an article titled "Architecture in the Landscape: Toward a Unified Vision," Anne Whiston Spirn complains, "Architects and even many landscape architects persist in perceiving the landscape as a visual setting for the built object, responding merely to the shape and color of hills, trees and flowers within the landscape, as opposed to the processes that animate it."[1]

In a parallel context, James Corner highlights tactile materiality as an important consideration in imagining culturally ambitious work in landscape architecture, because an emphasis on tactile experience helps us to resist:

143

> ...the commodifying impulse that reduces landscape to scenery or merely visual background.... Whereas the scenic gaze tends to objec-tify and distance the subject, the tactile engages, sublimates, and draws one nearer to the experience of place. The tactile returns us literally to the intimacy of things, the warmth of wood and the coldness of metal, the musk of damp leaves and the balm of humid air, or the coarseness of volcanic rock and the polish of fossilized rock.[2]

These repudiations of the notion of landscape as a visual setting can help clear the ground for discussing Chinese gardens, for they cannot be understood at all in scenic terms. The Chinese term *yuan* (garden) commonly refers to environments that integrate open-air spaces with buildings and covered spaces. This integrated understanding has been obscured in the twentieth century because, under Western influence, the modern Chinese study of gardens has been dominated by two positions; one stressed the architectural aspects of gar-dens and has been popular among scholars in architecture schools, while the other held that horticultural considerations were the most significant, a view propounded by scholars in institutes of forestry. Spirn's promotion of a "unified vision" of architecture and landscape seems helpful in displacing this common dichotomy between architectural and landscapist understandings, which is incongruent with traditional Chinese views. Also, Spirn's insistence on the processes that animate the landscape helps to restore a sense of temporality to Chinese gardens long obscured by imported modernist frameworks of under-standing that emphasized static space and depopulated images. Similarly, Cor-ner's emphasis on the tactile helps to restore a sense of this dimension of the experience of gardens that was prominent in Chinese garden writing but in this century has been marginalized by the scenic gaze operating in most publications on Chinese gardens.

It is also possible to imagine how Chinese notions of landscape can provoke fresh reflections on Spirn's and Corner's texts. For instance, one can contrast Spirn's discussion of process with the Chinese notion of propensity (*shi*).[3] This idea was originally articulated in Chinese discussions of military strategy and politics but came to be used in the domains of calligraphy, landscapes, painting, and history as well. The term *shi* oscillates between the static and the dynamic points of view; in any given configuration there is an inherent propensity for the unfolding of events. Like the water surging from a breach in the wall that had previous held it back, bringing everything tumbling downward with it, or like a crossbow, stretched to its limit, that can release a fatal effect from a distance, the skilful general achieves maximal effect with minimal effort from a distance by exploiting the strategic factors in play.[4] The field of propensity is charged with tension of forces (water held back by a wall, crossbow stretched to the limit). This sense of tension can be contrasted with the unified vision proposed by Spirn in which there is peaceful coexistence or a fundamental fit, for instance, between Glenn Murcutt's roofs and the canopy of eucalyptus that hovers above them, and between the torrential rains and the huge gutters that serve them.

Consider the following passage from Spirn's article:

> Landscape was the original dwelling.... The origins of architecture lie in making shelter, in creating refuge.... Architecture is a powerful tool of adaptation, but it has become an instrument of alienation. Most contemporary architecture, with its sealed windows, emphasis on facade and ignorance of landscape, divorces us both from the intimate processes of living and from nature, our fundamental habitat. Our power to transform the Earth has promoted the illusion that we control nature, that we are somehow separate from it.... Our survival as a species now depends upon whether we can adapt our environment in new ways. The resolution of this fundamental issue of our age will determine our viability as a species. We must adapt both our institutions and our buildings, landscapes and settlements to this end.[5]

One is struck by the Aristotelian language of means and ends in Spirn's text. The discourse of propensity, by contrast, never made explicit the relation between means and ends but operates in terms of a setup and its efficacy.[6] The strategic sensibility that might inform the alignment of means and ends is left implicit in Spirn's discussion, and in its place one finds a poetic description of exemplary works: Taliesin West, Sea Ranch, the houses of Glenn Murcutt.[7] Spirn's unified vision of architecture and landscape is exemplified by the work of noted professional designers; this still puts a premium on human agency and leaves much room for human subjectivity. By contrast, the Chinese emphasis on propensity leads to the view that efficacy does not depend on the personal merit of individuals.[8] My purpose in making these contrasts is not to arbitrate or to take sides but to show that fundamental issues in contemporary landscape architectural discourse can be interarticulated with Chinese concerns, and this opens up a sense of possibility for cross-cultural dialog.

145

A further level of cross-cultural resonance can be identified: among writers in landscape architecture, Spirn is notable for cultivating a poetic voice that carries an art of noticing. Her interest in the poetic is, in some basic ways, very different than the important role of literary cultivation in the transmission of values and sensibilities in the Chinese landscape tradition,[9] but it calls to mind a common predicament. Words and formulations that carry thoughts and convey a sense of agency can, over time, become merely comforting clichés. In traditional Chinese discussions of gardens, a poetic language rich in literary allusions is commonly employed, emphasizing the concrete and the particular and avoiding the abstract and theoretical. The seventeenth-century treatise on garden design, *Yuan ye*, is a well-known example.[10] In a recent essay, I argued that the atrophy of thought in this context takes the form of the repetition of clichés and the enumeration of facts, staying on the immediate level of information. In the 1980s, a new burst of Chinese scholarly writings on *Yuan ye* appeared. These tended to focus on a few selected phrases and ideas in the treatise and to comment on their importance by repeating the treatise's original framework of discussion. Over time, the tendency has been to focus on content at the expense of the meandering thinking that animates it.[11]

As one looks back on the last twenty years of landscape architectural discourse on ecology and process, one cannot help wondering about the extent to which the popularization of environmental ideas has dulled the possibility of developing refreshing insights at a cross-cultural level.[12] We can contrast popular rhetoric with the poetic works of writers such as Gary Snyder, whose syntax and diction hint at the intimacy and naturalness of a new relation to the land. In Snyder's poem "For All," a refreshing couplet is reminiscent of the emphasis that Corner places on tactility: "Rustle and shimmer of icy creek waters / stones turn underfoot, small and hard as toes." Here, the simile "hard as toes" figures inhabitation of the land as a matter of the fact of contact and intimacy.[13] But every thoughtful use of language and every refreshing insight, in the contemporary world as well as in traditional China, confronts the draining effects of popular usage. I call attention to this problem not because a general and definitive resolution is viable and plausible but because any thoughtful response in terms of its contemporary Western context might well be suggestive for the Chinese context, and vice versa.

Binary Thinking and Polarism

In Snyder's "For All," the line "stones turn underfoot, small and hard as toes" opens onto the lines "cold nose dripping / singing inside / creek music, heart music, / smell of sun on gravel." Tim Dean finds here a sense of reciprocity: Whereas "'hard as toes' assimilates the land to the economy of the human…the metaphor 'cold nose dripping' assimilates by its context the human to the economy of the land—the poet's nose (and his poetry) is like a stream in the northern Rockies."[14] The pattern of language therefore leads us to consider the patterning of thinking.

In a recent essay, Elizabeth K. Meyer offers an illuminating critique of binary thinking as a pervasive and detrimental pattern of thinking in landscape architecture.[15] She argues that landscape architecture is a "hybrid activity that is not easily described using binary pairs as opposing conditions."[16] Architecture and landscape, man and woman, culture and nature are some of the binary terms that Meyer considers part of an outmoded thinking that has been detrimental to the interests of landscape architecture in this century. In binary thinking, the landscape is designated as female or feminine "other" and subordinated to culture and architecture.

My interest in Meyer's critique arises from the Anglo-European philosophical and cultural basis of binary thinking. This is underpinned by a worldview characterized by an *ex nihilo* creation in which a fundamentally indeterminate and unconditioned power determines the meaning and order of the world.[17] This primary dualism, in various forms, is the source of dualistic categories— for example, knowledge/opinion, universal/particular, nature/culture, cause/ effect—that organized human experience. In Western architecture, this is related to the importance of "geometry and number, prototypes of the ideal, …their immutability contrasting with the fluid and changing reality of the sublunar world."[18] The Western conception of architectural and landscape design as the rational application of universal principles to particular sites and as the imitation of nature through the use of geometric and proportional principles is directly related to the predominance of such thought.

As the French intellectual Augustin Berque argued recently, the Chinese tradition developed notions of landscape without recourse to dualistic thinking. Fundamental to this tradition is the bipolarity of *yin* and *yang*, which indicates a relationship of two terms, each of which can be explained only by reference to the other. Unlike dualistic oppositions, each term in polar relation requires the other "as a necessary condition for being what they are."[19] But it is important to note that such terms are not dialectical. Unlike dialectic relationships, polar relationships are not involved in an oppositional play moving from contradiction through synthesis to sublation.[20] In the Chinese tradition, *yin* and *yang* are not dualistic principles of light and dark, male and female, where each term excludes its opposite, where each "logically entail[s] the other, and in their complementarity [the two] constitute a totality."[21] Rather, *yin* is becoming-*yang*, and vice versa. Further, *yin* and *yang* refer to the relationships of unique particulars and express:

> …the mutuality, interdependence, diversity, and creative efficacy of the dynamic *relationships* that are deemed immanent in and valorise the world…. In sum: *yin* and *yang* are *ad hoc* explanatory categories that report on interactions among immediate concrete things of the world…. Important here is the primacy of particular differences and the absence of any assumed sameness or strict identity.[22]

By contrast, dualistic oppositions such as nature/culture and man/woman involve terms that indicate essential sameness. It is important to recognize, therefore, that dualism and the polarism of *yin* and *yang* refer to different ways in which the relationships of binaries may be conceived. Elsewhere, I have developed a series of reflections on key Chinese terms in the treatise *Yuan ye*, showing how notions such as interdependence (*yin*), borrowing (*jie*), suitability (*ti*), and appropriateness (*yi*) follow a nondualistic logic.[23]

The contrast between dualism and polarism makes it possible to recognize that the critique of the dichotomy between architecture and landscape is part of the much larger critique of fundamental aspects of the Anglo-European tradition. Taken together with the recent work of Augustin Berque,[24] Meyer's essay opens the possibility of avoiding a dualistic reading of Chinese notions. This, in turn, leads to the realization that, once the normal modernist and dualistic assumptions that have commonly attended the reading of Chinese materials are set aside, Meyer's enterprise might be assisted by being brought into relation with Chinese reflections on landscape and gardens.[25]

Theory as an Occasion of Mutuality

"Does landscape architecture need theory?" "Does landscape architecture need a theory that is internal to it?" "Do you think landscape architecture should be developed with resources that lie outside its domain?" On most occasions when I am confronted by these questions, I find myself very much puzzled, lost for words, for the cultural agency of landscape architecture is rarely raised for discussion at the same time. I want to ask, "Why are we not attacking the cultural horizons that are tacitly called up by these questions? Why do these questions sound as though they are inviting us to debate whether, *in principle*, something is needed? Why are we not articulating the predicaments and asking whether these have, or conceivably can be, effectively addressed without the conceptual resources of 'theory'?"

Take, for instance, Rem Koolhaas's attempt to think about the future of cities in terms of the Generic City.[26] Koolhaas likens the Generic City to contemporary airports and argues against those who continue to think about cities and architecture solely in terms of local identity and traditional community. The Generic City is the result when identity is stripped away, Koolhaas says. In his discussion, "identity" is something associated with history that is deposited in architecture, and Koolhaas argues that "identity conceived as this form of sharing the past is a losing proposition."[27] By implication, the Generic City that Koolhaas promotes as a winning proposition is said to be "largely Asian."[28] If Koolhaas's text is meant to get under Asian skins, he is certainly successful. Writing in the Taiwanese architectural journal *Dialogue*, Weijen Wang observed that the Generic City was inspired by "the East in the eyes of the West" and steeped in a kind of neo-orientalism.[29]

Without undertaking a detailed reading of Koolhaas's text here, I nevertheless point out that this text is symptomatic of the limitations of thinking "globally" without refined theoretical resources. In traditional China, the physical survival of buildings has not been an integral part of the "identity" of cities. Unlike the European tradition of enduring monuments, Chinese buildings continue to be caught in a perpetual cycle of building and rebuilding.[30] If Koolhaas now finds that he has to contend with "identity" in Asian cities, this is because Asian cities have come to be thought of in terms of what Alois Riegl calls "age-value."

148

When Koolhaas opposes the Generic to "identity," he seems to be playing along with the standard Western opposition of the general and the particular. Readers familiar with the writings of the theorist John Rajchman are aware that, following Gilles Deleuze, the "Is" of attributive identity can be countered by the "'and' of disparate aggregation" instead of being opposed to the notion of the generic. Following Rajchman's terms, I have elsewhere explained how thinking in terms of categorization might be understood anew in questions such as the identity of the Chinese landscape architect without recourse to essentialist understandings of categories.[31] One gets the sense that Koolhaas is rightly critical of certain attitudes but, without following the cross-cultural differences in thinking that his critique implies, he ends up imposing certain European horizons in a universalistic manner. It is in instances like these, then, that "theory" might play a useful and important role.

149

The foregoing discussion demonstrates that theoretical reflection and writing can serve a role in revitalizing cross-cultural exchange in landscape architecture. My sense is that such theoretical activity can enrich our sense of the possibilities associated with such exchange and can be motivated by impulses that are kindred to those that motivate landscape interventions. Borrowing the words of Georges Descombes from his contribution to this volume, I characterize the thinking that has been outlined here as recovering something that

> entails a shift in expectation and point of view… achieving such shifts in complexity with minimal means… so that a preexisting place might be found, disturbed, awakened, and brought to presence…scraping the ordinariness of a situation and imposing a shift on what seems the most obvious… to make new forms, to create new feelings and associations.[32]

I hope it is evident that theoretical reflection and the work of practitioners can be related as activities that are motivated by the same kinds of impulses, searching after effects in domains of endeavor that are cognate with each other.

I discuss the cross-cultural thinking that I explore here in terms of "shuttling." This shuttling is a rhythmic unfolding, an open-ended to-and-fro that resists linear thinking and the teleological drive toward transcendental viewpoints and definitive pronouncements. The shuttling is between particular instances of writings rather than abstract categories of thought such as "East and West," "style and function," "space and time," and "landscape as language." It emerges out of specific configurations of ideas already in circulation. It is, in fact, not possible to imagine shuttling as a universally and indefinitely extendable thought, encompassing more and more within its movements without limit. There is a rarity of texts and landscapes among which one can spin out a cross-cultural web of relations.[33] Instead, the kind of shuttling I advocate evokes a sense of new associations and possibilities in landscape architecture that may be understood as the products (or processes) of "cultural mutuality."[34] It is the special role of educational institutions with multidisciplinary resources to help landscape architects articulate a sense of cultural mutuality and the possibilities this affords as they enter the global age.

Notes

I would like to thank James Corner, Michel Conan, Ufuk Ersoy, Mark Jackson, Carlos Naranjo, Michael Tawa, and Daryl Watson for their advice and comments on various aspects of this essay.

1   Anne Whiston Spirn, "Architecture in the Landscape: Toward a Unified Vision," *Landscape Architecture* 80 (August 1990): 39.

2   James Corner, "The Landscape Project," in *Designed Landscape Forum 1*, eds. Gina Crandell and Heidi Landecker (Washington, D.C.: Spacemaker Press, 1998), 33–36.

3   See François Jullien, *The Propensity of Things: Toward a History of Efficacy in China*, trans. Janet Lloyd (New York: Zone Books, 1995).

4   Students of contemporary landscape architecture will recognize some resonance between this Chinese notion with Corner's lecture discussions of "field operations."

5   Spirn, "Architecture in the Landscape," 37–38.

6   Jullien, *The Propensity of Things*, 37.

7   Spirn, "Architecture in the Landscape," 40–41. See also her recent *Language of Landscape* (New Haven, Conn.: Yale University Press, 1998).

8   Jullien, *The Propensity of Things*, 39ff. The issue of human agency can be related to recent discussions of the avant-garde in *Landscape Journal* 10, no. 1 (spring 1991).

9   See my "Word and Garden in Chinese Essays on Gardens of the Ming Dynasty: Notes on Matters of Approach," *Interfaces: Image, Text, Language* (Dijon) 11, no. 12 (June 1997): 77–90.

10 On this treatise, see my "The Interdisciplinary Prospects of Reading *Yuan ye*," *Studies in the History of Gardens and Design Landscapes* 18, no. 3 (July–September 1998); and "Here and There in *Yuan ye*," *Studies in the History of Gardens and Design Landscapes* (forthcoming).

11 See my "Self, Scene and Action: The Final Chapter of *Yuan ye*" (forthcoming).

12 On the need to reinvent the ecological imagination, see James Corner, "Ecology and Landscape as Agents of Creativity," in *Ecological Design and Planning*, eds. George Thompson and Frederick Steiner (New York: John Wiley & Sons, 1997), 80–108.

13 I follow the discussion of this poem in Tim Dean, *Gary Snyder and the American Unconscious: Inhabiting the Ground* (London: Macmillan, 1991), 4–6.

14 Dean, *Gary Snyder and the American Unconscious*, 5–6.

15 Elizabeth K. Meyer, "The Expanded Field of Landscape Architecture," in *Ecological Design and Planning*, eds. George F. Thompson and Frederick R. Steiner (New York, John Wiley & Sons, 1997), 45–79. See also James Corner, "A Discourse on Theory II: Three Tyrranies of Contemporary Theory and the Alternative of Hermeneutics," *Landscape Journal* 10, no. 2 (fall 1991).

16 Ibid., 50.

17 Roger T. Ames, "The Body in Classical Chinese Philosophy," in *Self as Body in Asian Theory and Practice*, eds. Thomas P. Kasulis, Roger T. Ames, and Wimal Dissanayake (Albany: State University of New York Press, 1993), 159.

18 Alberto Pérez-Gómez, *Architecture and the Crisis of Modern Science* (Cambridge, Mass.: MIT Press, 1983), 8.

19 Ames, "The Body in Classical Chinese Philosophy," 159.

20 David L. Hall and Roger T. Ames, *Anticipating China* (Albany: State University of New York Press, 1995), 129–130.

21 David L. Hall and Roger T. Ames, "The Cosmological Setting of Chinese Gardens," *Studies in the History of Gardens and Designed Landscapes* 18, no. 3 (July–September 1998).

22 Ibid., 261–262.

23 Stanislaus Fung and Mark Jackson, "Dualism And Polarism: Structures of Architectural and Landscape Architectural Discourse in China and the West," *Interstices* (Auckland) 4 (1996); Stanislaus Fung, "Body and Appropriateness in *Yuan ye*," *Intersight* (Buffalo) 4 (1997): 84–91.

24 See, for instance, Augustin Berque, "Beyond the Modern Landscape," *AA Files* 25 (summer 1993): 33–37.

25 For a further example of cultural mutuality, see my discussion of the Chinese use of Western techniques of architectural drawing in the spatial analysis of Chinese gardens, which I relate to the recent work of James Corner on issues of representation, "Longing and Belonging in Chinese Garden History," in *Perspectives on the Study of Garden History*, ed. Michel Conan (Washington, D.C.: Dumbarton Oaks and the Trustees for Harvard University, 1998).

26 Rem Koolhaas, "The Generic City," in *S,M,L,XL* (New York: Monacelli, 1995), 1238ff.

27 Ibid., 1248.

28 Ibid., 1261.

29 Weijen Wang, "Writing Between the Generic: Neo-orientalization and Deorientalization Reflected at the Harvard Asia-Pacific Design Conference," *Dialogue* 15 (June 1998): 101. See also Wang Chong Thai, "Cacophony: Gratification or Innovation?" in *Postcolonial Space(s)*, eds. Gülsüm Baydar Nalbontoglu and Wong Chong Thai (New York: Princeton Architectural Press, 1997), 131–139.

30 See Frederick W. Mote, "A Millennium of Chinese Urban History: Form, Time, and Space Concepts in Soochow," *Rice University Studies* 59, no. 4 (fall 1973): 35–65.

31 See my "Notes on the Architectural Education of Nomads," *Architectural Research Quarterly* (London) 2, no. 2 (winter 1996): 10–17.

32 Georges Descombes, "Shifting Sites: The Swiss Way, Geneva," in this volume. See also Elizabeth K. Meyer, "Landscape Architecture Design as a Critical Practice," and James Corner "Critical Thinking in Landscape Architecture," *Landscape Journal* 10, no. 2 (fall 1991): 156–159 and 159–162, for accounts of criticism that seem resonant with the cross-cultural thinking I propose here.

33 For a discussion of a postmodern temporality of thinking that is resonant with the kind of shuttling that I describe here, see Elizabeth Deeds Ermath, *Sequel to History: Postmodernism and the Crisis of Representational Time* (Princeton, N.J.: Princeton University Press, 1992), 45ff.

34 This term is taken from Wu Kuang-ming, *On Chinese Body Thinking: A Cultural Hermeneutic* (Leiden: E.J. Brill, 1997), chapter 9.

151

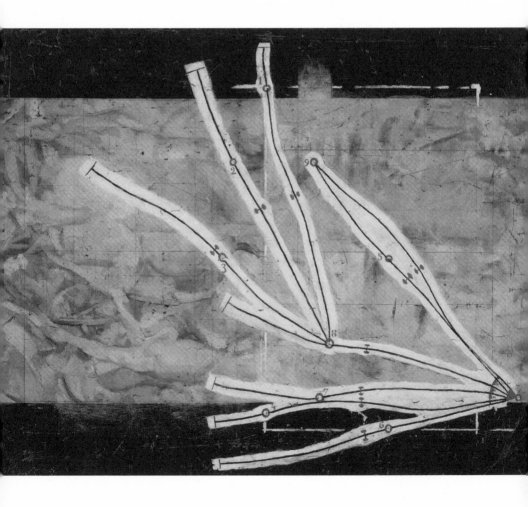

Chapter 10

Eidetic Operations and New Landscapes

James Corner

Landscape and image are inseparable. Without image there is no such thing as landscape, only unmediated *environment*.[1] This distinction can be traced back to the Old English term *landskip*, which at first referred not to land but to a picture of it, as in the later, selectively framed representations of seventeenth-century Dutch *landschap* paintings. Soon after the appearance of this genre of painting, the scenic concept was applied to the land itself in the form of large-scale rural vistas, designed estates, and ornamental garden art. Indeed, the development of landscape architecture as a modern profession derives, in large measure, from an impulse to reshape large areas of land according to *prior* imaging. Not only is a collective recognition of land as landscape made possible through exposure to prior images (a phenomenon central to both spectacle and tourist landscapes) but also the ability to intentionally construe and construct designed landscapes is enabled through various forms and activities of imaging.

Whereas imaging is central to forging landscape, the tendency of many contemporary landscape architects to assume that this prioritizes visual and formal qualities alone significantly limits the full eidetic scope of landscape creativity. I use the term *eidetic* here to refer to a mental conception that may be picturable but may equally be acoustic, tactile, cognitive, or intuitive.[2] Thus, unlike the purely retinal impression of pictures, eidetic images contain a broad range of ideas that lie at the core of human creativity. Consequently, how one "images" the world literally conditions how reality is both conceptualized and shaped. That representation exercises such agency and effect is precisely why images in design cannot properly be considered as mute or neutral depictions of existing and projected conditions of secondary significance to their object; on the contrary, eidetic images are much more active than this, engendering, unfolding, and participating in emergent realities. Far from the assumed inertia of passive and objective representations, the paper surfaces and computer screens of design imaging are highly efficacious operational fields on which the theories and practices of landscape are produced.[3] Any recovery of landscape in

Fig 1. *Réseaux des stoppages (Network of Stoppages)*. Marcel Duchamp. 1914. Oil and pencil on canvas, 148.9 x 197.7 cm. The Museum of Modern Art, New York © 1999, Artists Rights Society (ARS), New York/ADAGP, Paris/Estate of Marcel Duchamp.

contemporary culture is ultimately dependent on the development of new images and techniques of conceptualization.

However, another side of landscape, while still eidetic, has significantly less to do with pictures, or even with any obvious a priori imaging. Both J.B. Jackson and John Stilgoe have documented the complexity of the term *landscape* and draw distinctions between art-historical, representational versions and vernacular, geographical definitions.⁴ They describe the Old German *landschaft* as actually preceding *landskip* and as referring not to scenery but to the environment of a working community, a setting comprising dwellings, pastures, meadows, and fields, and surrounded by unimproved forest or meadow. Moreover, as Stilgoe writes, "Like the Anglo-Saxon *tithing* and the Old French *vill*, the word meant more than an organization of space; it connoted too the inhabitants of the place and their obligations to one another and to the land."⁵

154

In other words, the meaning of *landschaft* comprises a deep and intimate mode of relationship not only among buildings and fields but also among patterns of occupation, activity, and space, each often bound into calendrical time (Fig. 2). In this sense, *landschaft* is related to the German *gemeinschaft*, which refers to those forms and ideas that structure society in general. Whereas the scenery of *landschaft* may be picturable (that is, to the degree that scenery is a valid or knowable concept in the deeply habituated *landschaft*), its deeper, existential aspects circle more socially cognitive, eidetic processes. Spatial, material, and ambient characteristics are still here, but their essence is not necessarily that of Cartesian objecthood; they are present in sometimes foggy and multiplicitous ways, structured but not immediately visible—structured, in fact, more through use and habit in time than through any prior schematization.⁶

Distinctions between the designed landscape and the more evolved, working *landschaft* are further elaborated in cultural geography. As Raymond Williams remarks, "A working country is hardly ever a landscape."⁷ Here, Williams invokes the necessary detachment, contrivance, and focused attention

Fig 2. *October*, from *Les Très Riches Heures du Duc de Berry*. The Limbourg Brothers. 1413–16. Musée Condé, Chantilly, France.

necessary for the formation of landscape. Similarly, in distinguishing between "outsiders" and "insiders," Denis Cosgrove describes how:

> [t]he visible forms [of the land] and their harmonious integration to the eye, may indeed be a constituent part of people's relationship with the surroundings of their daily lives, but such considerations are sub-servient to other aspects of a working life with family and community. The composition of their landscape is much more integrated and inclu-sive with the diurnal course of life's events—with birth, death, festival, tragedy—all the occurrences that lock together human time and place. For the insider there is no clear separation of self from scene, subject from object.[8]

155

To the degree that everyday inhabitants experience *landscape*, they do so in a general state of distraction, and more through habit and use than through vision alone. Their eidetic image of place is bound into a greater phenomenal range of significance than vision or contemplation affords. By contrast, the outsider—the tourist, the spectator, the state, the administrative authority, the designer and planner—views landscape as an object, a thing to behold, and not only sceni-cally but instrumentally and ideologically. Enterprises such as tourism, plan-ning, and resource management are predicated precisely on such a synoptic management of land. Total vision affords a powerful set of instruments to not only describe the world but also to condition and control it. Just as there is no innocent eye, there is no neutral or passive imaging, meaning that landscape, too, as image, is neither inactive nor benign. If detachment and estrangement engender the very concept of landscape—as distanced prospect—then perhaps, too, landscape itself precipitates only further estrangement and withdrawal. This is landscape's dark side, alluded to in this book's introduction.[9]

As Michel Foucault and others have argued over the past twenty-five years, visual regimes—such as perspective and aerial views—are extremely effective instruments of power, enabling mass surveillance, projection, and camouflage. Synoptic, radiating vision extends a gaze that makes the viewer the master of all prospects, a scopic regime of control, authority, distance, and cool instrumental-ity.[10] Much of the so-called postmodern critique is targeted at exposing the authoritarian and alienating characteristics of synoptic objectification, includ-ing master planning (aerial regimes) and scenography (oblique and perspecti-val regimes). Extended to landscape, this critique suggests that a too-narrow concern for landscape as object (whether as formal composition or as quantifiable resource) overlooks the ideological, estranging, and aestheticizing effects of detaching the subject from the complex realities of participating in the world. Here, I want to echo Heidegger's "loss of nearness" as well as modern culture's withdrawal into privacy, as foreseen by Nietzsche and Marx.

Now, these remarks paint a perhaps too skeptical perspective that may be difficult for many to share. The scenic overlook, for example, is an apparently benign situation that presents a delightful view and transports one back into collective memory. One can survey the land with detached and distanced safety, caught momentarily in the dreamy and idealized presence of a harmonious and pleasing past. Many find escape from the ills of contemporary society in the scene and in their experience of recollection. That the scene itself displaces viewers, keeps them at a safe and uninvolved distance, and thus presents the landscape as little more than an aesthetic object of attention, escapes the attention of the gazing subject, as does the fact that the scenic moment literally transports viewers back in time, effectively decontextualizing them from the very real ills of the present. Obviously, looking at landscapes is a seductive and seemingly innocent affair, one that provides delight and pleasure for many, especially given the incredible and still-rising popularity of tourism, National Park attendance, and weekend drives in the country. Clearly, the public does not find landscape's scenic beauty at all a problem.

Indeed, scenic landscapes would not be a problem were it not for the sadly sentimental and escapist understructure that pervades their viewing; *there is simply nothing to look forward to*. Here, landscape is nothing more than an empty sign, a dead event, a deeply aestheticized experience that holds neither portent nor promise of a future. Both evil and invention are hidden, and the viewer is allowed to momentarily forget and escape from present and future difficulties, finding compensation in the recollection of earlier, "simpler" times. The net effect is personal withdrawal and nostalgia for the presence of the past, both of which are rooted in an aestheticized—rather than a productive, useful, or engaging—landscape experience.

Furthermore, the scenic landscape tends not only to displace the viewing subject in both space and time but also to displace the objects that it contains. As the geographer Jonathan Smith explains, the "durability" and autonomy of landscape causes its physical appearance to move further and further away from the agency and scene of its creation, and with this displacement "it loses the taint of intention and assumes the purity of nature."[11] In other words, because of the passage of time, landscape decontextualizes its artifactuality and takes on the appearance of something natural. Such enduring innocence may well herald great emancipating potential (as the landscape itself escapes the authority and control of its makers), but it also harbors a deceit that can be covertly appropriated by those who exercise power in society. For Smith, this point raises the question of "how the visible landscape might structure our regard of elements in that landscape...[and particularly] how it might, when judiciously styled, structure our regard of groups with certain social pretensions, privileged groups with a particular stake in the mode in which they are regarded."[12] Moreover, the seductive appeal of the "judiciously styled" visual landscape "may forestall reflection on the failure of society to furnish its members with the means to consume landscapes in more practical [and equitable] ways."[13] In other words, landscape can often obscure from its occupants the ideological impulses that motivated its formation and instead foster in them the feeling that they are in possession of a beautiful and innocent past, that they have escaped from the inequities and problems of the present.

It is through styling (design), of course, that one imbues the landscape with allusions to regional and cultural identity, enabling its occupants to believe that they are actually part of a collective, refined, and enlightened society. This is often an illusion, however, because the only real participation is that of the "little consumer" in the various aesthetic cultures of consumption. Here, think not only of the obvious references in real estate–driven suburbia and regal, colonial, and aristocratic images but also of the popular rise in the gardening and horticultural industry, or the recent trend in naturalist gardening and landscaping that inspires a sense of participation in the ecological and green movements. Landscape is bound into the marketplace and is available only at a price—the price of a package tour, an entry fee, a real estate view, or even the price of a scenic representation in souvenirs, photographs, and advertising.[14]

The veil of pretense that landscape erects is not, however, impermeable. In fact, its dominant, idealizing, and objectifying effects are broken every day. The erring realities of life contaminate the purity of any dominant master plan; an infinite number of "happenings" lend irony and disjuncture to a given scene. Machines in gardens, extermination trucks in countrified suburbs, homeless people in the civic center, and garbage on the church steps are examples of an ironic turn. Such everyday ironies reveal the pretension of representation and open social convention to critique and reflection. As Jonathan Smith writes,

"When closely observed, every self-image humans have written into the land-scape will betray its pretensions with ironic affirmations of an order that is both wider and weirder."[15] In other words, the landscape construct is inherently unstable, an indeterminate dimension that can be opened up through artistic practices and made to reveal alternative sets of possibility.

Consequently, to continue to construe the practice of landscape as the cre-ation of seductive and beautiful settings is only to forestall confronting the prob-lems of contemporary life. Veiling toxic sites or forest clear-cuts with buffer strips of hedgerow and wildflowers, while well intended, does not exactly address their causes and effects. Similarly, the largely scenic reconstruction of European-inspired streets and squares in today's modern cities does not guar-antee—and may actually retard—the performance of authentic public life (a point rendered even more ironic by the prevalence of surveillance cameras and security measures associated with many of these corporate-sponsored projects). As scenic or semantically encoded reserves, contemporary landscape expres-sions fail to activate anything more than the imagery of their own obsolescence, stylistic issues notwithstanding. The pictorial impulse denies deeper modes of existence, interrelationship, and creativity; it conceals the agendas of those who commission and construct it, and it seriously limits the design and planning arts in more critically shaping alternative cultural relationships with the earth. Whereas the architectural and planning arts work to improve the human condi-tion, they are reduced under largely representational regimes to simply express-ing or commenting on that condition. And, whereas the connoisseurs and the intelligentsia may enjoy the associative play of narrative references in high-art design, little that is socially emancipating and enabling results from authorial, representational landscapes.

The preceding paragraphs simplify the case greatly, but it is not my purpose here to outline a further critique of scenography. I am more interested in draw-ing a distinction between *landskip* (landscape as contrivance, primarily visual and sometimes also iconic or significant) and *landschaft* (landscape as an occu-pied milieu, the effects and significance of which accrue through tactility, use, and engagement over time). Both terms connote images, but the latter com-prises a fuller, more synaesthetic, and less picturable range than the former. Fur-thermore, the working landscape, forged collectively and according to more utilitarian demands than anything artistic or formal, has been more the tradi-tional domain of descriptive analysis by historians and geographers than of speculation by landscape architects.[16]

And yet, given the obvious limits of landscape as representation, not to mention the pathetic failing of most of what passes as landscaping today, is it possible to realign the landscape architectural project toward the productive and participatory phenomena of the everyday, working landscape? By this I mean to suggest a return neither to agrarian existence nor to functionalist practices but rather to emphasize the experiential intimacies of engagement, participation, and use over time, and to place geometrical and formal concerns in the service of human economy.[17] In this sense, the city is as much a participatory landscape as are the highly technological energy and agricultural fields of the Southwest, the worked plots of private gardens, and the activities circulating across vast urban surfaces. Similarly, we might say that gardens are defined less by formal appearances than through the *activities* of gardening, just as agricultural fields derive their form from the logistics of farming, and cities from the flows, processes, and forces of urbanization. In the working *landschaft,* performance and event assumes conceptual precedence over appearance and sign.

159

The emphasis here shifts from object appearances to processes of formation, dynamics of occupancy, and the poetics of becoming. While these processes may be imaged, they are not necessarily susceptible to picturing. As with reading a book or listening to music, the shaping of images occurs mentally. Thus, if the role of the landscape architect is less to picture or represent these activities than it is to facilitate, instigate, and diversify their effects in time, then the development of more performative forms of imaging (as devising, enabling, unfolding techniques) is fundamental to this task (Fig. 3).

A move away from ameliorative and scenographic *designs* toward more productive, engendering *strategies* necessitates a parallel shift from appearances and meanings to more prosaic concerns for how things work, what they do, how they interact,

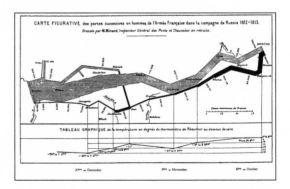

Fig 3. *Carte Figurative des pertes successives en hommes de l'Armée Francaise dans la campagne de Russia, 1812–1813.* Charles Joseph Minard. 1861. Taken from E.J. Marey, *La Mèthode Graphique* (Paris, 1885). This time-space map depicts the movement of Napoleon's army across Russia, the width of the band diminishing as the size of the army is reduced. The lower black line shows continued losses upon the retreat back to Poland owing to a bitterly cold winter.

and what agency or effects they might exercise over time. A return to complex and instrumental landscape issues involves more organizational and strategic skills than those of formal composition per se, more programmatic and metrical practices than solely representational.[18] Under such an operational rubric, issues such as program, event space, utility, economy, logistics, production, constraints, and desires become foregrounded, each turned through design toward newly productive and significant ends. This turning, as in *rhetorical turn* or the more interventionist *detournement*, is allied with the French term *dispositif*. This refers to the tactical but subtle and tempered disposition of parts (as in arrangement, complexion, management, and array). In setting up a well-disposed field, the designer stages the conditions necessary to precipitate a maximum range of opportunities in time, turning negatives and limits into positives and potentials.[19]

160

Although I am moving perhaps too quickly through this complex and important subject, I want to bring the question of image back into play, particularly the efficacy of imaging, or its agency in turning, forming, and enabling. To restate an important point, no matter how objective and descriptive the claims for it might be, imaging always exercises agency, actively unfolding, generating, and actualizing emergent realities. While theorists and historians focus on the object or the idea, designers focus on the actual activities of creativity, with the "doing" and with the often bewildering effects of bodying forth things neither foreseen nor predetermined. The question, then, concerns not so much the kinds of images designers should work with but rather what kinds of imaging *activities* should be developed and advanced. I am referring here to the actual durational experience of mapping, drawing, modeling, and making as a generative sequence in creative thinking (Fig. 4). This is where a clear distinction between imaging and picturing needs to be made.

W.J.T. Mitchell characterizes the distinctions between picture and image as:

...the difference between a constructed, concrete object (frame, support, materials, pigments, facture) and the vir-

Fig 4. *Water and mountain*. Sesshu. 1495. Ink on paper, 147.9 x 32.7 cm. Tokyo National Museum. This is one of a series of paintings derived using the technique of flinging ink onto canvas and spontaneously brushing the thrown pigment into an image. The emphasis is upon the generative process of seeing and creating rather than upon the painterly product.

tual, phenomenal appearance that it provides for the beholder; the difference between a deliberate act of representation ("to *picture* or depict") and a less voluntary, perhaps even passive or automatic act ("to *image* or imagine"); the difference between a specific kind of visual representation (the 'pictorial" image) and the whole realm of iconicity (verbal, acoustic, mental images).[20]

Mitchell describes this latter category as eidetic images, or:

>...*sensible forms*...which (according to Aristotle) emanate from objects and imprint themselves on the wax-like receptacles of our senses like a signet ring; the *fantasmata*, which are revived versions of those impressions called up by the imagination in the absence of the objects that originally stimulated them;...those "appearances" which (in common parlance) intrude between ourselves and reality.[21]

161

Thus, Mitchell identifies five families of image: the graphic (as in the picture), the optical (as in the mirror), the perceptual (as in cognitive sense), the mental (as in dreams, memories, and ideas), and the verbal (as in description and metaphor). Of course, each is never independent of the other categories; the mixing of synaesthetic senses and impressions is inevitable. Consequently, not all images are picturable, as in those mental ideas one "sees" but that bear no likeness to natural perception. One might speak here of an aesthetics of invisibility, a perception of essences. Speech, verbal description, gestures, and other rhetorical figures conjure up such otherwise invisible images, allowing one to see an idea. The ancient Greeks recognized the image aspect of ideas, as in the term *eidos*, which conjoins "idea" with "something seen." This is why imaging, understood as idea formation, is integral to the conception and practice of landscape. In *landskip*, the making of a picture participates in and makes what is to be pictured, whereas in *landschaft* the formation of synaesthetic, cognitive images forges a collective sense of place and relationship evolved through *work*.

This latter phenomenon can be likened to a kind of mental map, or diagram, a spatio-organizational image that is not necessarily picturable but is nonetheless laconic and communicable. As with all maps, such an image produces an appearance that is otherwise not visible, even though it rings true and eventually naturalizes into accepted convention. After all, space by itself is neither sensible nor imaginable, but is instead created in the act of imaging. Such eidetic constructs effectively bind individuals to a collective and orient them

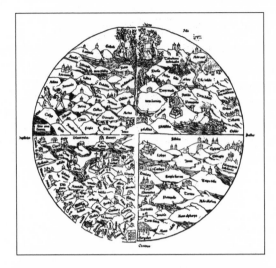

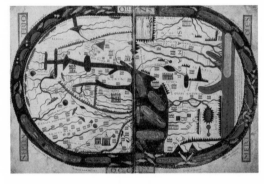

within a larger milieu. Thus, as highly situated and subjectively constituted schemata, eidetic mappings lie at the core of shaping an invisible landscape, one that is more an unfolding spatiality than surface appearance, more poetic property than the delineation of immediate real estate (Figs. 5 and 6).

Now, what does all this mean for landscape architectural practice? First, it points to both the difficulties and potentials that underlie representational technique in design, especially those conventions—such as plan, perspective, and rendering—that have become so institutionalized and taken for granted that we fail to appreciate their force and efficacy in shaping things. Second, it points to the limits exercised by the pictorial impulse over other aspects of knowing and belonging, highlighting the difficulty of representing other dimensions of being. And third, it suggests a need to revise, enhance, and invent forms of representational technique that might engender more engaging landscapes than the still-life vignettes of many contemporary landscapes. Those techniques that might prove most useful in this regard may be called *eidetic operations*—specific ideational techniques for construing (imagining) and constructing (projecting) new landscapes. These are partly

Fig 5. *Mappemonde Rudimentum Nivitiorum*, 1473. From the *l'atlas du vicomte de Santarém*. Bibliothèque Nationale, Paris.

Fig 6. *Beatus of Liebana from Saint-Sever*, c. eleventh century. From *Le commentaire sur l'Apocalypse*. Bibliothèque Nationale, Paris. This ovoid mappemonde shows the classical three continents (Africa, Asia, and Europe) and depicts the still mysterious Australia as a crescent separated by a sea. In this figure is the caption: "Next to the three parts of the world, there is a fourth beyond the Ocean, towards the south and unknown to us because the sun is too strong. In these areas live the Antipods."

akin, though not identical, to what Marco Frascari calls "technographies," composite images of three essential relationships defined as:

> 1) between a real architectural artifact and a reflected or projected image of it; 2) between a real artifact and the instrumental image in the mind of someone involved in a building trade related with its construction; and 3) between the instrumental image devised by the architect and the symbolic image that rests in the collective memory of a culture.[22]

Thus, explains Frascari, "technographies are enigmas that can only be solved in construction…images that are played in the world of construction but not necessarily explained."[23]

163

Designers need to more fully equip their arsenal of eidetic operations, in both the imaginative and efficacious senses of technographies. In reading analyses of image construction—whether E.H. Gombrich, Nelson Goodman, Rudolf Arnheim, Jean Piaget, Ernst Cassirer, Norman Bryson, or W.J.T. Mitchell, for instance—or in simply looking at the great works of art over the centuries—whether maps, paintings, collage, performance arts, or cinematic and digital media—I am struck by the range of types and forms of representation in comparison to the relatively small number of techniques used in the landscape, architectural, and planning arts. Imaging has a metaphoric agency in that the (mostly arbitrary) bringing together of two or more elements fosters a host of associative possibilities. When Picasso joins a bicycle handlebar to a down-turned seat, the new union is suggestive not only of a bull's head but also of a minotaur (as in part animal, part machine), an image that may be actualized by placing and using the assembly on a real bicycle. Similarly, such extension of association is achieved through the ideogram, or the pairing of two elements to produce a new image, a conception that is otherwise not picturable. This is exemplified, for instance, in Duchamp's *Genre Allegory (George Washington)*, 1943, where iodine-stained gauze bandage, speckled with military stars, constitutes the profile silhouette of Washington and invokes a tattered American flag, if not the rupture of the American sense of nationhood (Fig. 7).

Such eidetic images are fundamental stimuli to creativity and invention; they do not represent the reality of an idea but rather inaugurate its possibility. By contrast, images in conventional design practice tend more toward the wholly technological, the strictly denotative, the explicit, and the immediately intelligible. I am more than well aware of the increasing preponderance of unintelligible,

hermetic abstractions on the academic gallery and magazine circuits; however, a range of imaginative and demonstrative eidetic instruments greater than that the conventional practitioner currently employs must be developed if landscape and urbanism are to be recovered as significant contemporary practices. If landscape architects construct ideas, then the role of imaging in idea formation and projection needs to be better articulated than simply by opposing "artistic" renderings to "technical" working documents. In other words, perhaps a key to understanding eidetic imaging in design is found in a kind of thinking that in neither instrumental nor representational but simultaneously both.

It should be emphasized that such innovations do not necessarily have to be radical and completely new; they may derive equally from a subtle realignment of the codes and conventions of some convention or technique. In an essay on architectural drawing, David Leatherbarrow has argued that the primary mode of eidetic imaging in building belongs to the orthographic views of plan and section: "The plan view presents a simultaneity that prosaic seeing never enjoys; the section offers a penetration that is strikingly detective. Each translates depth by concentrating the temporality of its eventual unfolding."[24] The fact that orthography enables architectural insight and ideation in such fundamental and yet inexhaustible ways makes it perhaps the most powerful tool of eidetic imaging for spatial design. In recent years, the superimposition of multiple and sometimes incongruent layers in plan and section has led to the generation of new possibilities. Rem Koolhaas, for instance, effectively altered traditional large-scale planning and diagramming from simply composing form and organizing program to completely *reformulating* form and program into freshly hybrid conditions. The dismantling and isolation of layers and elements in plan not only proposes a productive working method, akin to montage, but also focuses attention on the logic of *making* the landscape rather than on its appearance per se. Bernard Tschumi's work with notation and combinatory indexes further exemplifies the reworking of certain orthographic and choreographic conventions.

Fig 7. *Genre Allegory (George Washington)*, Marcel Duchamp, 1943. Cardboard, iodine, gauze, nails, gilt-metal stars, 53.2 x 40.5 cm. Musée National d'Art Moderne, Paris © 1999, Artists Rights Society (ARS), New York/ADAGP, Paris/Estate of Marcel Duchamp.

In a similar vein, contemporary urban designers (such as Koolhaas, MVRDV, and a-topos) have developed a series of techniques they call "datascapes." These are revisions of conventional analytical and quantitative maps and charts that both reveal and construct the shape-forms of forces and processes operating across a given site (Fig. 8).[25] Not only are these imagings constructive and suggestive of new spatial formations but also they are so "objectively" constructed—derived from numbers, quantities, facts, and pure data—that they have great persuasive force in the hugely bureaucratic decision-making and management aspects of contemporary city design. Where they differ from the quantitative maps of conventional planning is in their imaging of data in knowingly rhetorical and generatively instrumental ways. They are

designed not only to reveal the spatial effects of shaping forces (such as regulatory, zoning, legal, economic, and logistical rules and conditions) but also to construct an eidetic argument in space-time geometry. The artistry lies in the *use* of the technique, how things are framed and set up. There is no assumption of truth or positivist methodology; instead, the datascape planner reveals new possibilities latent in a given field simply by framing the issues differently. Unlike the assumed and passive neutrality of

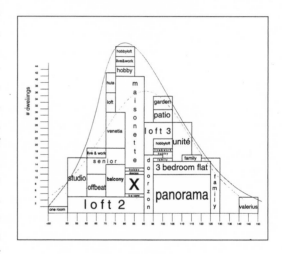

traditional data maps, datascapes reformulate given conditions in such a way as to produce novel and inventive solutions.

The revision of such fundamental imaging techniques as mapping, planning, diagramming, and sectioning effectively liberates the designer/planner from representation. In concentrating on how things work, how they go together, and how the project makes sense accords priority to the *working* of inhabited ground as opposed to the formalization of scenic landscapes.[26] Rather than a series of drawings that show what a finished project looks like or how all the different parts fit together, I am arguing for the thinking through a *program*—not a description—that outlines the performative dimensions of a

Fig 8. *Housing Silo,* Amsterdam: number of dwellings to area occupied. MVRDV, 1996.

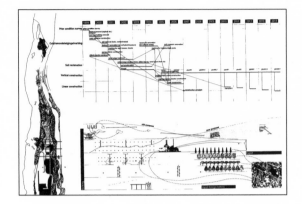

project's unfolding (Fig. 10). Sanford Kwinter has argued:

> diagrams do not themselves produce form...but rather [they] emit formative and organizational influence, shape-giving pressures that cannot help but be "embodied" in all subsequent states of the given region of concrete reality in which they act.[27]

166

Hybridized and composite diagram techniques will allow even further advances in landscape formation because of their inclusive and instrumental capacity. Techniques such as layering and separation, for example, enable a multiplicity of issues to be included and incorporated into the development of a project. Composite montage is essentially an affiliative and productive technique, aimed not toward limitation and control but toward emancipation, heterogeneity, and open-ended relations among parts. In particular, analytic and systematic operations can precipitate revelatory and rich effects. This point is as true for the dense sketches and notations inscribed and overlaid in the technical drawings of Carlo Scarpa, for instance, where multiple views and scales are developed as a sort of speculative yet systematic unfolding, as it is for the more strategic layer-diagrams by architects such as Koolhaas, Tschumi, and Eisenman. Whereas both these imaging types differ significantly in their formation and function, they share the same character of incorporating multiple levels of information; they avoid immediacy and reduction. Moreover, composite techniques focus on the instrumental function of drawing with regard to production; they are efficacious rather than representational. In other words, through utilizing a variety of analytic and analogous imaging techniques, otherwise disparate parts can be brought into productive relationship, less as *parts* of a visual composition and more as *means* or agents.

Other composite imaging operations include ideograms, imagetexts, scorings, pictographs, indexes, samples, game boards, cognitive tracings, and scal-

Fig 9. Site construction sequence, Venice Island, Pennsylvania. Wookju Jeong, 1998.

ings. Imagetexts, in particular, are conspicuously absent and underdeveloped in the design arts. These are synthetic and dialectical composites of words and pictures that together contain and produce an array of striking and otherwise unpicturable images.[28] As Mark Taylor describes, "The audio-visual trace of the word involves an inescapable materiality that can be thought only if it is figured."[29] Whereas most architectural and planning images combine words on drawings (as labels, keys, names, etc.), the sheer connotative power of this combination is rarely developed beyond what is, again, a merely descriptive function. And yet imagetexts by artists as divergent as William Blake, Richard Long, and Barbara Kruger, and by architects as divergent as Daniel Libeskind, Raoul Bunschoten, and Arakawa and Madeline Gins push the rhetorical and transfigurative force of synaesthetic imaging in extremely suggestive ways. To echo Mitchell, imagetexts, like ideograms, "must be construed not just as representations but as whole conceptions."[30]

The landscape imagination is a power of consciousness that transcends visualization. To continue to project landscapes as formal and pictorial objects is to reduce significantly the full scope of the landscape idea. If ideas are images projected into the political and cultural imagination in ways that guide societies

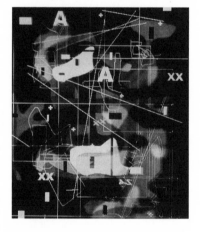

as they try to manage change, then their absence can only precipitate social regression into memory (nostalgia), on the one hand, or complete deference to technology (rational expediency), on the other. How one generates and effectuates ideas is bound into a cunning fluency with imaging. Similarly, the future of landscape as a culturally significant practice is dependent on the capacity of its inventors to image the world in new ways and to body forth those images in richly phenomenal and efficacious terms.

Fig. 10. Ideogram, Greenport Harborfront, New York. James Corner, 1996.

Fig. 11. Älsvjö Gameboard, James Corner, 1999.

Notes

1   To the degree that the term *environment* has assumed many meanings and values (as evidenced in the number and divergence of environmental philosophies), it is true to say that environment, too, in its various mediated forms, has become just as much a subjectively constituted and as sensible an *idea* as *landscape*. And, of course, here too lie the inevitable ideological strands inherent to any landscape formation. See Augustin Berque, "Beyond the Modern Landscape," *AA Files* 25 (summer 1993): 33–37. See also Alain Roger, *Court traité du paysage* (Paris: Gallimard, 1997).

2   *Eidetic* means "of a mental image." Such an image may be picturable but it may equally be acoustic, tactile, or otherwise imagined. See also notes 11 and 12.

3   I use the term *theories* here in the ancient Greek sense of *theoria*, meaning "to see."

4   John Brinckerhoff Jackson, *Discovering the Vernacular Landscape* (New Haven, Conn.: Yale University Press, 1984), 1–8; John R. Stilgoe, *Common Landscape of America, 1580 to 1845* (New Haven, Conn.: Yale University Press, 1982), 12–29.

5   Stilgoe, 12.

6   An important reference here is Maurice Merleau-Ponty, *Phenomenology of Perception*, trans. Colin Smith (London: Routledge and Kegan Paul, 1962), especially 3–63, and 207–298. See also Michel de Certeau, *The Practice of Everyday Life,* trans. Steven Rendell (Berkeley and Los Angeles, Calif.: University of California Press, 1988).

7   Raymond Williams, *The City and the Country* (New York: Oxford University Press, 1973), 36.

8   Denis Cosgrove, *Social Formation and the Symbolic Landscape* (1984; reprint, Madison: University of Wisconsin Press, 1998), 19.

9   See also John Barrell, *The Dark Side of Landscape* (Cambridge: Cambridge University Press, 1980); W.J.T. Mitchell, *Landscape and Power* (Chicago: University of Chicago Press, 1994); and eds. James Duncan and David Ley, *Place/Culture/Representation* (London: Routledge, 1993).

10   See Michel Foucault, *Discipline and Punish*, trans. Alan Sheridan (New York: Vintage Books, 1979); and Martin Jay, "Scopic Regimes of Modernity," in *Vision and Visuality*, ed. Hal Foster (Seattle: Bay Press, 1988), 3–23.

11   Jonathan Smith, "The Lie That Blinds: Destabilizing the Text of Landscape," in *Place/Culture/Representation*, 78–92.

12   Ibid., 82.

13   Ibid., 86.

14   See Alexander Wilson, *The Culture of Nature: North American landscape from Disney to the Exxon Valdez* (Cambridge, Mass.: Blackwell, 1992).

15   Smith, "The Lie That Blinds," 87.

16   See John Stilgoe, "J.B. Jackson, A Literary Appreciation," in *Land Forum* 1 (summer/fall, 1997): 8–10.

17   As in the Greek *oikonomia*, meaning "the management of a household or state," invoking ecological, economic, and productive responsibilities.

18   The term *metrical* is used here all its senses: numerical, spacing, instrumental, and poetic. See James Corner and Alex S. MacLean, *Taking Measures Across the American Landscape* (New Haven, Conn.: Yale University Press, 1996).

19   See François Jullien, *The Propensity of Things: Toward a History of Efficacy in China,* trans. Janet Lloyd (New York: Zone Books, 1995).

20   W.J.T. Mitchell, *Picture Theory* (Chicago: University of Chicago Press, 1994), 4 (n. 5).

21   W.J.T. Mitchell, *Iconology: Image, Text, Ideology* (Chicago: University of Chicago Press, 1986), 10.

22   Marco Frascari, "A New Angel/Angle in Architectural Research: The Ideas of Demonstration," in *Journal of Architectural Education* 44, no. 1 (1990): 11–18; quote on 15.

23 Ibid., 16–17.

24 David Leatherbarrow, "Showing What Otherwise Hides Itself," *Harvard Design Magazine* (fall 1998): 50–55. See also James Corner, "Representation and Landscape," *Word & Image* 8:3 (July–Sept. 1992): 243–275.

25 See interview with Winy Maas and essays by Stan Allen and Bart Lootsma in *El Croquis* 86: *MVRDV* (1997); and "Datascapes," in Winy Maas, Jacob Van Rijs, and Richard Koek, *FARMAX: Excursions on Density* (Rotterdam: 010 Publishers, 1998). See also James Corner, "The Agency of Mapping," in *Mappings,* ed. Denis Cosgrove (London: Reaktion, 1999), 212–258.

26 See also Stan Allen, "Diagrams Matter," in *ANY* 23: *Diagram Work* (fall 1998): 16–19; Julia Czerniak, "Challenging the Pictorial: Recent Landscape Practice," in *Assemblage* 34 (1998): 110–120; and *Architectural Design Profiles* 121: *Games of Architecture* (May–June 1996).

27 Sanford Kwinter, "The Geneaology of Models," in *ANY* 23: *Diagram Work* (fall 1998): 58.

28 This is a slightly narrowed definition. Mitchell, *Picture Theory*, extends the term to cinema, advertising, cartoons, and theater (for instance: "Artaud's emphasis on mute spectacle and Brecht's deployment of textual projections are not merely 'aesthetic' innovations but precisely motivated interventions in the semio-politics of the stage," p. 91). Also see Roland Barthes, *The Responsibility of Forms: Music, Art and Representation* (Farrar, Straus and Giroux, 1985).

29 Mark C. Taylor and Esa Saarinen, *Imagologies: Media Philosophy* (London: Routledge, 1994).

30 Mitchell, *Picture Theory*, 146.

169

Chapter 11

Leveling the Land

David Leatherbarrow

Earth, is this not what you want: to arise within us
invisibly?—Is it not your dream
someday to be invisible?—Earth: invisible!
What if not transformation is your urgent commission?

—*Duinesian Elegies,* R.M. Rilke

In a time when the basic premises of both architecture and landscape are being reconsidered, the topic of leveled land calls for attention because it is arguably the first and most fundamental act of topographical construction. Whether mounded up on an open plain or cut into the slope of a hillside, every terrain that has been transformed into a terrace serves as the physical and conceptual foundation for the accommodation and enactment of a broad range of topographical purposes, from the most mundane to the most elevated. Without this basis, most cultural practices are quite simply impossible. Certainly it is true that landscapes lacking level can be aesthetically pleasing, yet they may well be only that, which is to say they may well be useless and unlivable. This makes the platform a primary topic in the sort of site construction that envisages inhabitation. Yet, despite its primacy, leveled land is rarely given much attention in current discourse, perhaps because it is so commonly taken for granted.

The question this paper asks concerns the meanings conferred by topographical levels. Considerations of geometry and shape are important, but formal considerations of this kind are much more interesting when they are seen in connection with the cultural meanings they sustain. In the past, leveled land has symbolized attitudes toward gender, for example. Likewise, platform construction was, in some societies, accorded political significance on the premise that site building prefigures city building or sets the stage for public life.

In what follows, meanings of this kind are introduced in consideration of ancient, Renaissance, and modern cases. This range is invoked not to suggest the influence of one on the other but to differentiate ways of interpreting a topic

Fig. 1. Rising Earth (Semele?), red-figured krater. From H. Robert, *Archäologische Mährchen*, 1898.

of design that I see as fundamental in site building. Moreover, I do not suggest that these meanings should be revived or restored in our time (implying that we have none of our own) nor that they should be rejected (as a sign of contemporary enlightenment); rather, I suggest that analogous potentials should be sought and can be found within contemporary culture and current practices of terrain design—that we, too, can discover in topographical construction symbols of existence. I will achieve my purpose if I demonstrate the interplay of the technical and ethical aspects of leveled land, for that is where the real drama of place building is played out. There, too, we will find the possibility of recovering a fuller sense of landscape.

172

The word *terrain* is cognate with *terrace*, both deriving from the Latin *terra*, which not only signifies "earth" but also gives rise to a set of approximately synonymous terms—*parterre, terrestrial, territory,* and *terra firma*—as well as the names of some earthbound objects—*tureen* and *terrier*, for example. As above, so below; anything beneath the level of the terrace is *subterranean*, hence *interment*. Together with its designation of particular geological strata, the etymology of *terrain* connotes a particular material quality. *Terra* is related to *tersa*, which signifies in Latin "dry ground" and translates the Greek *tersesthai*, meaning "dried" or "to dry up," as soil is when baked by the sun. From this last set of terms derives the English word *terse*, which means "neat," "concise," and "abbreviated" as well as "clean and dry" or "wiped off"—hence the word *detergent*, the action of which leaves a shine, like the gloss of polished stone. Not just stone reflects light; leveled terrain can have these characteristics too. To understand why, we must try to imagine what is beneath its surface.

If the terrace is essentially a level, limited, and dry deck, the subsoil is, by contrast, unlimited and wet, or at least moist. This recognizes a vertical antinomy between what is dry above and wet below the level of constructed topography, an antinomy that has had great force and amplitude in the history of ideas about the nature of built sites. For present purposes, a topical reading of this history can begin with the ancient Greeks, for whom a number of polarities were associated with the contrast between all things wet and dry—unbounded and bounded, polluted and pure, feminine and masculine, and most broadly, content and form.[1] These pairs were differentiated in Pythagorean symbolism and restated by Aristotle, but they appeared even earlier in cosmologies that emerged out of archaic patriarchal social institutions. The stuff or matter of creation was symbolized as formless and wet, likely to leak, and lacking of lasting limits, which explained for Aristotle matter's "desire" for form, a desire consummated in the marriage between substance and shape.[2] Before this, in an age, time, or moment when the stuff of the world was without shape, matter was not only undefined and amorphous but *unknowable*, for it was only through edges that all things were defined.[3] Edgeless matter was, nevertheless, vital and procreative—a fertile fluidity from which all visible things arose.

Water exaggerates these qualities of shapeless territory. "Always below me is water," says the twentieth-century surrealist poet Francis Ponge.[4] We must lower our eyes to see its formless and fresh shine. Water has the virtue of unselfish willingness to sacrifice its present form for the shape of its next container, doing this continually and insistently, as if this act of humility were its lifelong task and highest purpose—as if its charge were to fill every space it enters the way sound does a room, pressing everything other than itself out of its new container. If passive, water is forcefully so, and therefore consequential. The pressure it exerts substantiates shape, serving as its underside energy and source. By contrast, the word *formal* identifies the dry and empty sort of figures that lack this expressive depth. Unfortunately, it is precisely this latter sort that is the subject matter of much aesthetic appreciation.

For the ancient Greeks, this substantiating force was generally thought to be female. Anne Carson, a contemporary classics scholar, poet, and feminist critic, observes that in the ancient Hippocratic treatises women, not men, were thought to be essentially congenial to water: "The female [writes the Hippocratic author] flourishes more in an environment of water, from things cold and wet and soft, whether food or drink or activities."[5] Further, subterranean soil and women were believed akin to one another by virtue of their shared vital liquidity, because both were thought capable of channeling the inexhaustible reservoirs of procreative power, often thought to be a dark liquid, but sometimes—and

173

Fig. 2. Dance of Maenads, white-ground pyxis; the Sotheby Painter. Walters Art Gallery, Baltimore, Maryland.

surprisingly—assigned a kind of transparency, especially after some poets and philosophers had transferred the creative potency of innards to the mind, determining it to be the source of ideation.

The seat of this power was not necessarily cranial, however.[6] The model for the body's productivity was the earth itself. Thus, the elaborate symbolism of the earth as the great receptacle should not be allowed to eclipse the correspondence between its withdrawal and emergence, for the two movements were always seen as reciprocal: if the earth receives it also makes itself manifest; it retreats and it arises. This transaction was symbolized compactly in the cosmology of Anixamander: "Whence things have their origin [*aperion*], there they must pass away, according to necessity, for they must pay penalty for their injustice [the injustice of wanting to linger in the light too long]."[7] According to Carson, men, in the mind and experience of the ancient Greeks, were divorced from this cycle of arising and withdrawal and, thus, from formlessness, because they were thought self-defined and defining, upright and dry.[8] Accordingly, marriage was thought the means whereby formed and unformed, or dry and wet, were united, in imitation of the earth, or as a way of participating in its renewal.

Being more exact about what the Greeks saw as the different sites of this union will return me to the subject of level land. To do so I propose abbreviating a story told by ancient Pherecydes of Syros, who was reputedly the teacher of Pythagoras. He explained that the world was formed when Zeus threw a matrimonial veil over the head of the goddess of the underworld. This nuptial textile instituted marriage: "When everything was ready," the story goes, "they held the wedding. On the third day Zeus made a great and fair cloth, and on it he wove the [lines or divisions of the] earth, the ocean and the houses of the ocean…. This they say was the first *anacalypteria* [wedding veil], from this the custom [of the veiled bride] arose both for gods and men."[9]

The marital veil, on this account, was really a map that entwined in its fibers the axes and ordinance of the world. It was not really a covering but a gauze, gossamer, or filigree framework that *disclosed* an inhabitable landscape, one that had been there but was unknown, meaning that the act of veiling resulted in an unveiling. Surely this is an outrage for logical thought, for nothing that covers can also uncover. But if we suspend for a moment the principle of noncontradiction we can see in this veiling-unveiling a reminder that every interpretation or disclosure presents itself through its own lens or framework, that the things themselves are always (and finally) inaccessible. The veil preserves or safeguards the earth's transcendence by singing it. The word *anacalypteria* derives from

anakalypto, to uncover, and is related to *an logous*, to use open speech; which suggests the following: the lines and light from the sky *articulated* the ground; Zeus-work served the soil by providing a framework for its voice. Veiled or praised in this way, Chthonia, who had been darkly parthenogenetic (engendered, but not through sexual union), became Gaia, still abundant after the veil, but no longer emergent (*parthenos*)—rather, emerged and, consequently, visible.

The veil, map, or woven cloth was thus a trace of the act by which soil appeared within an articulated framework. Until that time, while still unveiled, unwoven, and unlined, dark earth had been (and would have remained) uncharted and unnavigable, like the sea, expansive and absorbing. By means of this chart of horizontals, the earth was shown to be a livable horizon, matter having been abbreviated into a mat. A historical consequence of this act was the transformation of ageless latency into a present condition; the sketch of figures buried with the earth's vertical depth was rendered into something recognizable as a horizon of human affairs. Through patterned textile a livable *landscape* first emerged in light.[10] Yet, what emerged was neither pictorial nor scenic, as the "scape" of landscape might suggest; were neologisms acceptable, a better term for an appearance such as this would be *landscript* or *landgraph*.

The graph, map, or mat I describe was a constructed thing; through artistic work, Zeus fashioned this world-building weave. Because weaving was, in ancient Greek society, generally women's work, one detects in this myth some measure of envy; if not that, at least of emulation. Nevertheless, insofar as it was made by divine hands, this fabric served as the paradigm of any skinlike surface resulting from textile art. *Textile* is the English translation of the Latin word *texere*, which in turn derives from a family of Greek words cognate with *techne*.

Fig. 3. *Baulatura*, from Berti Pichat, *Instituzioni di agricoltura*, Bologna, 1863.

Especially important in this case is *tiktein*, which means to engender or give birth, and relates directly to the disclosing sense of *techne*, signifying the knowledge, energy, or work whereby something comes into appearance. In prephilosophical accounts, this potential was the upward or outward pressure to which I refer above, resulting in an outward shine, or showing itself as congenial to light.[11] The nuptial veil made by Zeus was an artifact that allowed the earth to become articulate because it—I mean the weave—united subsoil with sky.

I want to stress that in this myth the sky image, the combination of lines and light, was only half of the reality of leveled land, a half that we tend to take as the whole. Precisely because of its tendency to withdraw from the other, the native half is often neglected and, generally, taken to be nothing more than a resource, assuming the privative sense of matter as formlessness. To build a fuller sense of the landscape's underside and substantial part, reference to another map may be helpful, one presented by Homer that is much more famous than the tale of Pherecydes. This story, and the mapmaking it describes, elaborates Greek symbols of political order, specifically the balanced and just correspondence among people, the basis for civic intersubjectivity.[12]

In the eighteenth book of the *Iliad*, Homer describes the making of the shield of Achilles: "When Hephaestus fashioned Achilles' shield he wrought emblems of the earth, the heavens, and the sea." This shield/map was also a dance floor, a *choros*: on the shield/map the famed god wove a dancing floor like that at Knossos Daedalus fashioned for Ariadne. Homer did not describe the level, lines, or material of this radiant surface—instead, the choreography it traced out, for across its sectional arc he wove together the steps of young dancers: "Here young boys and girls courted…linking their arms, gripping each other's wrists…and now they would run in rings on their skilled feet…and now they would run in rows, in rows criss-crossing rows—rapturous dancing."[13] Making a dancing deck such as this meant making a *human* textile, a society, a city. In Homeric myth, people were woven together once the vertical parts of place had been sewn into one—that is, once an artificial platform joined subsoil and sky. One imagines that its golden polish resulted from the action of the sun and of the dancers' feet. In ancient Sparta, the *agora*, or town center, was called *choros*, or dancing floor.[14] On this level the decisions of the *polis* were acted out.[15]

No such dance is possible on a wet surface, nor, for that matter, is civil society. Surfaces are slippery when wet. The aim of terrace building is not to eliminate water, though, nor to escape it, for durable platforms are dry only on their sun-facing surfaces. Pavements, said the renaissance architect Alberti, "rejoice"

176

in being laid in damp or humid conditions, for moisture welds their parts into an entire solid.[16] This weld restates the ancient cosmologist's weave, this solid the permanent unity of the *polis*.

Let me proceed with Alberti. When describing the siting of a platform on which a town could be established, he stated that all platforms were to be built up and based on a level eminence. This was motivated by an interest in both dignity and convenience. Dirt and rubbish would accumulate on a site if it were not raised up, he said, and enemies would be a constant source of trouble if they had the opportunity to attack from higher ground. Much better would be a fight on equal footing. Just as uneven advantage made both fighting and victory unjust, level standing equalized or balanced combat. So, too, in city building—level footing justified encounters. Rectitude so conceived was charged with social, legal, and structural meanings.[17] On such a terrace city dwellers could stand and stay together in rows criss-crossing rows. Associated with the word *stand* are a family of indicative terms—*state*, *statute*, *statue*, *stance*, *standard*, *establish*, *stable*, *station*, *static*, and *status*—that in each case refer to an experience of physical and cultural uprightness. *Droiture* in French and *aufrechtung* in German convey the same sense. Similarly, the upright experience of leveled land was thought to *sustain* civil concord.

Leveled land is not flat, however. For Alberti (Book 7, chapter 1, section 6), platforms built under the sky should have a slope of 2 inches in 10 feet, to allow for rainwater to run off. This follows the recommendation of Vitruvius (an expert in plumbing) and conforms to ancient Roman practice, as Alberti knew it from his own surveys and measurements of ancient monuments. The floor of the Pantheon in Rome is slightly convex in section, a profile that sheds the rainwater that enters the interior from the oculus above. This gentle curve appears in Piranesi's accurate sectional drawings. Admittedly, nothing more pedestrian could be observed about the Pantheon than the way its base platform stays dry.

An exterior equivalent that merits thought is the mounded landscape that resulted from sixteenth- and seventeenth-century practices of land reclamation in the Italian Veneto and the agricultural practices around Bologna, in the Po valley.[18] The surface pattern of these earthworks was a weave of arable areas and drainage lines. Equally important was their profile, or section, which consisted of a series of convex curves, each conforming to the cross section of a sarcophagus lid or a large trunk (*baule*), although, obviously, much, much larger. The English word that expresses this compacted top surface is *bale*, whether of cotton or straw—a word that is cognate with *ball*, a circle or curve that can be read

177

in both plan and section. The Italian word *baule* and the profile it identifies serves as the root of the term that was used to name these dried-up sites: *baulatura*.

Another English word for such a storage trunk is indicative of its anthropological equivalent: *chest*. When the shape of a storage chest (or treasury) is compared to the bulge of a breastplate, a connection to the shield of Achilles can be inferred.[19] Dried land, sarcophagus, shield, breastplate, and chest—in each case we are presented with a section that reveals a slight upward or outward bulge, one that reconciles coordinate surface geometry with enlivening but unseen pressure (of the dark earth, in the case of a dry terrace, of breath in one's chest). Leveled land, in both the Venetian and Greek symbols, is neither unmarked nor flat; it is, instead, a subtle crossing-over or marriage of the two.

In Renaissance architecture the design that expresses this symbolism most eloquently is the piazza at the center of Michelangelo's Campidoglio in Rome. The connection I suggest between the breastplate or shield and the slight convexity of leveled earth was proposed in this case by James Ackerman: "The mound-like rise of Michelangelo's oval…[can be related to] a type of ancient shield upon which the zodiac was represented. The legendary shield of Achilles was adorned with the celestial signs, and Alexander the Great adopted the Achillean type along with the epithet Kosmokrator—ruler of the Universe."[20] This title, Ackerman continues, was adopted by the Roman emperors and was perfectly suited to Marcus Aurelius, whose equestrian statue stood as an upright at the center or on the top of this oval mound.

The Python usually appeared at the center of the type of shield to which Ackerman refers. This archaic figure introduces a rich and elaborate symbolism of underground genesis.[21] Related to it is the equally abundant imagery of *omphalos* or *umbilicus*, both seen as sites of the center of the world or cosmos, and both represented by an upward bulge of the earth, often covered with a weave or network pattern, and always symbolizing fecundity and emergence— and obviously female.[22] Varro defined it as follows: "What the Greeks call the *omphalos* is something at the side of the temple at Delphi, of the shape of a *thesaurus* [domical or mounded treasury], and they say it is the tumulus of Python."[23] Here one might recall the profile of the Pantheon floor, on the assumption that drainage was not all its designer was thinking about. The surface pattern of the Campidoglio pavement is more expressive, however, insofar as its geometry is stretched by the mound's upward push. Ackerman observes that the central boss on military shields was called the *umbilicus* or navel. One meaning of the python symbolism was victory over death, or reemergence, a meaning appropriate to the treasury (burial place) of the *kosmokrator*, by whose means dynastic continuity was assured. The pregnant profile of the site was shaped to express this subterranean potential for (re)emergence.

The curved line of leveled land is always apparent, visually, as a horizon line. The most eloquent twentieth-century testimony to such a formation was given by the architect Le Corbusier in his book *Precisions*. "I am in Brittany," he said, "[where] this line [of the horizon] is the limit between the ocean and sky; a vast horizontal plane extends toward me. I appreciate the voluptuousness of this masterly restfulness…The sinuousness of the sandy beaches like a very soft undulation on the horizontal plane delights me."[24] The image of a slightly curved horizon figures in the fore- or middle ground of many of his drawings— in the drawings of his North African projects, for example. A better-known instance, perhaps, is his exterior perspective drawing of Villa Savoye, shown rising from and articulating the crest of a landscape. In his Brittany encounter, Le Corbusier confronted the essential form of the site's counterprinciple:

179

> I was walking and suddenly stopped. Between my eyes and the horizon a sensational event has occurred: a vertical rock, in granite is there, upright, like a menhir; its vertical makes a right angle with the horizon. Crystallisation, fixation of the site. This is a place to stop, because here is a complete symphony, magnificent relationships, nobility. The vertical gives the meaning of the horizontal. One is alive because of the other.[25]

For Le Corbusier, the right angle was a symbol of the most basic truth of his art and of his creativity. It was also an image of his personal life, or at least his married life.[26] This last point is made evident in the centerpiece of the iconostasis of the *Poem to the Right Angle*, section E3, dedicated to his wife, Yvonne, affectionately known as Von. The day she died, Le Corbusier described her as "the guardian angel of the

Fig. 4. "The Point of all Dimensions," Le Corbusier, *Précision sur un état présent de l'architecture et de l'urbanisme* (Paris, 1930). Foundation Le Corbusier.

foyer, of my foyer." The term *foyer* means "hearth," in this instance, and stands for "home." The image in the *Poem* is accompanied by the following text:

> Categorical right angle of character the heart's spirit. I gazed into the mirror of character and found myself/there found in me found. Looking ahead horizontal, arrows. She is right she rules and knows height/does not know it. Who made her thus, where does she come from? She is rightness/child of limpid heart/present on earth/close to me. Daily acts of humility vouch for her greatness.[27]

180

The image has at its center a black horizon joining sky and water (also a spiral and mountain); the intersecting white-and-black vertical could be a flame, signifying the foyer.[28] It parallels the clasped hands (another symbol of joining) and stands above a pattern that could be the candle, but also the folds of an apron, or of plowed fields—it could just as well stand for a bed or table—each one of these figures providing an equivalent symbol of a base that is both geometric and generative.[29] Above these layers of horizon rises the twist of a white body into the foreground and back through an opening toward a watery sun appearing through a window.

Le Corbusier's first painting was called *Chimney*. It centers on a rectangular block emerging out of a layered field of superimposed terraces—terraces of books, it seems. The word *chimney* also directly refers to fireplace and to foyer.[30] Chiefly important, I think, is the mounding up. A useful later image to compare is the drawing of the Acropolis, in *Towards a New Architecture*, as a mountaintop summit with the Parthenon (concealing and containing the withdrawn *parthenos*) under the light. The famous photograph of the Mill Owner's Building across a watery foreground is also indicative of mounding. In views such as these one sees the raised level that appeared in Venetian landscape, the Homeric dance and archaic creation myth. In each case, leveled land serves as the correlate of upward movement and upright posture—ascent and *droiture*.

This is summarized most eloquently in Le Corbusier's principle of the fusion of opposites. The principle recurs throughout his work as spirit/matter, sun/moon, day/night (as in the famous twenty-four-hour drawing), man/woman, reason/intuition, action/rest. Fusion results in balance, equilibrium, and harmony. This appears in the bottom image of the *Poem* (section G3). In his symbolism of the right angle, the vertical is the spiritual axis and the horizontal the material. If vertical refers to the axis of creativity, horizontal refers to latent and uncreated order—primeval waters—the reflective stage of the creative process (gestation) out of which *droiture* arises. On this point the text and image in section A3 of the *Poem* is instructive:

> The universe of our eyes rests upon a plain edged with horizon/Facing at the sky/Let us consider the inconceivable space hitherto uncomprehended. Repose supine sleep—death/With our backs on the ground…. But I am standing straight! since you are erect/you are also fit for action. Erect on the terrestrial plain of things knowable you sign a pact of solidarity with nature: this is the right angle/Vertical facing the sea/there you are on your feet.[31]

181

This pact with nature joined vertical potentiality to horizontal articulation. The right angle, too, joined opposites in this way.

Yet, to think of leveled land as flat is to wrongly project the vertical onto the horizontal, mistaking the second as a mirror image of the first, neglecting all the differences Le Corbusier and the others I've considered have observed: that topographical depth is dark, not light; moist, not dry; engendering, not engendered; and formative, not formed. Mistaking each of these for its opposite leads to a sense of design that subordinates consideration of materials and construction to those of shape and form—the aestheticism to which I briefly referred already.

In contemporary discourse and practice, materials and construction are receiving renewed attention. We have come to realize that they are not only formed but also formative. Similarly, the idea that the earth is an objectifiable resource is under widespread and increasing criticism. To understate myself: Matter is no longer "mere." Renewed attention to the "things themselves" is, I think, to be welcomed and encouraged insofar as it challenges ways of working that neglect hidden potentials. I believe that care for existing conditions is the first premise of creative work. But when the art of making livable settings is conceived as the business of letting things "speak for themselves," we substitute one distortion of topography for another; a world that is capable of making itself

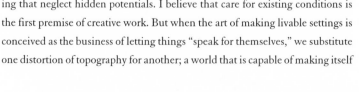

Fig. 5. *"Catégorique angle droit du caractére,"* Le Corbusier, *Le Poeme de L'Angle Droit* (Paris, 1955). Foundation Le Corbusier.

is allowed to take the place of one that we have made for ourselves. I suspect that in the long run this change of direction will lead to a dead end—something one senses in the physicalism of the current preoccupation with materials, the current assumption that the qualities of shine or rust are the full subject matter of architectural disclosure. Surely it is the interplay, fusion, or marriage of geometry and materials that is key. The task of both current thought and creative work is to develop images and symbols that free us from this ancient polarity by showing that a condition of reciprocal determination is more productive and revealing, perhaps even more basic.

Notes

1   A summary of these polarities as they bear on the form-content opposition is set forth in David Summers, "'Form,' Nineteenth-Century Metaphysics and the Problem of Art Historical Description," *Critical Inquiry* 15 (1989): 372–406. This distinction was also considered at great depth by Martin Heidegger. Most useful, perhaps, is "The Origin of the Work of Art," in *Poetry Language Thought* (New York: Harper Row, 1971), 26–31 especially. Also useful is his *What Is a Thing?* (South Bend, Ind.: Regnery, 1967). In contemporary language and practice, not all of these associations have survived, especially those about gender difference, nor would they be accepted.

2   Aristotle, *Physics*, trans. R.P. Hardie and R.K. Gaye (New York: Random House, 1941), section 192a.

3   See Anne Carson, *Eros: The Bittersweet* (Princeton, N.J.: Princeton University Press, 1986).

4   Francis Ponge, "Water," in *The Voice of Things,* trans. Beth Archer (New York: McGraw-Hill, 1972), 49–51.

5   Hippocrates, *On Regimen*, sect. 28 (Cambridge, Mass.: Harvard University Press, 1984); cited in Anne Carson, "Putting Her in Her Place," in *Before Sexuality*, eds. David Halperin, John Winkler, Froma Zeitlin (Princeton, N.J.: Princeton University Press, 1990), 137ff. See also Page duBois, *Sowing the Body* (Chicago: University of Chicago Press, 1990), 70–71 especially; Ruth Padel, *In and Out of the Mind* (Princeton, N.J.: Princeton University Press, 1992), 99–113 especially; and Ellen Reeder, *Pandora* (Princeton, N.J.: Princeton University Press, 1995).

6   Padel, *In and Out of the Mind*, 99–113.

7   For Anaximander, *aperion* was not identified with any single element, not earth, air, fire, or water; it was, instead, the principle of spatial indefiniteness. Other cosmologists symbolized the basic stuff of the world by elaborating the qualities of a single element. On the vast literature concerning these cosmologies, it is, perhaps, best to begin with the texts themselves, and a useful first source is G.S. Kirk and J.E. Raven, *The Presocratic Philosophers* (Cambridge: Cambridge University Press, 1971). For the subject of matter itself, see Ernan McMullin, *The Concept of Matter in Greek and Medieval Philosophy* (South Bend, Ind.: Notre Dame University Press, 1963), 66–69 for the matter-form distinction in Aristotle, and 83ff for ideas about the intelligibility of form. On the Anaximander fragment, the best text remains Charles Kahn, *Anaximander and the Origins of Greek Cosmology* (New York: Columbia University Press, 1960).

8   Carson, "Putting Her in Her Place." See also Gerda Lerner, *The Creation of Patriarchy* (New York: Oxford University Press, 1986), 205–11.

9   Cited in G.S. Kirk and J.E. Raven, *The Presocratic Philosophers* (Cambridge: Cambridge University Press, 1957), 60, fragment 54.

10 Indra Kagis McEwen, *Socrates' Ancestor* (Cambridge, Mass.: MIT Press, 1993), 54.

11 David Farrell Krell uses this etymology to redefine architecture itself; see his *Architecture* (Albany: State University of New York Press, 1997), 11–37. See also McEwen, *Socrates' Ancestor*, 54.

12 It is possible that there is a common root for both grammatical forms of the word *inter*: (1) the intransitive verb in the *terra* family, signifying burial, and (2) the prefix meaning *between* or *among*, like the French *entre* and the Latin *in terus*, from which the English word *interior* derives. Accordingly, the earth platform can be seen as the topographical premise for permanent public space. Alberti made this argument, as I show below.

13 Homer, *The Iliad*, trans. Robert Fagles (New York: Viking Penguin, 1991), 487.

14 In the prelude to Theogony, Hesiod used the word *choroi* to name the dance floors of the muses, referring to terraces on Mount Helikon, which was the birthplace of memory. The most recent consideration of this term's bearing on topographical matters, particularly architecture, is Maria Theodorou, "Space as Experience," *AA Files* 34 (fall 1997): 45–55, which relies greatly on Jacques Derrida, "Khora," in *On the Name* (Stanford, Calif.: Stanford University Press, 1995).

15 In Pindar's poetry, citizens danced on such a surface to raise up into propitious attention the "nymph of the city" (*chthonia phren*). For a discussion of this, see William Mullen, *Choreia: Pindar and Dance* (Princeton, N.J.: Princeton University Press, 1982), 79–89 especially.

16 Leon Battista Alberti, *On the Art of Building in Ten Books* (Cambridge, Mass.: MIT Press, 1988), book 3, chapter 16.

17 On the philosophical anthropology of rectitude, see Erwin Straus, "Upright Posture," in *Phenomenological Psychology* (New York: Basic Books, 1966), 137–165.

18 On this practice, see Emilio Sereni, *History of the Italian Agricultural Landscape* (Princeton, N.J.: Princeton University Press, 1997), 298–303 especially. For this reference I am indebted to Tom Beck.

19 In both Greek and Roman military iconography, the breastplate, like the shield, displayed ornaments that conferred on its bearer the status of *cosmocrator*. On this iconography, see both Otto Brendel, "The Shield of Achilles," in *The Visible Idea* (Washington, D.C.: Decatur House Press, 1980), 72, and Franz Cumont, *Die orientalischen Religionen* (Stuggart, 1959), 276ff.

20 James Ackerman, *The Architecture of Michelangelo* (London: A. Zwemmer, 1961), 167–169.

21 See Marie Delcourt, *L'Oracle de Delphes* (Paris: Payot, 1981); Joseph Fontenrose, *Python: A Study of Delphic Myth and Its Origins* (Berkeley: University of California Press, 1959); and Jane Harrison, *Themis* (London: Merlin Books, 1963).

22 On *omphalos*, see J.P. Vernant, *Myth and Thought Among the Greeks* (London: Routledge and Kegan Paul, 1965), chapter 5 especially; Hans Herrmann, *Omphalos* (Münster: Aschendorff, 1959); and Louis Gernet, *The Anthropology of Ancient Greece* (Baltimore, Md.: John Hopkins University Press, 1981), especially chapter 15. On parallel ideas of *umbilicus*, see G. Dumézil, *Archaic Roman Religion* (Chicago: Chicago University Press, 1970). For the impact of symbolism on the making of landscapes and buildings, see Joseph Rykwert, *The Idea of a Town* (Princeton, N.J.: Princeton University Press, 1976); and E.B. Smith, *The Dome: A Study in the History of Ideas* (Princeton, N.J.: Princeton University Press, 1950).

23 Varro, *On the Latin Language*, 2 vols., trans. and ed. R.G. Kent (Cambridge, Mass.: Harvard University Press, 1967), book 7, section 17.

24 Le Corbusier, *Precisions* (Cambridge, Mass.: MIT Press, 1991), 75.

183

25 Ibid.
26 This connection, and many others I discuss, is made in Peter Carl, "Le Corbusier's Penthouse in Paris, 24 Rue Nungesser-et-Coli," in *Daidalos* (1988): 65–75.
27 Le Corbusier, *Poem to the Right Angle* (Paris: Foundation Le Corbusier, 1989), 65. On the *Poem* and the theme of upright posture in Le Corbusier, see Daphne Becket-Chary, "Droiture," M. Phil. Dissertation, Cambridge University, 1989.
28 Carl, 65.
29 See deBois, 65–86.
30 Carl, 67.
31 Le Corbusier, *Poem*, section A3.

Part Three: Urbanizing Landscape

Chapter 12

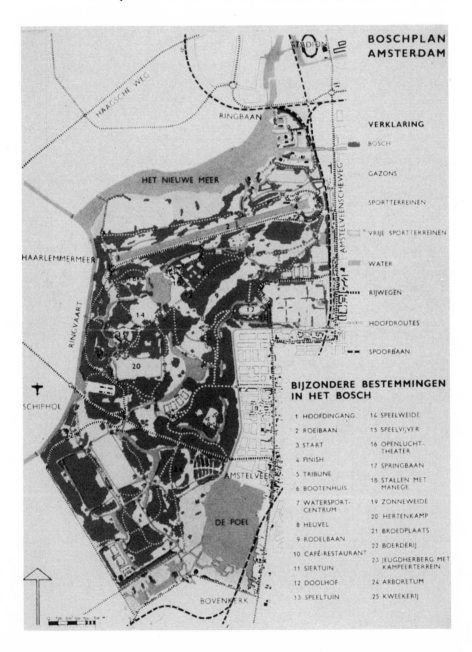

BOSCHPLAN AMSTERDAM

VERKLARING

- BOSCH
- GAZONS
- SPORTTERREINEN
- VRIJE SPORTTERREINEN
- WATER
- RIJWEGEN
- HOOFDROUTES
- SPOORBAAN

BIJZONDERE BESTEMMINGEN IN HET BOSCH

1 HOOFDINGANG	14 SPEELWEIDE
2 ROEIBAAN	15 SPEELVIJVER
3 START	16 OPENLUCHT-THEATER
4 FINISH	
5 TRIBUNE	17 SPRINGBAAN
6 BOOTENHUIS	18 STALLEN MET MANEGE
7 WATERSPORT-CENTRUM	19 ZONNEWEIDE
8 HEUVEL	20 HERTENKAMP
9 RODELBAAN	21 BROEDPLAATS
10 CAFÉ-RESTAURANT	22 BOERDERIJ
11 SIERTUIN	23 JEUGDHERBERG MET KAMPEERTERREIN
12 DOOLHOF	24 ARBORETUM
13 SPEELTUIN	25 KWEEKERIJ

The Amsterdam Bos: The Modern Public Park and the Construction of Collective Experience

Anita Berrizbeita

The urban park has been traditionally understood as the place that mitigates the debilitating effects of congested urban life. This mitigation is typically achieved by transposing certain characteristics of the rural and natural environment into the city, establishing the park from the outset as the city's counterpart. In "Public Parks and the Enlargement of Towns," Frederick Law Olmsted proposed that extensive woods ought to surround the park, deep enough "to completely shut out the city from our landscapes" and so achieve "the greatest possible contrast with the restraining and confining conditions of the town."[1] Thus, as a place to escape from the overrationalization of the routine operations of the modern metropolis, the park offers the opportunity to restore and protect the individual's subjective and spiritual life against the impersonal forces that surround them.

The nineteenth-century public park was largely conceived as bourgeois territory. This was a place where the individual could exercise the intellectual and social freedoms afforded by liberal political thought. The very forms of the park supported the pursuit and cultivation of individualism: its naturalistic composition of layered, transparent spaces open to a multiplicity of readings, its aestheticized representation of nature, and its conceptual distance from the city around it. For the most part, individuals engaged in the passive, reflective contemplation of scenery, enjoying moments of quiet solitude that served to restore a sense of self. Thus, although a public space, the experience of the park was essentially private, "domestic and secluded"[2] in nature.[3] Nestled within a metropolis dominated by standardization, the public park of the 1800s marked a disjunction between everyday urban life and aesthetic practices, between a society that was ruled by mass production and its modes of cultural thinking inherited from eighteenth-century Enlightenment culture.

In what follows, I present a moment in the history of the public park when this disjunction ceases to exist, when there is no longer an antithetical

Fig. 1. Plan of the Bos Park. Cornelis Van Eesteren and Jacopa Mulder, 1930. Source: RIBA, vol. 45, Series III (May 1938).

relationship between the idea of the park and the idea of the city. The Bos Park, an 875-hectare forest-park built in Amsterdam between 1929 and the 1950s, breaks with the tradition of the nineteenth-century bourgeois park (Fig. 1). Its designers, the architect Cornelis Van Eesteren and the landscape architect Jacopa Mulder, adopted a program of "productivism" proposing landscape architectural design as *technique* (or a set of techniques) rather than as inspired aesthetic creation. Moreover, they made the productive program for the park explicitly visible in its physical form, connecting it to the processes of the industrialized city around it.

Reconceptualizing the relationship between the park and the city necessarily results in fundamental aesthetic and social shifts that both recover and transform the traditions of the urban park. It also restructures the relationship between the perceiving subject and the park itself (the object), and between the object and its creator. This is a materialist interpretation of the modern public park that looks for signification not in an aesthetic ideal achieved through mimetic representation but in the relationships among modes of material production and evolving social and political structures.[4] This view moves from an emphasis on aesthetic experience as an isolated, abstract, and autonomous instance in individual experience to one in which those experiences are fundamentally rooted in the realities of modern life.[5]

The Bos Park

In 1929, when the city council of Amsterdam approved the beginning of the Bos Park project, Cornelis Van Eesteren and Jacopa Mulder had two precedents to consider: the picturesque park, represented at that time by Olmsted and the English examples, and the *volksparks* (people's parks) built in Germany during the first two decades of this century. Van Eesteren and Mulder traveled to England and Germany to study examples of each type. They also had the recommendations of the exceptional report produced by the Boschplan Committee, which included images of landscapes that were desirable models for the Bos Park.[6] These were a swimming facility in Hanover, Germany, a playground in Berlin, a forest in Breda, and another in the Hague. These pictures suggested a remarkable synthesis of two as yet unpaired landscape types: the athletic facility with the native forest.[7]

Even before the park was finished, it was lauded as a remarkable innovation. The author of an article published in the *Journal of the Royal Institute of British Architects* in 1938, seven years after construction began, openly admitted the impossibility of naming the style of the park. It is described as "neither...Beaux Arts...nor even the genuine English landscape style...and the roads, rivers and canals do not run in snaky lines, returning on themselves in formally informal curves of tiresome and unnatural symmetry..... There is also no trace of the new German forms.... " The author goes only so far as to say that the scale of the meadows remind him of a Reptonian landscape and that the "landscape forms the link between the various component parts.... All these are *plainly* [my emphasis] linked together by long stretches of meadow of irregular contour and generally happy proportions."[8]

It is interesting that the critic was not able to describe the park according to established stylistic categories. Clearly, the appearance of this new park was quite different from that of its predecessors. Indeed, Van Eesteren's and Mulder's conception of the design and construction of the park as a process rather than as an aestheticized composition demanded that a critic understand its value less in terms of "how it looks" and more in terms of "how it works." It is precisely this conceptual shift from composition of form to process of production that negates[9] the traditional idea of the public park and connects the park to the city by presenting it as just another of the city's multiple productive operations. Ultimately, this shift in the conceptualization of landscape redefined the psychological space of the park as one that is not private and subjective but civic and public.

Built under the aegis of unemployment relief, the Bos Park was constructed entirely by men and horses, with little or no aid from machinery.[10] Nevertheless, the adoption of a series of rational design and construction techniques meant that there was a high degree of instrumentalization of natural processes commensurate to that of any other industrial procedure; the conceptualization of processes, such as drainage and plant growth, as productive entities allowed the park to be conceived as a site of production.

The first operation entailed dismantling the existing structure of orthogonal dikes and rectilinear drainage channels (Fig. 2). These had been laid 50 meters apart and compartmentalized the site into a series of rectangular agricultural fields typical of the Dutch polder landscape.[11] One dike was retained—the park boundary at the Schinkelpolder—in order to protect the site from surface drainage from the southwest.[12] The elimination of the original grid of dikes and channels was followed by smoothing out the terrain. This was necessary because the polders that constitute the site were formed and "de-peated"[13] at different times between 1858 and 1925, meaning that their elevations varied (Fig. 3)

Regularizing the topography allowed the restoration of a continuous ground plane on the site, uninterrupted by channels and earthen walls.

The second operation dealt with the management of water on the site, which averages 4.5 meters below sea level. The establishment of a forest rendered the windmill technique for eliminating excess water from the site ineffective. More importantly, programming the site as a forest required a concept for draining the soils that would allow for the planting and growth of a new forest. Thus, a massive drainage operation involving two separate systems was undertaken. The first system comprised a network of pipes laid between 1.5 and 2 meters below grade. This system continuously lowers the water table and thus enables the roots of the forest trees to develop. The second system comprised a series of canals evenly dispersed across

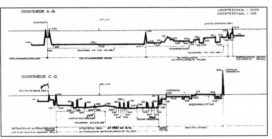

the site. These canals gradually convey the water to the northeast corner of the site, where a sluice pump releases it into a lake, the Nieuwe Meer. The numerous watercourses visible on the site are nothing other than an efficient drainage system.

The third operation involved the adoption of a planting system for the construction of the forest. The designers used a well-established practice of industrial forestry that is entirely dependent on a process of vegetational succession. Randomly distributed in a grid, two forest types were planted: a "provisional" pioneer forest of fast-growing alders, willows, poplars, and birch, and a "permanent" forest of the slower-growing ash, maple, oak, and beech (Fig. 4). In addition to helping further drain the site through evapotranspiration, the pioneer forest provided the necessary shelter for the seedlings of the permanent forest,

Fig. 2 (top). Plan of existing conditions. Source: *Rapport van de Commissie voor het Boschplan* (Amsterdam, 1931).

Fig. 3 (bottom). Site section.Source: *Rapport van de Commissie voor het Boschplan* (Amsterdam, 1931).

which require shade during their initial years. After fifteen years of growth, the pioneer forest, with the exception of the alder, was cut down, allowing the established permanent forest to grow. The remaining alder was pollarded to produce a horizontal branching habit and provide shade on the forest floor to prevent understory growth.

Finally, the landscape elements were distributed across the site in a spatial structure that is nonhierarchical, open-ended, and reiterative. Forest, open lawns, and water are distributed evenly across the site in a mosaic-like pattern that is more accurately described as a "fabric." Of the total 2,235 acres, 775 are devoted to woodlands, 625 acres to open lawns, and 835 roads and water.[14] That is, they exist in a more or less 1:1:1 relationship with each other.[15] This even but intermingled distribution of landscape conditions recalls the spatial distribution in De Stijl paintings, which typically give equal weight to all elements of the painting while filling the space of the canvas evenly all the way to its edges.[16] Similarly, at the Bos Park, the forest, lawns, and watercourses spread across the site all the way to its perimeter. There is no spatial differentiation between a center and an edge condition on the site, reflecting the continuity of the ground plane (Fig. 5).

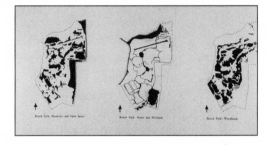

Three areas of the site were treated differently than the overall strategy described above. The southern third of the Buitendijksche Buitenveldersche polder, which is adjacent to densely populated neighborhoods, was devoted to game courts. The northern edge of the site, along the Nieuwe Meer, and the southeastern corner of the site, known as the Poel, were existing wetlands that the committee felt should not be forested. It would have been too costly to alter the soil and drain the water in these areas; in addition, their ecological value, as

Fig. 4 (top). Planting diagram. Source: Alan Ruff, *Holland and the Ecological Landscapes* (Manchester: Department of Town and Country Planning, University of Manchester, 1979).

Fig. 5 (bottom). Diagram showing the distribution of landscape elements. Drawn by Mitch Rasor.

well as their beauty, was recognized as an aspect of the site to be preserved, especially given its immediate vicinity to the city. The committee also suggested the preservation of several of the existing farms on the site. Presently, one of these remains near the marshland to the north, by the Nieuwe Meer. Over the fabric of woodland, water, and open lawns were superimposed the "exceptions" to the system: the rowing course, the sailing pond, and the bobsleigh hill, formed with the fill obtained from digging for the water bodies on the site.

Thus, although the construction of the park was systematic, it is evident that existing and new conditions were overlaid upon, or embedded into, the overall system. This is less an indication of a concern for the "genius of the place," which derives from a visual and an experiential interpretation of the site, and more of an interest in objectifying the landscape as living matter and in intensifying the raw materiality of the varying conditions of the site: the soft, spongy forest floor, its cycles and scents; the irreversible wetness of the marsh—but not of the fields; and the sense of sky and weather that is fundamental to Dutch landscapes.

Previous, traditional construction techniques in landscape architecture were subsumed under the stylistic intentions of the designer. The production of a scene that had integrity as a visual composition was of utmost importance. From the simplest technical innovations, such as the ha-ha,[17] to the most elaborate schemes of water control, the picturesque landscape was underlaid with myriad works of engineering, silently and secretly contributing to the production of an aesthetically naturalized view. Similarly, Frederick Law Olmsted resisted the introduction of program and utility into his parks and, when it became inevitable, program was folded into the internal, autonomous necessities of his aesthetic, picturesque agenda. Program, he argued, diminished the contemplative function of the park and impoverished its spiritual value for the individual.[18]

Conceiving landscape as program, or ascribing functional value to parkland, is the first radical break from a pictorial conceptualization of landscape. But in its inception in the German *volksparks* of the first decades of the twentieth century, functionalism did not provide the freedom from established rules of composition in landscape that, say, architectural functionalism allowed for buildings. In Lebereght Migge's and Martin Wagner's *Jugendpark* on the Pichelswarder peninsula in Berlin, for instance, the plan is organized in a traditional manner: around a central axis for marching youth formations, with a symmetrical distribution of program on either side, such as open lawns for military exercises.[19] Wagner's radical contribution, though, was to eliminate the traditional conceptual distance between work and leisure by incorporating both in equal terms: as productive, functional aspects of the city. For him, the health benefits that parks provide for people had an economic value akin to capital generated by other productive functions of the city.[20] This interpretation of parkland in the city was later adopted by CIAM's 1928 Declaration of La Sarraz and again in its 1933 Charter of Athens.[21] However, while reconceptualizing a landscape strictly in terms of its functional value displaced the prevalence of scenic approaches to design, it had not yet provided new techniques of design and construction. There were no new technologies in nature, so to speak, only new ways of putting nature to use.

In its provision of a dense programmatic plan (rowing, canoeing, water ski-ing, speedboating, equestrian sports, cycling, trails, winter sports, and court games such as hockey, football, and cricket), the Bos Park is clearly the offspring of the German *volkspark*, but it represents a break with that tradition in its expression of the landscape as functioning biological *material*. The strategy at Bos Park concretizes the differences among the elements in terms of the specific contribution of each to the overall ecological structure of the landscape, and among their functions (water for drainage, for example, is expressed differently than water for sports). This constitutes, in effect, a division of labor, "understood in its widest sense to include the division of production, the differentiation of work processes and specialization."[22] Drainage, forest production, and the open lawns are highly specialized operations, carrying out objectively prescribed tasks that enable human use of the site: drainage for reclamation, forest for wind protection, and open lawns for play.

The differentiation of landscape types is also carried through to the pro-gram. Those aspects of the program that require specific dimensions, such as game courts, are not blended into the form of the forest. On the contrary, they are densely laid out, extending the organiza-tion of the adjacent neighborhood into the park. The 2-kilo-meter rowing course (originally 72 meters wide, expanded to 92 meters in 1964), on the north of the site, is sited perpendi-cular to the direction of drainage flow, immediately distin-guishing itself functionally from the other water bodies on the site (Fig. 6). Likewise, park buildings, traditionally rustic in

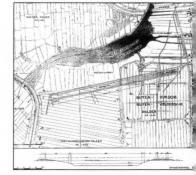

Fig. 6. Bos Baan study. Cornelis Van Eesteren and Jacopa Mulder, 1930.
Source: *Rapport van de Commissie voor het Boschplan* (Amsterdam, 1931).

order to "blend in" with "nature," are here made of concrete, steel, and glass. All elements are shown to be simply what is demanded technically of them. Their function resides primarily in their material properties rather than in any aesthetic value or quality.

Perhaps the most meaningful break that the Bos Park makes with the pictorial tradition is, then, the proposition that design itself is the establishment of a *working method*, a system of operations informed by scientific analysis (hydrology, forestry, social sciences) and aimed toward concrete applications (reclamation, shelter, recreation). What is significant here is that the working method and the technical means themselves are unveiled and incorporated into the final appearance of the park, giving it its artistic logic and meaning. Composition as a passive practice is rejected in favor of construction as an active process.[23] The park is the result of the conditions of its own making.

Landscape as System of Production

In traditional mimesis, meaning is generated by isolating some aspect of the world and expressing that reality in the art object by manipulating the conventions of the medium. But when the impulse of the work is not about representation of outside reality but the articulation of its system of production, the work induces what Michel Foucault called a condition of "exteriority."[24] By this he meant that the perceiving subject does not focus on discerning a hidden content manifested in the work but, instead, his or her attention is directed toward the external conditions of its existence. The meaning of the work, normally lodged in an aestheticized, mimetic representation of a previously understood reality, is now relocated "to the outside," in the nexus of relationships that derive from the process and system of production.[25]

I draw five implications from this relocation of meaning from object-as-representation to object-as-system-of-production:

Loss of Form. The distribution of forest, open lawn, and water in an all-over pattern that fills the space of the site results in a "loss of form"—that is, in a loss of figuration of the voids (open lawns) against the mass (forest).[26] Instead, there is a superimposition of four systems—woodland, lawns, water, and elements—that equally contribute to and reiterate the spatial experience. No layer is subordinate to the others; each is coopted to have equal presence in the landscape.

Multiple Meanings. Another formal implication is the absence of spatial narratives (as at Rousham, for instance) and of processional spaces that may culminate in a monumental climax (such as the sequence from the Mall to the Ramble in Central Park). Instead, the visitor moves from area to area with the impression of never having quite arrived. The park is understood through the accumulation of reiterative experiences in time and space. This spatial strategy impedes the possibility of aesthetic contemplation from a distance and of a private, personal engagement with the park.

Anti-Aesthetic. As a corollary to this, the park does not fall into any of the aesthetic categories of landscape we know; it is neither beautiful nor picturesque nor sublime (Figs. 7, 8, 9). It resists all attempts at aesthetic categorization—a radical conceptual shift in itself, given the pervasive burden of having to be "beautiful" that has historically been placed on landscape. Instead, the park asks to be understood as a transcription into form of a program that has been determined according to a set of scientific and social criteria.

Reciprocity of Park and City. The park is stripped of metaphorical content and spiritual intention. It is demystified. The emphasis on materiality and the unveiling of the technical means of construction eliminate the transcendental in the park and invalidate the conceptual separateness of the park from the city. Rather than being presented as isolated and protected from technology and capitalism and, in turn, offering the individual shelter from these forces, the park is understood as one of many productive entities within the metropolis. Like the subway system or the stock exchange, the park is a piece of a system that contributes to and strives for maximum productive efficiency. In its multiplicity of functions, organized rationally according to function and production, the park is akin to an overlay of activities of the city. It no longer stands against the world but is one worldly thing among others.[27]

Index. Because meaning does not depend on the park as a symbol for a referent but on the congruence of the system of construction and existing standards of production in society at large, the park is not a fully resolved object.

Fig. 7 (top). View of park—forest interior. Photograph by Kate Orff.

Fig. 8 (middle). View of park—meadow. Photograph by Kate Orff.

Fig. 9 (bottom). View of park—canal. Photograph by Kate Orff.

Instead, it operates as an *index*. As Rosalind Krauss notes, indexes work differently from symbols in that they relate to their referent "along an axis of physical relationships. They are the marks or traces of a particular cause, and that cause is the thing to which they refer, the object they signify. Into the category of index, we would place physical traces (like footprints), medical symptoms...."[28] As an index, the park becomes a *trace* of a specific procedure rather than a completed, static, totalized object. Thus, the presence of the forest points to the continuously lowered water table, the trees themselves to ongoing succession, and the hill, an atypical landform in this landscape, to the massive digging operations that were necessary to construct the watercourses and the lake. These are registration marks, records on the site of those procedures and modes of production used for the park's construction.[29] As a result, the engagement of the subject with the park is not predicated on the aesthetic comprehension of its forms but on thinking through the processes that are at work behind those forms.

Object/Subject[30]

A reconceptualization of the landscape object is, by necessity, accompanied by a reconceptualization of the subject with which it is engaged. More specifically, the renunciation of formal composition in favor of an emphasis on the system of production induces a change in the relations between the designer and the work and between the perceiving subject and the park.

At the core of a materialist critique of social relations under capitalism, the theory of commodity reification provides a framework for understanding the transformations in the conceptualization of objects during modernism. Reification is a process through which human activities become diminished as a result of their analysis and fragmentation into rational components, conceived solely as a dialectic of means and ends. According to Fredric Jameson, what is important about reification is that its instrumentality foregrounds the organization of the means themselves over any particular aesthetic end.[31] Seen through this framework, the elements of the Bos Park landscape are not invested with qualitative values in themselves but "only insofar as they can be 'used.'"[32] In other words, the differentiation and specialization of procedures at the Bos Park transformed each landscape element into a *means* to a particular end, and they are therefore stripped of subjective value. The park is thus transformed into a system of production that is inherently reproducible in any given context.

Moreover, because the system of production prevails as the basis for design and for achieving signification, the designers' role is transformed into one in which they set in motion the processes that will complete the construction of the park. In the case of the Bos Park, Van Eesteren and Mulder relinquished control of the final form to processes of succession and hydrology. As a result, the park bears few, if any, traces of the subjectivities of the designer, resisting the appearance of having been manipulated or mediated by a particular artistic personality.[33]

The fundamental shifts in the conceptualization of the park explained earlier and, no less important, in the role of the designers, are supported by changes in the conceptualization of the perceiving subject. Who is, then, the subject that the modern park seeks to address?

A democratic social agenda motivated the Bos Park project from its inception and appeared frequently in the Bos Park Committee's report, which states that the park is intended for the proletariat "in its new emancipated status."[34] Most notably, the removal of the dikes is explained in ideological terms: leveling the site releases it from the tyranny of the rectilinear dike structure, which makes people walk in straight, confined lines. A site of continuous ground, not disconnected by the dikes' earthen walls, allows the individual to roam freely throughout and across the site. Movement is here endowed with signification because it represents social mobility and the emancipation of classes from old social and religious bonds as a result of the rise of capital. The pairing of this kind of loose but systematic spatial structure with a shift away from mimetic representation suggests that meaning in the park is no longer contingent on the passive contemplation of scenery but on the construction of open social practices.

The pamphlet published on the occasion of the opening of the park reiterates these shifts.[35] On its cover is depicted an array of activities offered at the park and no sense of its physical appearance at all. At the bottom of the cover, an assembly line of men, trees and shovels in hand, reiterate the forest as construction. Not shown is the introspective, meditating subject of the traditional park. Inside the pamphlet, sketches show individuals engaged in various forms of social exchange and physical activity. The park is presented as a place where the individual can share in collective public life.

There is not, however, a complete rejection of contemplation in the park. The pamphlet features several sketches, drawn by Mulder herself, of what seem to be views of the wetlands from the forest edge, suggesting the possibility of contemplation and solitude in the park. Van Eesteren and Mulder describe the predicament of the modern subject, one who is formed as much by an instinct for cultivating individuality as by the requisites of the new collective nature of modern life.[36] The Bos Park proposes the emancipation of private individuals by

197

giving them a public role. It introduces the possibility of new forms of shared civic life in the park, where the private individual exists in a dialectical relationship with the social. Here, one may reconcile his or her existence as individual subject with the larger collective, shifting from one to the other, existing within and yet retaining the possibility of making purposeful interventions in society at large. It is in accomplishing this shift in the status of the landscape vis-à-vis the subject that the Bos Park can be understood as a negation of the picturesque park tradition and of its associated ideas of representation, of authorial mediation, and of the park as auratic, transcendental space.[37]

Landscape as Process

Landscape as process is one of the paradigms of postmodern practice in landscape architecture, supported by theories of phenomenology and hermeneutics, among others. These theories, as well as the landscapes they inspire, value once again the individual over the collective. In landscape, these values are expressed through a system of open-ended design that is also largely based on setting up a biological process, such as erosion by wind or water, or plant succession, and letting the process, through time, show its effect on the site, constructing its landscape. Desvigne and Dalnoky in France and Hargreaves Associates in the United States are two of several practices that take on this agenda in their work. How is the idea of landscape as process different in contemporary practice than it was more than sixty years ago, at the time of the construction of the Bos Park, when practitioners such as Van Eesteren and Mulder also took a stand against pictorialism?

The difference can be found at the level of representation.[38] Time and process, and their corollary of open-endedness, are taken on as the subject matter of these practices. Yet, specifically in the work of Hargreaves Associates, process is aligned with an aesthetic and expressive agenda that does not entirely originate in the biological and the programmatic but in the formal. Hargreaves sculpts and manipulates form until it achieves congruence with a predetermined meaning, such as invoking "aeolian forces" on the land.[39] In its inception, the work is concerned with form for the sake of form, at least to the extent that this *represents* ecological processes. This representational agenda reintroduces subjective values and narratives into the work and recovers the subjective, individual vision of landscape. In terms of relations between subject and object, then, this work is closer to the nineteenth-century ideal of the urban park than the project for the Bos Park.

At the Bos Park, the idea of process derives its meaning specifically as it relates to production. Thus, whereas time and process are often invoked as aesthetic dimensions of landscape in contemporary practice, they were more technical and material dimensions of landscape at the Bos Park. Process at Bos was understood as technique, as a way of understanding and articulating a project in terms of its material determinants. This emphasis on those physical aspects of constructing urban landscape that had remained secondary in the realm of eighteenth- and nineteenth-century landscape aesthetics became, for the modernist vanguard, a strategy to expand the polemic beyond representation and to focus on questions of the collective reception of the work, to address a newly constituted mass culture.[40] In other words, a logistical concern for process as a way of objectifying the material in landscape, stripping it of narrative and mimesis, can be construed as a mechanism for pursuing the collective and enhancing shared social relations. Unlike the aestheticization of process during postmodernism, invoked to engage subjectivity, the Bos Park redirects attention beyond the individual subject and toward those processes that undergird modern life, that generate the social conditions of its making.

The work of contemporary Dutch designers OMA/Rem Koolhaas and West 8/Adriaan Geuze continues to engage process and materiality in landscape in the same conceptual way that Van Eesteren and Mulder did for the Bos Park. Their proposals are strategies specific to site and program rather than designs that are the product of formal, aestheticized visions.[41] But, unlike bland functionalism, where the logistics of a project come across as habitual, unexamined aspects of a site, Koolhaas and Geuze redirect the rational demands of a project toward a creative end. Logistical issues such as zoning and program become driving forces for innovation and transformation in design. In their work, landscape emerges as a matrix or framework for development, as living material in the functional sense, as site of production, as structural tissue that supports often contradictory programs, and as a territory that is indistinguishable from the city. Signification in these works is found in their modes of production, especially those that deal creatively with the identities, lives, and necessities of individuals participating in collective life.[42]

Notes

1   Frederick Law Olmsted, "Public Parks and the Enlargement of Towns" (1871), reprinted in Donald Worster's *American Environmentalism* (New York: John Wiley & Sons, 1973), 111–132.

2   Ibid.

199

3   For a description of the private nature of the early public park, see Richard Sennett, *The Fall of Public Man* (New York: Alfred A. Knopf, 1987), especially chapter 4, "Public Roles," 64–88.

4   See Umberto Barbaro, "Materialism and Art," in *Marxism and Art: Writings in Aesthetics and Criticism,* eds. Berel Lang and Forrest Williams (New York: David McKay, 1972), 161–176. See also Lang and Williams' introduction to the book.

5   In formulating this view and others in this essay, I am particularly indebted to K. Michael Hays's *Modernism and the Posthumanist Subject* (Cambridge, Mass.: MIT Press, 1992).

6   *Rapport van de Commissie voor het Boschplan Amsterdam* (Amsterdam, 1931). The committee was established in January 1929 and produced its report more than two years later, in May 1931. The list of consultants contributing to the report is extensive, and included subcommittees on hygiene, sports and relaxation, soil, and flora and fauna, among others, and experts on bathing and swimming installations. There is also extensive discussion in this report about the significance of the parks. This document is available from the Department of Public Works in Amsterdam. Claudia Swan, Ph.D., translated this document for the author.

7   Although all forests in Holland are man-made, the Dutch have a tradition of forest making that is at least five centuries long. By native forests I mean those that are composed of species that existed in the Netherlands before the waters of the Atlantic rose. See IR.T.W.L Scheltema, "Holland's Man-Made Forests," in *American Forests* 50 (November 1944): 540–541.

8   "The Amsterdam Boschplan," in *Journal of the Royal Institute of British Architects* 45, series III (May 1938):681–689. See also Antonio Cerdena, "Attrezzature verdi di Amsterdam," *Casabella* 277 (July 1963): 34–49. An excellent description of the political and legal events that led to the approval of the project is Sergio Polano, "The Bos Park, Amsterdam, and Urban Development in Holland," in *The Architecture of Western Gardens*, eds. Georges Teyssot and Monique Mosser (Cambridge, Mass.: MIT Press, 1992): 507–509. For this paper, I derived most of my information directly from the *Rapport van de Commissie voor het Boschplan Amsterdam*, wherein a great deal of site analysis and technical information appears.

9   On negation: it is commonly held that the emergence of new ways of conceptualizing objects (their role in society as well as their appearance) is prompted by a reaction against the norm. When a society can no longer justify the inevitability of its artistic practices, new and more adequate ones arise from a critique of the institutions that had thus far provided the social base for those practices. In modernism, this critique is called the *practice of negation*. What the modernist vanguard repudiated were two fundamental assumptions about the institution of art that had become entrenched in nineteenth-century bourgeois society. First was the assumption that there is an individual author who is the originator of meaning, who engages in the activity of design intending to inscribe in its forms his or her own subjectivities. Second was the belief that the perceiving subject enters the realm of the work seeking a space apart from life in which the mind is free to develop its own subjectivities, free to make its own connections. See T.J. Clark, "More on the Differences Between Comrade Greenberg and Ourselves," in *Modernism and Modernity*, eds. Benjamin H.D. Bochloh, Serge Gilbaut, and David Solkin (Halifax: University of Nova Scotia Press, 1983). Industrialized mass production, already a fact of life by the end of the nineteenth century, lay at the core of the modernist critique of bourgeois art. The mass-produced object, devoid of traces of authorship, of claim to uniqueness, and, therefore, of aura, naked of any representational cloak that might hide its genesis in repetitive, standardized, mechanized production presents itself to the vanguard artist as the locus for the critique of the auratic work of art. To engage in an aesthetic practice that used tech-

niques and objects of mass production was, therefore, to engage in a practice of negation. Note: I use the term *modernism* to refer to those changes in the conceptualization of objects that occurred at the beginning of the twentieth century as a result of a
skepticism that developed about the nature of representation in art. I adapt this definition from T.J. Clark, *The Painting of Modern Life* (Princeton, N.J.: Princeton University Press, 1984), 10.

10   Gerrie Andela, "The Public Park in the Netherlands," *Journal of Garden History* 1,
no. 4 (October–December 1981): 391.

11   Like the majority of land in the Netherlands, the site of the Bos Park lies several
meters below sea level. Historically, the Dutch have dealt with this condition by
building polders, extensive tracts of lowland that are reclaimed from the sea and
remain protected from it by dikes. Windmills convey the water that collects in the
channels within the enclosed lands "uphill" to sea level in order to drain the polder
fields.

12   Groundwater was estimated to be 60–70 centimeters higher southwest of the
Schinkelpolder due to heavy rains and winds coming from the southwest.

13   To depeat is to remove the thick layer of peat from the surface of the terrain. At the
Bos Park site, this layer was about 50 centimeters deep before the conversion of the
site to polders. Because peat is highly acidic and retains water, removing it was necessary to improve drainage of the soil and reduce its acidity in order to cultivate it for
agriculture. Also contributing to the irregularity of the terrain were "peat ridges"
caused by pushing around the peat layer and leaving it piled at the edges of fields.

14   *Het Amsterdamse Bos: The Amsterdam Forest Park* (Public Parks Service Guide), 48.

15   See Alan Ruff, *Holland and the Ecological Landscapes* (Manchester, England: Department of Town and Country Planning, University of Manchester, 1979), 10.

16   Cornelis Van Eesteren joined De Stijl in the 1923 and collaborated with Van Does-
burg on many projects. Although clearly this is not a plan that recalls the form of De
Stijl paintings or architecture, the strategy of distributing elements in a nonhierarchical way throughout space is one that Van Eesteren must have derived from his work
with De Stijl.

17   A ha-ha is a physical boundary, such as a ditch or a retaining wall, between two properties designed in such a way that it is concealed from within, making the landscape
seem physically continuous.

18   Alexander von Hoffman, "'Of Greater Lasting Consequence': Frederick Law Olmsted and the Fate of Franklin Park, Boston," *Journal of the Society of Architectural Historians* 47, no. 4: 339–350.

19   Marco De Michelis, "The Red and the Green: Park and City in Weimar Germany,"
Lotus International 30 (1981): 111.

20   Ludovica Scarpa, "Quantifying Parkland: The Standards of Happiness in Social-
Democratic Berlin," *Lotus International* 30 (1981): 119–122.

21   Van Eesteren was president of CIAM from 1930 to 1947.

22   Georg Simmel, "The division of labour as the cause of the divergence of subjective
and objective culture," in *The Philosophy of Money* (1900), trans. Tom Bottomore and
David Frisby (London: Routledge and Kegan Paul, 1978), 453–463.

23   I borrow this formulation from Benjamin Buchloh's description of the Soviet avant-
garde's concern for *faktura*, "the mechanical quality, the materiality, and the
anonymity of the painterly procedure," in "From Faktura to Factography," *October:
The First Decade, 1976–1986*, eds. Annette Michelson, et al. (Cambridge, Mass.: MIT
Press, 1987), 81.

24   Michel Foucault, "The Discourse on Language" (1971); reprinted in *The Archaeol-
ogy of Knowledge* (New York: Pantheon, 1972), 229.

25   Hays, *Modernism,* 154–160.

201

26 Yves-Alain Bois, *Piet Mondrian, 1872–1944* (Boston: Little, Brown, 1994). I borrowed this term from Bois's description of Mondrian's work.

27 Hays, *Modernism,* 172.

28 Rosalind Krauss, "Notes on the Index: Seventies Art in America," in *October: The First Decade, 1976–1986*, eds. Annette Michelson et al. (Cambridge, Mass.: MIT Press, 1987), 4.

29 Ibid.

30 *Subject* refers to individual as well as collective consciousness. The term is inherently equivocal because the two seemingly contradictory meanings depend on each other. The individual self is always understood within the context of a larger ideological or institutional framework. Conversely, a generalized concept of the subject would suppress differences that distinguish an individual from others, differences that constitute a vital aspect of social practices. *Object* refers to the artifacts of culture, their formal organization, as well as the forces that produce them. Because those forces are manipulated by the subject, both concepts are mutually dependent and exist in a dialectical relationship with each other. See Theodor W. Adorno, "Subject and Object," in *The Essential Frankfurt School Reader*, eds. Andrew Arato and Eike Gebhart (New York: Continuum, 1982), 497–569.

31 Fredric Jameson, "Reification and Utopia in Mass Culture,"in *Social Text* 1 (1979): 130–148.

32 Ibid.

33 The distance that develops between the object and its producer as a result of the division of labor is explained by Georg Simmel: "Whenever our energies do not produce something whole as a reflection of the total personality, then the proper relationship between subject and object is missing….The internal nature of our achievement is bound up with parts of achievements accomplished by others which are a necessary part of a totality, but it does not refer back to its producer….Its meaning is not derived from the mind of the producer but from its relationships with products of a different origin….The significance of the product is thus to be sought neither in the reflection of a subjectivity nor in the reflex of a creative spirit, but it is to be found only in the objective achievement that leads away from the subject….The broadening of consumption…is dependent upon the growth of objective culture, since the more objective and impersonal an object the better it is suited to more people….Such consumable material, in order to be acceptable and enjoyable to a very large number of individuals, cannot be designed for subjective differentiation of taste, while on the other hand only the most extreme differentiation of production is able to produce the objects cheaply and abundantly enough in order to satisfy the demand for them. The pattern of consumption is thus a bridge between the objectivity of culture and the division of labour." Excerpted from "The Division of Labour as the Cause of Divergence Between Objective and Subjective Culture" in *The Philosophy of Money*, 454–455.

34 There are many references regarding the appropriate uses of the park vis-à-vis society, especially in part two of the report, titled "General Significance of the Bosch plan." In addition to the need for extensive kinds of program, the committee clearly stated that for the new parks "visual consumption is not enough." *Rapport van Commissie voor het Boschplan Amsterdam*, 9.

35 *Bosch-Plan. Tentoonstelling* (Amsterdam: Public Works Department, 1937).

36 In "The Metropolis and Mental Life," Georg Simmel guides us through the historical development of this condition. The eighteenth-century belief in liberty and equality was corollary to that in an individual's freedom of movement in social and intellectual relationships. Another ideal arose in the nineteenth century through the economic division of labor, in which "individuals liberated from historical bonds now wished to distinguish themselves from one another." The division of labor, central to

all capitalist production, causes, on the one hand, the dissolution of the individual as free and autonomous and, on the other, the emergence of a kind of individualism that arises out of a need to assert one's uniqueness amid the vast machine of the metropolis. Simmel even proposes that the metropolis ought to provide the arena where the struggle between individualism and collectivity may be played out. See Georg Simmel, "The Metropolis and Mental Life" (1904); reprinted in *The Sociology of Georg Simmel*, trans. and ed. Kurt Wolff (New York: Free Press, 1964), 423.

37 *Aura* is defined by Walter Benjamin as a distance that exists between the work of art and the perceiving subject as a result of the authenticity value placed on the object because of its uniqueness in the world. Aura is drained from the object through its mechanical reproduction and through the processes of advertising it, displaying it, and fixing a price for its consumption. See Walter Benjamin, "The Work of Art in the Age of Mechanical Reproduction" (1935); reprint in *Illuminations*, ed. Hannah Arendt (New York: Schocken, 1969), 217–251. Aura in terms of the landscape can also be thought of as a distance between the perceiving subject and the landscape. Although it is possible to argue that no two landscapes can be identical (and that therefore all landscapes are auratic), uniqueness may not be a sufficient condition for the definition of an auratic landscape. Rather, it needs be further qualified in more specific terms, as a function of the landscape's contrast with its context, whether physical (i.e., Central park versus the city around it), or ecological (an endangered ecosystem), or cultural (the Hudson River Valley of the luminist painters, which does not exist any more), which renders that landscape in some way unique and transcendental, imbued with mysticism. My point is that when processes of mass production are applied to the making of landscape and made visible in their form, they also remove the possibility of aura from those landscapes and, therefore, restructure relations between the perceiving subject and the landscape.

38 Representation is generally taken to mean the construction of a resemblance of a previously existing reality in a work of art. I assume there is representation in all forms of aesthetic production, including in modernism, and thus I bracket the term as *mimetic representation*. By this I mean one that specifically seeks to reproduce another landscape, such as an existing naturalistic scene.

39 See *Process: Architecture* 128: *Hargreaves: Landscape Works* (January, 1996).

40 In this sense, the Bos Park differentiates itself from projects of the more recent ecological movement, the advocates of which focus their energies on the amelioration of an external environment rather than on representational and social concerns. See James Corner, "Ecology and Landscape as Agents of Creativity," *Ecological Design and Planning*, eds. George Thompson and Frederick Steiner (New York: John Wiley & Sons, 1997), 80–108.

41 For instance, the planting strategy of Koolhaas's proposal for the Parc de la Villette recalls the forest management attitude employed at Bos Park.

42 See Bart Lootsma's essay "Synthetic Regionalization" in this collection.

Chapter 13

Neither Wilderness nor Home: The Indian *Maidan*

Anuradha Mathur

As cities and towns across India continue to both expand and grow denser, wide open areas are still an integral part of the urban fabric. Often more than a square mile in area, these public lands are neither cultivated parks nor neglected wastelands. They are something other. In Calcutta, one of the most congested cities of the world, a vast open landscape still occupies over two square miles in the heart of the city despite encroachments by buildings, parks, clubs, and monuments. Similarly, in Bombay, a series of grassy plains stretches across the city center; at their narrowest, these open spaces measure about 600 feet and in all constitute at least 150 acres of open ground.

The character of these spaces is modest and devoid of embellishment. Their simple emptiness stands in stark contrast to the intricate urban fabric surrounding them. Rarely thought of or described as designed landscapes, these places do not call attention to themselves, yet they continue to support a wide spectrum of urban life from cricket, football, and other sports to trade fairs and circuses, from political rallies and religious congregations to the grazing of goats. These anonymous and accommodating grounds are called *maidans*.

A *maidan* is commonly described as a "large plain," an "open field," or a "vast ground." While such spaces do not appear to be obviously constructed territories, acts of leveling and clearing extend their limits to distant horizons and establish a clear domain. The simple clarity and openness of the *maidan* is under threat, however, as modern development pressures seek to reformulate these territories according to functional, economic, and aesthetic criteria.

Maidans can be traced in Indian cities following the influence of Islam. Even though the Arab armies reached the borders of India in the eighth century, sustained contact with the new religion of Islam occurred after the Afghan invasion in the eleventh century.[1] The early Muslim rulers from Central Asia and, later, the Mughals from Persia, brought with them the space of a vast open landscape enclosed within a settlement. They called these spaces *maidans*. Distinct evidence of Islamic *maidans* dating back to the fifteenth century can be found today in Indian cities such as Ahmedabad, Agra, and Shahjehanabad.

Fig. 1. Maidan-i-Shah, Isphahan, as nomadic site. Source: Mme Dieulafoy, *La Perse* (1887).

The advent of the British during the seventeenth century brought to India new attitudes toward military protection and urban patterns. These patterns included vast open grounds within the urban fabric. The notion of commons and recreational space was, of course, traditional to English ways of life.[2] The memory of these public spaces, refracted through the military and political requirements of colonialism, encouraged the emergence of another form of open ground in colonial towns like Bombay, Calcutta, and Madras.[3] The word *maidan* became part of colonial Indian vocabulary during the eighteenth century to describe these spaces. Although the Islamic and colonial maidans were the result of different spatial, cultural, and political histories, there is little physical difference between the two today.

In what follows, I trace the development and evolution of the Indian *maidan*. I argue that the *maidan* is both nomadic and collective. It is what Ivan Illich calls "commons," or:

> ...that part of the environment that lay beyond a person's own threshold and outside his own possession, but to which, however, that person had a recognized claim of usage—not to produce commodities but to provide for the subsistence of kin. Neither wilderness nor home is commons, but that part of the environment for which customary law exacts specific forms of community respect.[4]

These places that are neither wilderness nor home are being threatened today by the demands of modern urbanization, and yet they offer the only real hope of individual freedom and collective engagement in the enclosure of the city. They are as relevant today, and for cities other than those in India, as they have ever been.

The Nomadic and the Collective Landscape: Camp and City

Maidan is a word of Persian origin. It conjures up images of a plain, a meadow, a ground, or a field. As a battleground it is called *maidan-e-karzar*; as a branding ground it is *dag-gah*; as a military camp it assumes the name of *lakshar*; as a sports field it is a *maidan-warzish*, and as a parade ground it is called a *maidan-e-mashq*. *Maidans* were primarily associated with pilgrims, traders, and militia, and today the *maidan* has come to embrace all these and many other uses.[5]

One early recorded manifestation of the *maidan* derives from the ninth century. Ahmad Ibn Tulun (868–906)[6] is remembered for his creation of a very large *maidan* in the military extension of the town of Fustat just outside Cairo. Later *maidans* were usually attached either to the pleasure palace on the outskirts of the city or in front of a citadel within the city.[7] Travelers to this region through the fifteenth and seventeenth centuries gave fragmented accounts of other *maidans*. The most striking and well documented of these is in Isphahan (Fig. 1).[8]

"Let me lead you," wrote a traveler at that time, "into the Maidan… without doubt as spacious, pleasant and aromatic a bazaar as any in the Universe."[9] The Maidan-i-Shah was part of the extension to the town of Isphahan by Shah Abbas (1587–1629) and built during the seventeenth century. Besides being a "pleasant and aromatic" marketplace covered with temporary stalls that displayed wares ranging from food and spices to mules and horses, the Maidan-i-Shah was also used for public processions and religious festivals. At other times the *maidan* was a polo ground, the exclusive domain of horses and their riders. The ground was often under water in winter, while in "summer men with watering cans laid the dust, which was never excessive because the ground was covered with fine river sand." [10] Variously described as a "park," "square," and "market," even "hippodrome,"[11] the *maidan* appeared to be all yet none of these. The Maidan-i-Shah that survives in Isphahan today has gone through several "beautification" schemes, with paving and planting that fragment it into parterres. Neither a *bagh* (Persian garden) nor a *maidan*, it is today a generic site for garaging automobiles in the city.

The Muslim city of Ahmedabad was laid out in 1411 by the Mughal ruler Ahmed Shah on the banks of the Sabarmati river in what is today northwestern India. Ahmedabad is probably one of the few historically Muslim cities in India where it is still possible to trace under layers of urban fabric the outlines of a *maidan* that had once been at the center of its life. Due to the lack of cartographic documents, the evolution of the city can only be constructed from brief descriptive accounts in memoirs, travel documents, and archaeological records. A fort and the Jumma Masjid (or Friday Mosque) formed the two dominant foci of the settlement. The area between them was structured along a monumental axis extending from the entrance of the fort past the mosque. It included the main bazaar street (also referred to as the processional way) and a vast rectangular *maidan* that connected and separated the religious and royal centers of the city. A triple-arched gateway, the Teen Darwaza, formed a threshold between the bazaar street and the *maidan*.

Visited by many travelers during the sixteenth and seventeenth centuries, Ahmedabad was praised for its wealth and grandeur, although Emperor

Jehangir was less impressed. Following his visit in 1617, the Emperor wanted to rename it Gardabad, or "abode of dust."[12] A traveler from northern Germany, Albert J. de Mandelslo, who visited Ahmedabad twice in 1638, leaves a more enthusiastic account of the various sights of the city, including the Maidan Shah:

> The Maidan Shah, or the King's Market, is at least 1600 feet long and half as many broad, and beset all about with rows of palm-trees and date-trees, intermixed with citron trees and orange-trees, whereof there are very many in the several streets; which is not only pleasant to the sight by the delightful prospect it affords, but also makes walking along them more convenient by reasons of the coolness.[13]

A French traveler, M. de Thevenot, who was in Ahmedabad twenty-eight years later in 1666, provides a different account. He describes the *maidan* as the "King's Square" and as measuring "400 paces in breadth and 700 in length [2,100 feet by 1,200 feet] with trees planted on all sides. The gate of the Castle is on the west side opposite to the three arches, and the gate of the Caravanserai on the South."[14] Despite these varied descriptions, the surface of the *maidan* was recognized as a flat plain of earth and at its center was a *karang*, or water tank or well.

During the reign of the Muslim kings, the *maidan* was a place where "great feudatories or foreign embassies assembled before approaching the presence," according to historian Sir Theodore. Hope. Whereas the *maidan* was acknowledged as a place outside the royal center, it was used as a ceremonial place by the ruler who "enthroned on the terrace, mustered the troops for martial enterprises and gala day reviews, or held splendid court in the cool of the evening besides the splashing fountain."[15] In spite of this royal patronage, the *maidan* was a place open to all for gathering and thoroughfare, where the royalty and commoners met. A site for temporary markets as well as the Khas Bazaar, the *maidan* was also the venue for the weekly Gujari (gypsy) fair. This fair still takes place today on the dry bed of the Sabarmati river, and remains a popular feature of Ahmedabad.

Based on a survey conducted by the English in 1825, one of the earliest maps available of Ahmedabad shows the *maidan* as no longer a vast rectangular plain but now a triangular space, the land near the Teen Darwaza having been steadily claimed for permanent structures. As recalled by the elders of the city,

the *maidan*, though much diminished, remained an important place for political meetings, games of cricket, and temporary bazaars. The only traces of the
existence of a once large plain in the heart of the city are the Teen Darwaza,
which still stands majestic amid the roaring traffic and ruins of the fort. One can
still measure between these relics the original extent of the Maidan Shah.

Intrinsically one of the main institutions of the city, the *maidan* was articulated as a geometric space. Its surface was barren earth or fine sand. Its center
was free of any monument or pavilion, unlike the *char bagh* (Persian garden),
although, as already mentioned, it was frequently marked by a well or water
tank. Trees were not common, but where they did exist they were arranged on
the periphery so as to contain and not fragment the essentially empty quality of
the plain.[16]

Often described by Western travelers and historians as a "great square,"[17] the
maidan cannot be described as a spatial entity in the hierarchy of squares and
streets. The *maidan* is not a distinct enclosure, like a courtyard. Although
attempts were made to maintain a visual structure, the peripheral boundaries of
the *maidan* are more decorative frames than spatial figures. In other words,
although it is a bounded space within the city, the *maidan* does not exist as a per-
ceptible room. This lack of definition is, perhaps, appropriate, for in a landscape
where horizons are broad, the *maidan* is a place born of a desire to establish
human domain by marking boundaries while maintaining a sense of immen-
sity—a phenomenal landscape quality retained from nomadic ways of life.

As a ground for pitching tents, the *maidan* accommodates the nomadic
spirit within the city. Conversely, as temporary reference points within a disorienting expanse, the tent structures make bearable the uncertainties of the
maidan. The tent is a form of shelter that allows for the migratory existence of
caravans, military camps, and religious pilgrimages. It was a natural form of
dwelling for the Muslim rulers, who often found themselves "in camp" as pilgrims and warriors. The palaces of the Sultans were often comparable to glori-
fied tents; Ali Qapi, the name of Shah Abbas's palace on the edge of the
Maidan-i-Shah at Isphahan, literally means the "royal tent" (Fig. 2).

The tent is a mode of construction that is found across time and territories
whenever there are migratory events and the need for temporary dwellings. It is
commonly described as "a portable shelter of skin, coarse cloth, esp. canvas supported by one or more poles and usually extended by ropes fastened to pegs in
the ground."[18] The portability of a tent and its ease of installation draws attention to the nature of the ground it is pegged into. The temporary nature of this

209

attachment is complemented by the permanence of the ground, which is made of leveled and compacted soil or sand. The ground accommodates trampling, pegging, riding, and thoroughfare via its capacity to remain level and firm. Soil that also allows for the absorption of water and other urban traces makes this vast and expansive ground also *deep*.[19]

210

The notion of depth and material become as significant as the vast horizon for the embodiment of nomadic ground. Before the science of geology presented the depth of soil as a naked transect, depth was experienced through the sounding of wells. While monuments in a *maidan* might be said to oppose its expansive spirit, wells reinforce its sense of limitlessness. The well in a *maidan* connects ground and sky through water. Further, the presence of water, however scarce, allows this sometimes dreary and parched ground to be temporarily habitable. As the vertical axis, the well anchors the horizontal expanse. Its presence is often hidden from a cursory glance and revealed only as one traverses this ground as a *nomad*.

The *maidan*, then, can be seen as the outcome of a need for the nomads-turned-settlers to establish an endurable slice of the infinite desert in their settlement. This brings us to the aspiration for anonymity—the anonymity of the vast horizon that accommodates not just the nomadic spirit but the collective as well.

Pilgrimage and Prayer

Islam literally means "subjugation to Allah," thus propagating the equality of all persons before Him. It perpetuates a sense of collective gathering as the basis of its liturgical practice. Prayer that comprises mental, verbal, and physical subjugation is performed in a hierarchical range of services: by the individual, the community, the entire population of a city, and the whole Muslim world. The primary institution for prayer in the Islamic world is the *Jami Masjid*—the name means "collective" or "assembly mosque"—which is the site of weekly prayer every Friday, the day of assembly (*Yawn-al-Jama*). The plan of the mosque, reflecting its congregational nature, consists of a large hall preceded by an

Fig. 2. Maidan-i-Shah, Isphahan, as market and campground. Source: C. deBruyn, *Travels* (1737).

immense courtyard. The congregation, oriented toward Mecca by the *mihrab* (niche) in the *qibla* (wall), focuses on the speaker.

The *mussalla* (or *idgah*) is used for prayer during the two major festivals, *id-al-Fitre* and *id-al-Adha*, for the assembly of the entire population of the city. The *mussalla* consists of the essential components of a mosque: the *qibla* wall and a *mihrab* bordering a vast expanse of ground and providing a sense of orientation. The *maidan* is used on these two days of the year, with a canvas *qibla* temporally erected as the venue for prayer. Here, all Muslims of the city gather and face Mecca, standing shoulder to shoulder, to pray.

According to Islamic creed, the doctrine of resurrection is second only to that of Allah's creation of the world. The Resurrection (*Al-Qiyama*) and the Judgment (*Hisab*) will take place on a plain of assemblage called the Maidan-e-Hashr, where multitudes will gather for the final divine decision. It is interesting to note that a similar assembly is held every year at the time of the annual pilgrimage to Mecca at the Maidan-e-Arafat. Pilgrims still trek to Arafat, where Prophet Muhammed delivered His farewell sermon, as Muslims have done for centuries. Here is the greatest single assembly of people from all corners of the world ever to meet at one place, on one day and for one purpose.

The Maidan-e-Arafat is enclosed by low mountains encircling an enormous barren plain, in the midst of which rises one solitary mount: the Mount of Mercy. During the Pilgrimage, this plain transforms into a tented city of more than two million people. As far as the eye can see, the Maidan-e-Arafat is a moving mass of pilgrims, the ultimate gathering place for the entire Islamic world. Here, the nomadic grounds of the pilgrim and the collective grounds of faith come together explicitly in a physical landscape that accommodates both.

Sport and Commons

There is yet another expression of *maidan* that emerged out of a context very different than the ones previously discussed, but which has nonetheless influenced the modern notion of *maidan* in India. In a landscape that was so thickly vegetated that one had to either raise or level the ground in order to broaden one's horizon, the *maidan* appeared as a clearing. The limits of this clearing established a defensible territory that remained at the threshold of an infinite domain.

In the early English settlements in India, vast clearings appeared in front of the city's fort more out of military concerns than a sense of community. In Bombay and, later, in Calcutta, these grounds were constructed outside the fortifications; trees were cut, swamps were drained, and ground was leveled to form a vast plain. This feature was called the Esplanade. *Esplanade* derives from the Latin *esplanare*, which means "to level" and commonly implies open space designed for public walks or drives. *Esplanade* is also a military term used to signify "an open level space of ground, separating the citadel of a fortress from the town, and intended to prevent any person approaching the town without being seen from the citadel."[20] Esplanades that later formed some of the great *maidans* in India were thus first constructed as a distancing device, a no-man's-land (Fig. 3).

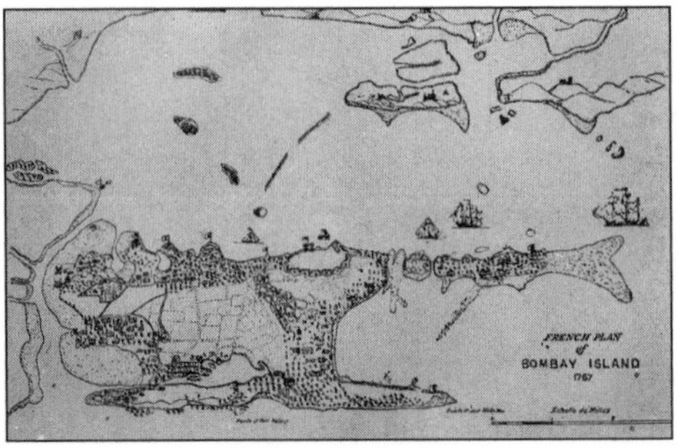

Due to military requirements, no permanent structures could be erected on the *maidan*. An unenthusiastic commentator in Bombay once wrote that "the dreary, treeless sun-burnt wilderness of the Esplanade during the hot season with its few dusty narrow roads leading to the native town is appalling."[21] In time, however, the wind-swept open expanse of the *maidan* acquired social as well as military significance for both the European and the Parsee populations of Bombay. It was most likely the oppressive climate, together with a desire for nomadic freedom, that drove the population of the overcrowded and airless Fort of Bombay to the *maidans*.[22] Here they pitched camp—sometimes elaborate bamboo bungalows—to spend long summer (for shade) and winter(for shelter) months. These esplanade tents became a distinctive feature of Bombay. Even into the late 1890s, long after the destruction of the Fort walls, "tents still rose like mushrooms…every cold weather."[23] For the English, with their enthusiasm for outdoor recreation, the *maidan* became a primary venue for gatherings, promenading, and sports (Fig. 4).

In the evolution of many colonial towns, the vast clearings of the *maidans* played a pivotal role in the transition from a static pattern of the fortified enclave to a more dynamic one of open settlement. Although many *maidans* were partially built over, large parcels were retained and formed a major structuring element for the new developments that tended to grow around or across its expanse. By the early twentieth century, the *maidans* in Bombay had lost their

Fig. 3. French plan of Bombay Island, 1767, showing the clearing of the esplanade outside the Bombay fort. Source: *The Bombay Gazetteer*, 1.

sea view as well as their evening recre- ators, but sportsmen continued to be the most zealous supporters of the open ground. Their enthusiasm encouraged gymkhanas, which during in the Bom- bay Presidency described any club with outdoor facilities for sport. A number of gymkhanas for Europeans catered to specific outdoor sport such as golf, cricket, and pigeon shooting. Most of these had modest beginnings in tempo- rary pavilions erected on the *maidan*.[24]

213

Unlike Bombay, Calcutta was at no time of its development a fortified town. The old Fort William was merely a token structure. A gigan- tic new fort was built in the 1780s; jungle was cleared, swamps were drained, and existing Indian dwellings were removed to create a clear range of fire around this new Fort William. Thus, Calcutta, like Bombay and Madras, acquired an esplanade as a consequence of military requirements. There was, however, a fundamental difference in the struc- tural pattern of Calcutta compared to the other settlements of the East India Company. The new fort at Calcutta was purely a military construction and did not accommodate the princi- pal buildings of the township as they did in Bombay. The offi- cial buildings as well as the houses of the inhabitants were allowed to be constructed across the wide expanse of the esplanade (Fig. 5).

"Ostensibly we the British…were no more than merchants…. But slowly and surely we were changing the role of a purely mercantile community for that of a great political power," wrote an unnamed author at the turn of the nine- teenth century.[25] The growth of imperial power, as well as the desire and need to express this power, added other dimensions to the perception and use of the

Fig. 4 (top). Engraving of the Bombay Green as *maidan* within the Fort, 1767. Source: James Forbes, *Oriental Memoirs IV* (1813).

Fig. 5 (bottom). *Maidan* as no-man's-land between fort and town, circa 1792. Source: "Calcutta and Its Environs, 1792–93: From an Accurate Survey in 1792 and 1793 by A. Upjohn," in Kath- leen Blechynden, *Calcutta Past and Present* (London: Thacker, 1905).

maidan. The grassy plains provided grand vistas and became critical spaces of expression for the new role acquired by the East India Company. The monumental value of the *maidan*'s vast expanse proved more significant for Calcutta than Bombay as the *maidan* evolved into a symbol of the British Raj, supporting its pageants and parades besides its grand monuments.

For the English recreators in Calcutta, the *maidan* became the venue for regular pleasure drives. The *maidan* offered little shelter or solace, except for an occasional bandstand. Its surface was usually grassed over or made from earth that could be trampled, played, ridden, or camped on. Trees appeared more as something left behind in the clearing than an embellishment added to its structure. As a venue for sport however, the *maidan* continued to retain its significance, especially after Calcutta initiated Indian cricket in 1804.

With the rapid and chaotic growth of this city, the *maidan* has often been referred to as the "lungs of Calcutta." Even today, long after the colonial occupation, the *maidan* remains at the heart of the bustling city and provides an important place for collective and diverse gatherings. In the words of the town planner Gordon Cullen:

> [The Maidan] has been able to absorb in its broad acres a multitude of activities, together with an astonishing variety of landscapes, and still remain vast and ocean like. Possibly due to its complexity and diversity as one characteristic dissolves into another, the Maidan retains a universal quality, a quality big enough to open a window in the vast compression of this fantastic city. Somewhere in any big city you have to punch a hole right through and let people breathe with the spirit as well as the lungs.[26]

For the majority of the Indian population, recreation was centered around family and religious celebrations, for which a tent would often go up in the *maidan*. For the British, by contrast, the concept of recreation was interpreted as "one involving physical activity and which should preferably take the form of organized 'sport'."[27] Besides physical fitness, sport also carried moral connotations: team games and team spirit were encouraged as means of character building. A number of field games, including hockey, cricket, football, and polo, first found their way onto the *maidan* in the early nineteenth century. As a collective ground for recreation and sport, the *maidan* accommodated a kind of anonymity. Within the stratified colonial world, sport became a socially accepted means by

214

which "individuals segregated by sex, social rank, and race could interact and communicate without compromising their individual position."[28]

The Idea of *Maidan*

Maidans have emerged as a result of human intervention directed not toward the addition of identity, events, or character to a level ground but rather toward keeping land free and indeterminate. In landscapes where topography is uneven and horizons limited, mounds are leveled, ditches are filled, and vegetation is cleared to create open and unobstructed plains. Conversely, in landscapes where the horizons are broad, an expanse is marked and cordoned off to be protected as a generous, unfragmented space. In both cases the aspiration is to maintain an anonymous expanse that extends the human horizon beyond capture. Such scale and simplicity is almost inconceivable to many that envision public space in more hierarchical and formal terms.

215

Though *maidans* were used by two very different regimes in India as a tool for power, it would be an error to construe these spaces as expressions of power (as in a fort or palace). Rather, *maidans* reflect the collective aspirations of a people. Though partly encroached upon today, *maidans* still remain vast and ocean-like within the density of many Indian cities. The need for an indeterminate no-man's-land, a nomadic field, and a shared collective space continues to be important. In the plan of the contemporary Indian city, the *maidan* is still an unspecified part of the urban program; it is left free of any permanent structures or claims, a vast plain in the heart of the city. As a recent writer noted, "It might be a dangerous place for someone with a touch of agoraphobia."[29]

In cities of increasingly circumscribed social, racial, or economic enclaves, the *maidan* has come to both symbolize and provide neutral territory, a ground where people can gather on a common plane. It is a place that offers freedom without obligation. This ability to accommodate a diverse range of social and political structures makes the *maidan* an extremely significant space in the city. It is a place where people can "touch the spirit of commonness."[30]

The freedom afforded by the *maidan* has limits, however, regarding its occupation by the individual. The vast, nondescript void and lack of focus can be disorienting and appear purposeless. Yet the expanse and anonymity of the place is transformed daily by cricket games and visiting fairs or circuses (Fig. 6). At other times, the *maidan* gathers the full scale of the city, be it a religious congregation on Ramzan Id, a large political rally, or Gandhi launching his Quit India movement. Here, the *maidan* transforms into a sea of humanity

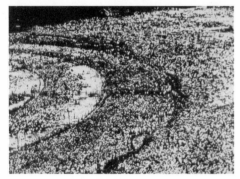

before receding once again into quiet emptiness (Fig. 7).

The constructed ground of Indian cities has for centuries accommodated the *maidan* and its changing functions. The modern zeal for economic development and objectification of commodities is making the *maidan* a less welcome phenomenon, however. Even so, the *idea* of *maidan* still has significant power in the collective imagination of Indian cities. Thus, following the disappearance of many historical *maidans*, people continue to appropriate landscapes that lend themselves to both nomadic and collective life. For the citizens of the crowded city of Ahmedabad, which has expanded far across the banks of the Sabarmati river, the riverbed itself is today the *maidan* (Fig. 8). This is a vast, dry plain for most of the year, except during the monsoons. The flat, ephemeral territory offers freedom within the enclosure of the city and extends the limits of the horizon in time (Fig. 9).

Engaging Landscape

There is much that the *maidan* can offer those who are concerned for the public realm today, not only in Indian cities but in Western cities as well. City landscapes are being increasingly commodified, monitored, and constructed in ways that discourage spontaneous appropriation and unplanned transformation. In resistance to this over-determinism, a few contemporary landscape architects and urbanists are seeking to promote qualities of indeterminacy, open-endedness, and temporality in their work. Their aim is to engender and support engagement rather than objectification. These efforts are particularly applicable

Fig. 6. Temporary habitation on the Oval *Maidan*, Bombay, c. 1900. Source: The Victoria and Albert Archives, Bombay.

Fig. 7. A galaxy of people during the Congress Party Centennial Celebrations on the Azad *Maidan*, Bombay, 1986. Source: *The Afternoon* 9 (January 1986).

to large-scale public, decommissioned, and marginalized lands within or at the edge of cities. Such spaces
resist popular prescriptions of use, identity, and meaning.[31] Is this shift from form to events, permanence to
change, identity to void, a recognition for the need to
recover essential territories in the city that are "neither
wilderness nor home?"

Maidan exemplifies engagement and negotiation
between built claimed ground and shifting fluxed
ground, the nomad and the sedentary, the collective and
the individual human spirit. The spirit of the nomad,
untempered by the collective aspirations of the city,
could be as destructive as a collective spirit that does not
allow a person freedom to wander. Can we still accommodate and value the anonymity of the nomadic and the
aspiration of the collective spirit within a constructed
landscape? Can we nurture and reinvent the idea of
maidan in the enclosure of cities elsewhere as on the dry,
dusty plains of India?

Notes

1   The first to arrive was Mohammed Ibn Kasim, who conquered the Indus Valley up to
Multan. This remained the extent of the Arab conquest for several hundred years.
The invasion of Mahmud of Ghazni in the eleventh century was more significant for
the spread of Islam in India. Toward the end of the twelfth century, a fresh wave of
invasions came from the northwest, headed by the Afghan chief Shahab-ud-din
Ghuri, who decisively established Muslim rule in India. The Sultans of Delhi, called
the "Slave Kings," followed him and together consolidated the Muslim Empire. Following them was Allaudin Khilji, who conquered Gujarat and for a while overpow-
ered a great part of the south. The disintegration of the Muslim Empire, however,
came in the fourteenth century following the reign of Mohammed bin Tuglaq and an
attack by the Afghan chief Timur from Samarkand. One hundred fifty years lapsed
before the Mughals from Persia gathered the Empire again.

2   See Steen Eiler Rasmussen, *London: The Unique City* (Victoria: Penguin Books,
1934).

3   The English first arrived in India as merchants. The East India Company was established by London merchants in 1612 at Surat, a city on the west coast then under

Fig. 8 (top). The vast plain of the Sabarmati riverbed, Ahmedabad, 1985. Photograph by Anuradha Mathur.

Fig. 9 (bottom). Gathering on the Sabarmati riverbed on the eve of Mahatma Gandhi's Salt March
to Dhandi, c. 1930. Source: The Gandhi Ashram Archives, Ahmedabad.

Mughal rule. This was followed by other trading posts at Madras (1639), Bombay (1661), and Calcutta (1690). Mughal strength was collapsing by the mid-eighteenth century in the face of Hindu rebellion, and a power struggle between Mughal provincial governors gave the British and the French, the only contenders then for dominion in India, an opportunity to forward their own political ambitions. The fight for dominion was decisively won at Plassey in 1757. The British, spreading inward from their trading posts, became successors to the Mughals.

4   Ivan Illich, *Gender* (New York: Pantheon Books, 1982), 18, n.10. Even though the *maidan* and the English commons cannot be merged with respect to their specific history and evolution, the idea of the commons as discussed by Illich is very similar to that of *maidan*.

5   Some of these usages were shared with me by Professor Momin at Bombay University.

6   Ahmad Ibn Tulun belonged to the Abbasid dynasty, the Caliphs of Baghdad from the mid-eighth to mid-thirteenth centuries A.D.

7   See Doris Behrens-Abouseif, "A Circassian Mamluk Suburb North of Cairo," *Art and Archeology Research Papers* 14 (December 1978).

8   For most Islamic cities besides Isphahan, only fragmentary visual evidence exists of historic *maidans*. One has to rely on descriptions and observations of curious travelers or contemporary chroniclers to imagine and reconstruct the presence of these *maidans*.

9   Wilfred Blunt, *Isfahan—Pearl of Persia* (London: Elek Book, 1966), 63.

10   Ibid., 64.

11   See Behrens-Abouseif, 20.

12   M.S. Commissariat, *A History of Gujarat*, vol. 2 (Bombay: Orient Longmans, 1957), 351.

13   Quoted in Commissariat, 351.

14   Quoted in Commissariat, 352. Both Albert de Mandelslo and M. de Thevenot describe the *maidan* in Western terms that came close to defining the temporary function it accommodated during their brief visits there.

15   Sir Theodore C. Hope, *Architecture at Ahmedabad* (London: John Murray, 1866), 42.

16   According to Nesar Alsayyad, the dimensions of *maidans* were determined by the surrounding monuments to provide for their appropriate viewing. He, however, concludes that this remained the only *raison d'être* for the *maidan* besides being a thoroughfare, as a result of which they have little significance as open space in the Islamic city. See Nesar Alsayyad, "Space in an Islamic City: Some Urban Design Patterns," *Journal of Architectural and Planning Research* 4, no. 2 (1987): 109.

17   This is most often expressed in descriptions, both old and recent, of the Maidan-i-Shah in Isphahan.

18   *Webster's Encyclopedic Unabridged Dictionary* (New York: Portland House, 1989), 463.

19   See David Leatherbarrow's essay "Leveling the Land" in this collection for a discussion on depth.

20   J.H. Stocqueler, *The Military Encyclopedia* (London: W.H. Allen, 1853), 97.

21   Samuel T. Sheppard, *Bombay* (Bombay: Times of India Press, 1932), 111. Sheppard presents this description from Milburn's "Oriental Commerce in Bombay."

22   Sir D.E. Wacha, *Shells from the Sand of Bombay—My Recollections and Reminiscences 1860–75* (Bombay: K.T. Ankelesaria, 1920). An extensive account of the "air-eaters" and others on the *maidan* is given by Wacha in his personal recollections of the early nineteenth century. The northern portion of the *maidan*, he notes, was chiefly used for military purposes and executions. The southern section, which was exposed to Back Bay, was visited at eventide by the inhabitants of the Fort, specially the Parsis,

who occupied a special part of the *maidan* for their exclusive groups and evening prayers. Other areas were dotted with squatting groups involved in sedentary pastimes.

23 Sheppard, *Bombay*.

24 In 1876, the various clubs amalgamated to form the Bombay Gymkhana Club. This was given a more permanent status as well as a structure on the *maidan*. The club was started with a concession from the government to erect upon the *maidan* "a pavilion of such a construction as will admit easy and speedy removal" (Sheppard, 146). In 1879, the club got permission to enclose a plot of land on the condition that the land would be reclaimable on seven days' notice. In 1905, the club was granted a ninety-nine-year lease on the land and a new pavilion was built that stands today in a cordoned portion on the southern portion of what is now known as the Azad *Maidan*.

25 Quoted in S.M. Edwardes, *Rise of Bombay* (Bombay: Times of India Press, 1902).

26 Gordon Cullen, "The Steamroller and the Flower," *Architectural Review* 150, no. 898 (December 1971): 377.

27 Anthony D. King, *Colonial Urban Development—Culture, Social Power and Environment* (London: Routledge Kegan Paul, 1976), 56.

28 Ibid., 57. Also see Charles Allen, *Plain Tales from the Raj: Images of British India*. (London: Andre Deutsch, 1975), 109.

29 Geoffrey Moorhouse, *Calcutta* (New York: Harcourt Brace Jovanovich, 1972), 214–215.

30 This is a misquote of Louis Kahn by Sten Nilsson in *The New Capitals of India, Pakistan and Bangladesh* (Lund: Studentlitterature, 1973), 195. Kahn wrote of the "spirit of community," not "spirit of commonness." The word *commonness*, however, opens a new dimension in the understanding of anonymity that is crucial to *maidan*. John Stilgoe, in his essay "Town Common and Village Green in New England: 1620 to 1981," in *Common Ground: Caring for Shared Land from Town Common to Urban Park*, eds. Ronald Lee Fleming and Lauri A. Halderman, (Cambridge, Mass.: Harvard Common Press and the Townscape Institute, 1981), writes: "'common' is an old word, rich in meanings and acquired over centuries. Yet it is not easily defined. The word denotes something that is readily accessible and openly shared, something that has a general, nonprivate nature. It can, however, also mean something ordinary, undistinguished, almost vulgar."

31 The reader is referred to designers as diverse as Adriaan Geuze, George Hargreaves, Mario Schejtnan, Georges Descombes, Paolo Burgi, Peter Latz , and James Corner, where emptiness and restraint undergird the structuring of large landscapes for open-ended futures. See also an instance of this in my own work with Dilip da Cunha in James Corner, ed., *Governor's Island* (University of Pennsylvania, Graduate School of Fine Arts Document, 1996).

Chapter 14

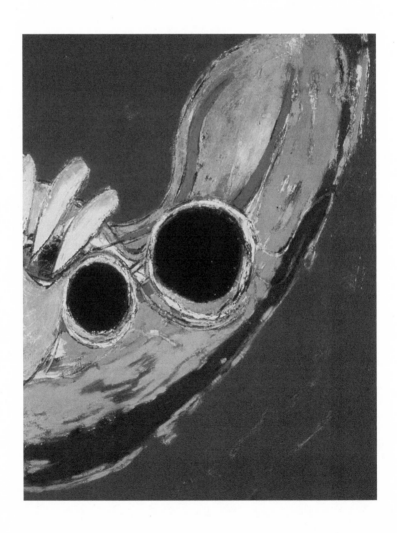

Airport/Landscape

Denis Cosgrove (with paintings by Adrian Hemming)

While the recovery of landscape highlights the newly discovered richness, complexity, and intellectual fertility of landscape as a theme in contemporary thought, design, and practice, it also suggests connections with the past and with historical landscapes. The excitement of recovery springs, in large measure, from stretching landscape's meanings beyond conventional attachment to a delimited and consciously designed section of the natural world and to spaces subtended to the surveying eye: framed, selected, picturesque. Landscape today is unbounded, flexible, and mobile, composed of forms, connections, and spaces that can neither be contained within conventional frames nor pictured according to the scopic conventions of a distanced, authoring eye. Landscape mobilizes both material and mind, nature and imagination, space and technique, in novel and imaginative ways.

Landscape's meanings broaden especially in the designed spaces of edge cities—industrial parks, shopping malls, highway intersections—and virtual landscapes stretch into immaterial space on the computer screen, the television advertisement, and in the tourist brochure. But in holding on to the word *landscape* to designate such diverse spaces, connections with older meanings are sustained, reflecting a desire to insert contemporary experience into a longer historical trajectory of meaningful connection between land and life, space and meaning.

This essay explores this dual meaning of recovery as both retrospective and prospective through the juxtaposition of images and words stimulated by London's Heathrow Airport. Mapping through these two media, the contrasting approaches of an academic geographer and a professional painter are brought together to investigate a space that may initially seem to lie well beyond the conventional understanding of what constitutes a landscape. Yet in doing so, we seek to recover one of landscape's oldest historical associations—that between landed estate and painting—in order to throw light on one of the most

Fig. 1. *Big Bird #2*. Adrian Hemming, 1995. Oil on canvas, 4 x 5 feet. (All paintings in this chapter by Adrian Hemming, with thanks to Louisa Howick, Howick Fine Art, and to David Cummings and the B.A.A. Art Committee.)

characteristic spaces of the late twentieth-century world: the airport. We are not here concerned with such design issues as *landscaping* the terminals, runways, or public open spaces but rather with conceiving the airport as a complex functional, spatial, and, to a degree, visual whole. Working from immediate, formal parallels between the modern airport and the Georgian landscape park, and paralleling the written analysis with drawn and painted images produced for a commission to make public artworks in one of Heathrow's terminal buildings, we pursue a single idea: that of *recovering Heathrow as landscape*.

In England, *landscape* popularly denotes an artistic tradition of painting and garden design, historically associated, above all, with the parkland vistas of the eighteenth-century landed estate. The Georgian park aesthetic is, for many observers, the paradigm and measure of English scenic taste, for some the supreme expression of the English artistic genius. While the larger part of lowland rural England has always lain outside the bounding walls of such estates, and despite the effect of agribusiness on English agrarian scenery—removing field hedges and turning bucolic pastures to monocultured grain spaces—readings of the English landscape remain closely tied to the Georgian landed aesthetic.

Although, at first sight, the distance between the sights, sounds, and smells of a late twentieth-century international airport and the eighteenth-century landscape park seems unbridgeable, a little reflection suggests rather closer formal parallels between hypermodern and georgic spaces than might initially be expected. With its air of "improvement," the landed estate was the economic engine of Georgian England—locus of its capital accumulation, technical innovation, and social modernization.[1] The international airport acts increasingly as the motor of contemporary metropolitan life, central to the prosperity and growth of any major urban region with pretensions to participation of a global economy. Workplace to more than fifty thousand people, Heathrow airport is edge city's most dynamic focal point,[2] as critical a motor for London's

222

Fig. 2. *Feersum Enginn #2.* Adrian Hemming, 1995. Oil on canvas, 4 x 5 feet. The commission: the word *aviation*. The brief: to paint four large paintings to be installed inside the new Terminal One at Heathrow Airport. In arriving at the final work, hundreds of drawings and studies were made. How to make sense of so much visual material: man, machine, complexity? The works entailed sifting, editing, building up, and scraping down all sorts of possibilities. Mapping, accumulating insights; painting as investigation.

economic growth and prosperity, for technological change and for cultural interaction today, as the city's eastern docklands were to Victorian London, or the agricultural estate—in Bedfordshire or Barbados—to eighteenth-century England.

In scale and area too, Heathrow may be compared to a Georgian landed park. The 2,750 acres within its perimeter fence approximate the shape and area of a substantial Georgian estate. It is as securely guarded from poaching intruders. The terminal buildings grouped at the center of its open green vistas gather personnel and functions in the manner of a Palladian country house and outbuildings located at the heart of an organized farming operation. The plan and operation of surrounding spaces are recorded at the center and displayed on interior walls in the form of charts, maps, and paintings. Such display was, of course, one of the most important roles played by landscape survey, drawing, and painting in Georgian England.[3]

From the central control tower, movements and transfers of aircraft are observed, plotted, and coordinated so as to maximize flow across the continuous surfaces of the airfield and its immediate surroundings. As design characteristics of the airport, continuity of surface and the ease of visual and physical movement across and through large-scale spaces echo the concerns of eighteenth-century landscapists: to hide boundaries within the estate—for example, by using the sunken fence or ha-ha—to give the eye an uninterrupted surface, to connect house and grounds across a single sweep of green, smoothed slopes, across whose gently contoured topography a serpentine carriageway led to the entrance.

There are obvious limits to any such comparison between airport and Georgian park. But bringing the two together within the conceptual frame of landscape allows one to recover some of the language of landscape in application to the spaces of the airport. In recent critical thought, landscape is approached as a spatial, environmental, and social concept rather than as a primarily aesthetic term. It denotes not only the ensemble of forms and features resulting from human interventions on the earth's surface but also the cultural, economic, political, and technical processes that produce and sustain such spaces. Landscape is thus much more than a visual descriptor of the natural world as shaped by human agency. Landscape is best understood as a way of seeing, imagining, and representing the external world.

The history of landscape as a European idea and practice is related to changing modes of economic, social, and political authority over land and

223

territory.[4] The fertility of the landscape idea lies above all in its synthetic capacity, its ability to collect and frame all aspects of a given area—the aesthetic and the functional, the social and the ecological, the spatial and the environmental—and to achieve this within a single representation. As a mode of picturing, landscape obeys formal conventions that structure these relations; it is selected, composed, and framed according to rules of design and order. Survey, map, and painting have been the principal technical modes of designing human environments as landscapes. Understanding landscape in any medium, whether on the ground or in a graphic or textual representation, is thus an interpretative process demanding attention both to design criteria of formal structure, composition, and technique and to the range of environmental and social processes that give it meaning.

224

As a landscape, Heathrow's structure and composition may first be considered cartographically. Within the frame of the perimeter fence, its space is dominated by a regular geometry of grassed areas and concrete pathways structured around the central terminal buildings. These areas are dominated by elemental considerations of physical geography such as topography, wind, temperature, and rainfall. Flat land is a primary requirement for any airport, and Heathrow's location on the gravel of the Thames floodplain meets this demand within reasonable distance of the central metropolis (Westminster and the commercial City of London). It is immediately accessible to the elite western residential sector from which the airport's original passenger market largely derived.

Aircraft requirements to take off and land into the wind determined the original geometry of runways, which can still be traced within Heathrow's landscape structure. A compact Star-of-David pattern of concrete ribbons ensured two parallel runways in each of the six major wind directions together with a vacant central space available for terminal constructions (Fig. 4). Cartographically, the landscape structure of runways and terminals resembles a giant compass or wind rose. Indeed, geometric and carto-

Fig. 3. *Touchdown #1*. Adrian Hemming, 1995. Oil on canvas, 4 x 5 feet. Moments of touchdown, moments of takeoff. Moments of power as thrust begets lift and lift translates into grace. Curving trajectories, mobile bodies. The problem: how to fix so many dynamic activities onto a two-dimensional surface, a static surface that remains, ultimately, self-referential.

graphic orientations provide a leitmotif of the airport landscape generally. Not only is Heathrow located on the spot
where the Ordnance Survey—the national topographic
map system—originated its triangulation, but a key point
within the airport space was for many years the "compass
area," a flat circle of concrete located at maximum distance
from the distorting influence of buildings, a point where
aircraft could correct their magnetic navigational instru-
mentation before takeoff.

If we were to pursue the conceit of comparing Heathrow to a Georgian
park, we might see the compass area as the equivalent to the obelisk, or Tower of
Winds, that commonly acted as a gnomon or sign of the seasons within parkland designs. Today, the original geometrical harmony of runways has been distorted by the extension of the parallel east-west runways constructed to handle
the longer takeoff and landing distances of large jetliners, while the angular
arms of the landing bays reach out from the terminals like marine wharves, providing a more complex and intricate geometry.

225

Temperature governs the airport landscape in ways equally fundamental to
topography. Runway lengths are determined by the greater takeoff distances
required in hot weather. Grass growth and, thus, mowing are also conditioned
by temperature. The margins of grass blade length are tightly circumscribed by
the countervailing needs for sufficient vegetation to prevent dust and earth
removal by jet blast, yet insufficient length for nesting and cover, to avoid bird
strikes. The result is short-cropped lawn as the dominant cover, as in a grazed
landscape park. Water presents equally demanding constraints: flat land and the
high water table of this riverine site reduce natural runoff speeds and volumes,
so balancing reservoirs are located around the airport. The deicing fluids used to
enable aircraft to take off in winter weather produce formidable problems of
pollution in groundwater. For both sets of reasons, water sluicing and pumping
systems at Heathrow must be highly sophisticated. It is worth recalling that
water management and pumping schemes have been a controlling feature of
landscape design from the spectacular baroque waterworks at Lante and Versailles to the New Deal regional landscapes of the Tennessee Valley Authority
and Washington State. Heathrow's topographic adjustments to the elements are
as finely calculated as those on any farming estate or pleasure garden.

Fig. 4. Heathrow Airport, London. Original Star-of-David runway pattern.

Considered from an oblique rather than from a vertical perspective,[5] from the perspective of the air traffic controller or the airline pilot, for example, Heathrow's landscape is a virtual network of sightlines and flight paths. Intervisibility is equally crucial for aircraft, radar antennae, and control tower. Not only do the invisible spaces of air traffic control determine the height and disposition of buildings, producing an essentially flat, treeless landscape marked by a series of aerial valleys whose only visible expression is the stepped-back heights of buildings adjacent to runway axes, it results in an equally virtual but critical matrix of intersecting sightlines. The technical requirements of vision govern airport space more completely than any composition and perspectives of a landscape painting or park, yet they do not compose a formal image.

Thinking of Heathrow's location offers a further set of historic references to landscape. The airport's geographical position lies midway along an extended axis of designed landscapes stretching west out of London from the Royal Parks of Westminster through the seventeenth- and eighteenth-century aristocratic villa and royal palace grounds that follow the River Thames from Chelsea through Chiswick, Richmond, and Twickenham to the Surrey and Berkshire landscapes of Virginia Water, Runnymede, and Windsor Great Park. The swooping arc described by aircraft landing and taking off from the airport traverses this axis, tying Heathrow visually to the chain of powerfully symbolic designed English landscapes whose iconography is national and monarchial. In this sense, Heathrow, as a landscape, integrates with what has been called the Crown Heartland of Britain, and thus resonates with a deep national tradition of designed landscape.[6]

While such formal considerations allow retrospective connections to be made between the airport and designed parkland landscape, the spatialities of Heathrow allow a more progressive sense of landscape to be engaged, one that places less emphasis on the scenic, naturalistic, and pastoral associations of landscape than on its synthetic capacities, its ability to capture and recompose

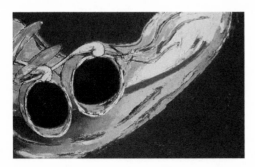

Fig. 5. *Big Bird*. Adrian Hemming, 1995. Oil on canvas, 8 x 5 feet. *Landside* refers to the hermetically sealed terminal buildings, a miniature city designed for the ergonomic flow of people mass. But here power is subjugated, controlled by the semiotics of directional signs—signs to shops, signs to gates, signs to taxis and buses. It is outside that the real glory of the airport takes place, in Airside, viewed through giant plate-glass windows.

the distinctive spatialities of the contemporary world. As the world's busiest international airport, Heathrow represents a global node where space, time, and cultural diversity concentrate into a single point. If the erasure of conventional boundaries is the most salient spatial feature of the late-twentieth-century condition,[7] the airport may be taken as its most perfect landscape expression.

The airport exists for the mass transgression of the most enduring and demanding topological boundary faced by humans: that between earth and air. To do this demands massive inputs of energy and the most sophisticated coordination of people and machines, both across extended distances and within highly specialized zones of activity. At the international airport, the fixity of longitudinal boundaries between the world's time zones that make routine the budgeting of daily life across the globe dissolve away, ceding place to a universal space-time adjusted to the speed and connectivity of airline timetables.

Conventionally, political borders between territorial sovereignties have been linear features: coastlines, rivers, mountain ridges, frontier fences. At the international airport, such frontiers concentrate into a point location deep within sovereign territory. The resulting boundary condition means that the airport landscape has become ever more elaborated over the past three decades as the primary location not only for transnational population transfers but also, in consequence, as the principal focus of security concerns surrounding such activities as illegal immigration, drug smuggling, terrorism, money laundering, and claims for refugee status. Thus, the airport has become the paradigm surveillance landscape monitored by the latest CCTV and video recording systems, an endlessly subdivided space on both land and air sides, a labyrinth of gateways and channels filtering and directing movements of personnel who are ever more finely differentiated by complex identification procedures. A more processual and mobile meaning of landscape is generated by these features of the airport's spaces, uses, and movement patterns.

In fact, a high proportion of those passing through the airport are characterized, in terms of the airport landscape, by nothing more than their spatial and temporal mobility and liminality. They are transit passengers who merely touch down into this space, connect briefly with other people and objects, and leave, with no trace other than, perhaps, a purchase in the ersatz boutiques that fill the commercial spaces of the airport. In these open-currency and duty-free malls, the world's cultures are reworked into marketable simulacra and retailed through an insistent appeal to the exotic, often expressed in landscape images of other places.

227

At Heathrow's International Terminal Three, global and national landscapes are ruthlessly compressed into graphlike eruptions along a single penciled line running the length of the arrival-departure corridor. Outbound, one passes into a world quoted through iconic landscape markers: the Taj Mahal, the pyramids of Egypt, the Eiffel Tower, the Statue of Liberty. Inbound, one arrives in Britain through a similarly shorthand procession of landscape markers: Nelson's column, Liverpool Cathedral, Stonehenge. Elsewhere in the airport, a similar corridor frieze names twenty-six global cities outbound and the same number of British places inbound, each listed by alphabetical order of their first letter. Boundaries between cultural identities are thus endlessly manipulable and permeable within the airport as free-floating signs marking the otherwise featureless internal landscapes of terminal buildings. In landside spaces, color, sound, and movement are hermetically sealed from the natural elements on the airside where, in dramatic contrast, nature's authority over the external landscape remains insistent. These paired landscapes exist in parallel, their former connection via plate-glass observation windows or aircraft steps now severed by closed walls and the extendable jetway.

In Heathrow's internal and external spaces are reminders of the convention of trompe-l'oeil landscape scenes that once decorated Roman, Renaissance, and Georgian villas, perhaps the oldest conceit of landscape representation.[8] Those illusionary landscapes created a cornucopian world of the imagination, whose references to arcadian perfection and sensual pleasure contrasted with scenes of productive space on the actual estate viewed through porticos or framed windows. In the airport, fast-food kiosks themed to the world's culinary cultures, mock-authentic pubs and bars, and an ever-expanding number of tax-free retail outlets offering international designer-labeled merchandise produce spaces of perfected consumption. As in the similar consumption landscapes of the out-of-town mall, visual pleasures are stimulated through brand recognition, seductive

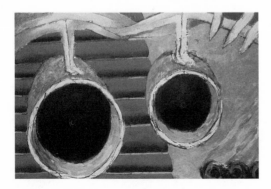

Fig. 6. *Feersum Enginn*. Adrian Hemming, 1995. Oil on canvas, 8 x 5 feet. Airside: the asphalt, man dwarfed by machines, buffeted and blasted by noise and wind. The forbidden areas. The monotony of grayness until a single color breaks—primaries, vibrant. Flatness and space the size of the sky, all dominated by invisible sightlines. A sublime beauty, a coupling of raw power—*feersum enginn*—with ultimate grace as the plane curls around the edge of a huge cumulus and sparkles briefly.

advertising images, and lifestyle association to create a complex landscape of imagination and illusion.

Complex visual pleasures are synthesized in the airport landscape through the collusion of supersophisticated technology, a hyperdeveloped capitalist marketplace, and a knowing public. Finally, therefore, let us consider the modes whereby this landscape is actually *seen*. The eighteenth-century park was designed to be viewed from the windows of the house or from a carriage turning slowly through the curves of its drives, or in relaxed perambulation across its lawns. The modern airport challenges ways of seeing landscape in many ways, erasing conventional boundaries in vision, as in so much else. Flight has been the twentieth century's most radical challenge to conventional ways of viewing the earth. Landscape architects such as Geoffrey Jellicoe and Garrett Eckbo, and planners such as Le Corbusier and E.A. Gutkind, reveled in flight's capacity to alter the ways we see and experience the world. The airport concentrates and conflates diverse experiences of linear and aerial perspective; from the stacked airliner above Heathrow we see the spaces of West London and the airfield itself spread below as flattened landscape geometry. Perception, clarity, and color alter with the descending aircraft as we enter the landscape at a progressively lower angle of sight. This changing angle of vision and the speed and trajectory of descent make for a continuous kinesis as relations among landscape elements shift. Dramatizing such changes in the formal relations between objects and pathways in landscape was always part of landscape art. Indeed, it was not uncommon for garden designers to control the viewer's movement through the landscape in order to enhance the aesthetic effects of perspective.

Similar effects are achieved within the airport's interior spaces by the functional requirements of passenger security and safety. For the traveler, lines of movement and viewpoints are strictly controlled. One enters Heathrow at ground level, either direct from the aircraft or, outbound, via a road or rail tunnel; both of these open into the heart of the terminal area. Transfer from outside to inside is often unremarked, through the jetway or a wide, sliding door in a glazed wall, by underground passage from subway train or car park, for example. Between and within the terminal buildings, sets of blind walls and automatic doors control sight as well as movement from concourse to departure lounge, from customs hall to concourse. The limits of built space are rarely felt.

Passage through the airport itself is repeatedly marked by the technology of seeing; video cameras, announcement screens, and X-ray machines simultaneously extend and delimit vision. Scenes are revealed theatrically by sliding pan-

229

els, darkened passageways, and arched portals. In all these respects, the airport is a space of controlled vision and movement, gathering and dispersal. Its design deploys for practical ends many of the techniques traditionally used in landscape design for aesthetic purposes. In all these ways, the term *virtual landscape* begins to take on a degree of experiential meaning within the airport.

As a final comment on seeing, we might further consider the *virtuality* of the airport as landscape. Perhaps the closest most passengers get to seeing the airport landscape from the viewpoint of the pilot, for whom its open spaces are primarily designed, is through on-board video screens showing takeoff and landing from cockpit-positioned cameras. In fact, most of those organizing and controlling airport spaces and movements do so through screens rather than the unaided eye: flight simulators, air traffic controllers, check-in staff, booking agents, security personnel. At the risk of overextending, as I reverse my analogy,

I might suggest that landscape is always virtual space. Daniele Barbaro at the Villa Maser before his Veronese frescoes and the Duke of Devonshire at Chatsworth among his Claudes moved no less than the Heathrow passenger among landscapes of virtual space seen in flights of fancy.

But if the airport reworks ideas of landscape as a scenic, naturalistic experience, it also extends and

Fig. 7 (top). *Touchdown #2*. Adrian Hemming, 1995. Oil on canvas, 4 x 5 feet. The siting of the paintings is crucial. They are viewed from two aspects: the terminal concourse some 50 meters away, and the upper walkway where staff walk right alongside the pictures. Thus, the paintings must be bold so as to read from a distance and convoluted on their surface for close examination. They summarize my response to the Heathrow environment, but in the end—as with so much twentieth-century art—they are self-referential.

Fig. 8 (bottom). Drawing: *Heathrow Series*. Adrian Hemming, 1995. Mixed media on paper, 11 x 13 inches. The painter is, in a sense, like the geographer. Geographers must synthesize what they find in the field; they collect information, itemize and cross-reference it, fitting it into a particular scheme while expanding it to other horizons. The painter condenses similar information into a single object—the painting—which is, paradoxically, infinitely expandable, depending on the spectator's point of view.

recovers landscape as a synthetic idea, a flexible concept capable of containing and, perhaps, synthesizing diverse but connected spatial practices in the context of a world entering a new millennium. Landscape is recovered for an age in which the visual image and ocular experience have achieved extraordinary salience in daily life, yet one in which invisible connections and networks of communications technologies shape and continuously transform the territorialities that underpin and give form to experience.

Notes

1 Much of the revised historiography of English Georgian landscape in the past decade has focused on its relations with agrarian modernization and colonial agrarian settlement. See, for example, Stephen Daniels, *Fields of Vision* (London: Polity, 1993); John Barrell, *The Dark Side of the Landscape: The Rural Poor in English Painting 1730–1840* (Cambridge: Cambridge University Press, 1980); W.J.T. Mitchell, ed., *Landscape and Power* (Chicago: University of Chicago Press, 1994).

2 Joel Garreau, *Edge City: Life on the New Frontier* (New York: Doubleday, 1991); see also the contributions to *Architectural Design Profile* 135: *Consuming Architecture* (1998).

3 On the historical relationship between mapping and landscape, see Denis Cosgrove, *The Palladian Landscape: Geographical Change and Its Cultural Representations in Sixteenth-Century Italy* (State College: Pennsylvania State University Press, 1993); see also Denis Cosgrove, ed., *Mappings* (London: Reaktion, 1999).

4 Denis Cosgrove: *Social Formation and Symbolic Landscape*, 2nd ed. (Madison: University of Wisconsin Press, 1998). See also Martin Warnke, *Political Landscape: The Art History of Nature* (London: Reaktion, 1995).

5 The distinction between vertical and oblique perspective is critical, historically, in shaping the landscape vision and differentiating painting from mapping as distinct modes of spatial representation. Modern computer imaging techniques, in CAD, for example, allow manipulation across this divide.

6 The significance of the middle Thames valley landscape in the national consciousness is perfectly expressed in the location of "national" sporting events whose landscapes extend along this axis: Twickenham (rugby football), Hammersmith, Fulham, Henley (rowing), Ascot (horse racing), Wentworth (golf). On the concept of Crown Heartland, see Peter Taylor, "The English and Their Englishness: A Curiously Mysterious, Elusive and Little Understood People," *Scottish Geographical Magazine* 107, no. 3 (1991): 146–161.

7 See David Harvey, *The Condition of Postmodernity: An Enquiry into the Origins of Cultural Change* (Oxford: Blackwell, 1989).

8 See Cosgrove, *Palladian Landscape*, chapters 4 and 9.

Chapter 15

Programming the Urban Surface

Alex Wall

In recent years, a number of urban projects in Europe have fallen between the traditional categories of landscape and urbanism. These works signal a shift of emphasis from the design of enclosed objects to the design and manipulation of larger urban surfaces. They also indicate a renewed interest in the instrumentality of design—its enabling function—as opposed to representation and stylization. Here, the term *landscape* no longer refers to prospects of pastoral innocence but rather invokes the functioning matrix of connective tissue that organizes not only objects and spaces but also the dynamic processes and events that move through them. This is landscape as active surface, structuring the conditions for new relationships and interactions among the things it supports.[1]

In describing landscape as urban surface, I do not mean to refer to simply the space between buildings, as in parking lots, planted areas, and residual spaces. Neither do I want to limit the use of the term *landscape* to wholly green, natural, or recreational spaces. Instead, I refer to the extensive and inclusive ground-plane of the city, to the "field" that accommodates buildings, roads, utilities, open spaces, neighborhoods, and natural habitats. This is the ground structure that organizes and supports a broad range of fixed and changing activities in the city. As such, the urban surface is dynamic and responsive; like a catalytic emulsion, the surface literally unfolds events in time.

In this sense, the urban surface is similar to a dynamic agricultural field, assuming different functions, geometries, distributive arrangements, and appearances as changing circumstance demands. This adaptability derives in part from the planar character of the surface, to its smooth and uninterrupted continuity, but also from the equipment and services embedded within it. Thus, if the goal of designing the urban surface is to increase its capacity to support and diversify activities in time—even activities that cannot be determined in advance—then a primary design strategy is to extend its continuity while diversifying its range of services. This is less design as passive ameliorant and more as active accelerant, staging and setting up new conditions for uncertain futures.[2]

Fig. 1. The contemporary metropolis—an endless cityscape.

233

The Contemporary Metropolis

Much of the reason for revising practices of landscape and urbanism today derives from the changing nature of cities. The traditional notion of the city as a historical and institutional core surrounded by postwar suburbs and then open countryside has been largely replaced by a more polycentric and weblike sprawl: the regional metropolis (Fig. 1). Here, multiple centers are served by overlapping networks of transportation, electronic communication, production, and consumption. Operationally, if not experientially, the infrastructures and flows of material have become more significant than static political and spatial boundaries. The influx of people, vehicles, goods, and information constitute what urban geographers call the "daily urban system," painting a picture of urbanism that is dynamic and temporal.[3] The emphasis shifts here from *forms* of urban space to *processes* of urbanization, processes that network across vast regional—if not global—surfaces.[4]

The effects of urbanization today are multiple and complex, but three are of particular significance with regard to planning and design. First is the rise of new kinds of urban site. These are the ambiguous areas that are caught between enclaves. They may even be so extensive as to constitute entire generic zones. These might be called *peripheral sites*, middle landscapes that are neither here nor there, and yet are so pervasive as to now characterize the dominant environment in which most people actually live.[5] In contrast, the old city centers are becoming increasingly themed around tourist and entertainment functions. A second effect of modern urbanization is a remarkable increase in mobility and access. This refers not only to the increase of private automobiles and transportation alternatives—that, for many, encompasses a fully fledged lifestyle—but also to the rising density of population, the increased instability of capital and investment, and to the abundance of information and media.

A third effect, and a consequence of the above two, involves a fundamental paradigm shift from viewing cities in formal terms to looking at them in dynamic ways. Hence, familiar urban typologies of *square*, *park*, *district*, and so on are of less use or significance than are the infrastructures, network flows, ambiguous spaces, and other polymorphous conditions that constitute the contemporary metropolis. Unlike the treelike, hierarchical structures of traditional cities, the contemporary metropolis functions more like a spreading rhizome, dispersed and diffuse, but at the same time infinitely enabling.[6]

These emergent conditions demand that designers and planners revise their approaches toward the making of urban projects. A renewed concern with infrastructure, services, mobility, and with the provision of flexible, multifunctional surfaces promises a revitalized role for the design professions. The grafting of new instruments and equipment onto strategically staged surfaces allows for a transformation of the ground-plane into a living, connective tissue between increasingly disparate fragments and unforeseen programs.

There is, of course, a recent history to these shifts. In the 1950s, architects and critics already were increasingly preoccupied with the larger urban environment. The rapid spread of cities and the atomization of buildings across vast landscapes reduced the distinctions between city and countryside as well as the differences between places.[7] During the Aspen Design Conference in 1955, the architect/planner Victor Gruen exhorted architects to look beyond the limits of the individual building to the environment, to the context in which the building was to function. He proclaimed:

235

> Architecture today cannot concern itself only with that one set of structures that happen to stand upright and be hollow "buildings" in the conventional sense. It must concern itself with all man-made elements that form our environments: with roads and highways, with signs and posters, with outdoor spaces as created by structures, and with cityscape and landscape.[8]

Gruen's context for these remarks was his view that it was less individual buildings that needed the attention of design and more the landscapes that were emerging as cities dispersed across the region. His work was aimed toward resisting decentralization and undifferentiated sprawl by creating new nodes of concentration and focus. Perhaps it was his European background that made it impossible for him to accept the idea of a continuously settled, dispersed landscape.

By the mid-1960s, the programs for rebuilding European cities following the second world war and American cities as part of urban renewal policies stimulated new thinking about large-scale urbanism and landscape. Some of the more radical speculations proposed new forms of settlement type. The Florentine group Superstudio envisaged a continuously developed, artificial surface. In their project *Supersurface 5*, the formal device of the grid was inscribed across a pure, planar landscape, providing both a metaphor and an instrument for the networks of energy and information that could extend to every corner of the earth (Fig. 2).[9] In contrast, the projects drawn by the British group Archigram showed concepts of plug-in communities and new infrastructural support landscapes.[10] Their agenda was not only to empower the individual but also to stage

event-structures that could bring about new metropolitan dynamics. Depicted in many of Archigram's ideas were individuals plugging into larger networks of interactive information, education, and entertainment. While projects such as *Rokplug* and *Logplug* proposed a transitory and flexible existence on the surface, others such as *Instant City* proposed large-scale infrastructures to support mass events and activities—an image inspired, perhaps, by the emerging technology of rock concerts and festivals (Fig. 3).

The strategic aspects of Archigram's work derive from the inherent flexibility of the designed system; parts can be added, removed, or rearranged at will, accommodating a range of uses at different times, from mass exhibitions and festivals one day to individual mobile homes and gardens the next. These radical speculations demonstrated tangible, urbanistic techniques for making urban environments that used emerging technology to achieve individual freedom within new collective structures.

A Field of Social Instruments

Many of the above themes provided an early inspiration to Rem Koolhaas and the Office for Metropolitan Architecture (OMA), based in Rotterdam. Since the 1970s, Koolhaas and his colleagues have continuously and critically developed the role that program plays in the making of a project. More than aware of the highly changeable and unpredictable characteristics of the contemporary

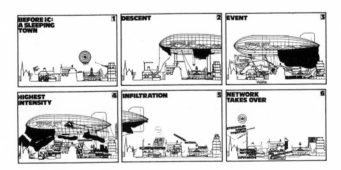

Fig. 2 (top). *Five Tales.* Superstudio, 1971–1973. Source: *Superstudio and Radicals* (Tokyo: Japan Interior, 1982), 13.

Fig. 3 (bottom). *Instant City: Sequence of Effect.* Archigram, 1970. The descent of the event-structure "instant city airships" on a typical English town intensifies, infiltrates, and stimulates new networks in the old, sleeping city. Source: Peter Cook, ed., *Archigram* (London: Studio Vista, 1972).

metropolis, these architects have attempted, in a number of ways, to push ideas of program toward more dynamic and productive ends. Program is viewed as the engine of a project, driving the logic of form and organization while responding to the changing demands of society. If the problems of urbanization had been identified in the 1950s and 1960s and the new technologies for rethinking these issues were developed during the late 1960s and into the 1970s, then the specific development of new design strategies has occurred since that time, largely under the vision and direction of Koolhaas and OMA. A seminal moment in this trajectory of ideas occurred in 1982, during the competition for the Parc de la Villette along the industrial periphery of Paris.

One of the first and most daring of President Mitterand's *Grands Projets*, the Parc de la Villette awoke designers to the difficulties of dealing with large-scale abandoned tracts of land in the city, especially when the intentions of the commissioning agency were both ambitious and uncertain.[11] The 121 acres of land were left over from the old nineteenth-century slaughterhouse complex that once occupied the site. There were many logistical problems, especially in terms of site reclamation and modernization of services. This was further complicated by a bewildering and exhaustive list of programmatic demands by the client, together with a sense of uncertainty about what, how, and when different parts of this program would be developed.

The problem, then, was less one of design in terms of styling identity, representation, or formal composition, and much more one of strategic organization. The surface had to be equipped and staged in such a way as to both anticipate and accommodate any number of changing demands and programs. OMA responded with the superposition of four strategic layers for organizing different parts of the program: the "east-west strips" of varying synthetic and natural surfaces, the "confetti grid" of large and small service points and kiosks, the various "circulation paths," and the "large objects," such as the linear and round forests (Fig. 4). The designers described their multilayered project as a "landscape of social instruments," where the quality of the project would derive from the uses, juxtapositions, and adjacency of alternating programs over time.[12]

Rather than a fixed design, the project offered the city a framework for developing flexible uses as needs and desires changed. The strips and grids

Fig. 4. Plan, Parc de la Villette, competition entry. Office for Metropolitan Architecture, 1983.

across surfaces, the point services, and the larger structures were designed to be both responsive and adaptive. The action of sliding one thing over another allowed for quantitative changes without loss of organizational structure. This framework of flexible congestion, whose character and efficacy lies in its capacity to adapt to change, set a significant precedent in later formulations of urbanism.[13]

One such formulation was proposed by Koolhaas and OMA in 1987 for the new town of Melun-Senart, France.[14] This project reverses the formal and structural roles of figure and ground, building and open space (Fig. 5). Rather than concentrating on the planning and arrangement of buildings, variously programmed voids are outlined. These derive from a careful analysis of existing conditions, habitats, historical fragments, existing infrastructure corridors, and new programs. Together they form a sort of massive hieroglyph, isolating various islands for future development.

The voids exercise a greater effect on the subsequent built environment than does the design of particular building layouts. They provide a resilient structure that can withstand the unpredictable political and economic pressures that architects and urban designers are rarely able to influence. Melun-Senart continues a logic that progressively reverses the significance normally attached to buildings and directs attention instead to the spaces in between. By incorporating the character and potential of the urban plan in the designed characteristics of the voids, the designers leave the building sites open and undetermined. Basically, anything can take place on the island sites as long as the void framework is preserved. As with the Parc at la Villette, the design is first a tactical strategy, anticipating the uncertainties of future development.

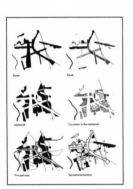

Mobility and Access: Surface as Collector and Distributor

The design and integration of new transportation infrastructure is central to the functioning of the urban surface. The importance of mobility and access in the contemporary metropolis brings to infrastructure the character of collective space. Transportation infrastructure is less a self-sufficient service element than an extremely visible and effective instrument in creating new networks and relationships. Whereas the railroad station and the airport offer a centralized infrastructural condition—a density that almost resembles the city, in terms of

238

Fig. 5. Planning diagrams, Melun-Senart new town. Office for Metropolitan Architecture, 1987.

services and programs—the more amorphous connective web of roads has rarely been recognized as a collective space unto itself. As the Italian architect Vittorio Gregotti argues:

> We are trying to return a positive morphological value to the road…in an attempt to revive it as a component of the settlement event and by restoring the road to the architectural realm [while] forcing one's discipline to consider the problems it implies as its own specific ones.[15]

One very clear example, in answer to Gregotti, is the second beltway of Barcelona, completed for the 1992 Olympics. The northern arc, the Ronda de Dalt, extends between the interchanges at the Diagonal Avenue (northwest) and the Trinitat Park (northeast) and was designed by a team of architects and engineers led by Bernardo de Sola (Fig. 6).[16] The Ronda de Dalt was conceived to achieve not the highest through-capacity of vehicles but the highest capacity of collection and distribution among local and regional transportation networks. The design also created opportunities to reconfigure the local conditions for new programs and open space. This is especially the case at the interchanges, where new typologies between landscape and building have begun to emerge.

Thus, the significance of the design of this highway is less its scenic and efficiency value than the road's actual capacity to stimulate and support new forms of urban space. This is achieved partially by the segregation of the sectional character of the road, with faster (regional) lanes in the center, flanked by slower (local) lanes that connect with new frontage and neighborhood streets. In some places, the space above the highway is occupied by new public buildings, especially high-volume structures such as sports venues. New parks and recreational areas are also designed into the system, linking once isolated housing estates to larger public spaces. The Ronda de Dalt thus demonstrates, in contemporary terms, the forgotten idea of the 1920s parkway as an instrument of connection, convenience, and mobility.

A second example of new infrastructural design demonstrates how the space of mobility may also be a collective space. Among the northern suburbs of Paris, between St. Denis and Bobigny, is a mix of industrial zones, large social housing estates, cemeteries, hospitals, and areas of waste ground. Existing transportation infrastructure reflects the nineteenth-century pattern of radial

239

Fig. 6. Aerial view, Ronda de Dalt, Barcelona. Bernardo de Sola, I.M.P.U.S.A., 1982.

extension and effectively divides communities into separate sectors. Between 1990 and 1995, the landscape architect Alexandre Chemetoff and the Bureau des Paysages implemented the design of a new trolley line running between St. Denis and Bobigny (Fig. 7).[17] This is a nine-kilometer line with twenty-one stations, and it is the first tangential boulevard in this area of Paris, initiating new relationships among once isolated sectors. Because of this new transportation line superimposed across the urban fabric, the project forms the basis for a host of other urban interventions.

The tramline is, literally, a link that provides a coherent system across an otherwise fragmented field. It comprises three series: the material of the surface; the vegetation structure of hedges, trees, and plantings; and furnishings, such as bollards, fences, lamps, trellises, and seating. Organized in different configurations, the families of surface, vegetation, and furnishings produce a contrapuntal effect in relation to the untidy irregularity of the surrounding fabric. The integrity and continuity of these elements produces not only an image of public space but also the necessary environmental conditions to support public activities. On a Sunday morning, for example, the line is crowded with French families of African, Arabic, and Asian background making their way to and from the street markets along the length of the line.

Chemetoff's design is a prime example of how infrastructure engages social and imaginative dimensions as much as it does engineering concerns. It effectively integrates parts of the city, reduces the marginalization and segregation of certain social groups, and stimulates new forms of interaction.

An Inhabitable Surface

The design of large-scale infrastructures such as those discussed above provides new conditions for other kinds of surface project. One such example is Eduard Bru's Vall d'Hebron Park in Barcelona, completed in 1992 (Fig. 8). This is a 26-hectare site in the inner suburbs, formerly dominated by an oppressive landscape of postwar social housing. Located directly north of the Gothic center and its nineteenth-century extension, the park spans the buttresses of the mountain chain to the north of the city. Bru understood that the beltway is the best location for leisure facilities that serve local and metropolitan users. Thus,

Fig. 7. St. Denis-to-Bobigny Tramway, Alexandre Chemetoff, 1988–1993.

240

the park is a collage of sports surfaces, routes, and park elements. In particular, the elaboration of the routes creates an intermediate landscape between the Ronda (Paseo Vall d'Hebron) and the surrounding neighborhoods. As Bru describes:

> This movement means that when existing elements permit, the streets become whirlpools, widening and forming what we might call deltas in the public areas of the park. The streets are asphaltic flows; they find geometries contained between the interstices and move according to circle arcs and clothoids.[18]

241

Bru describes a dynamic and changing landscape, one where the demands of changing programs lead to a different reading of the site. Moreover, he reflects many of these uses through new techniques of material fabrication. In using grass, wood, metal, concrete, asphalt, and recycled rubber tires in new and unusual ways, Bru creates a lively surface that promotes a diversity of functions. The automobile, too, is not excluded from this park, but rather fully incorporated into its design. As the designer describes:

> Driving to a super-market car park, and spending Sunday with the car door open, listening to the radio while the children play in the car park is a highly respectable custom. Here, the users surround themselves with those objects most dear to them: the car, the children, the radio. And they spend their Sunday placidly.[19]

Waiting for Appropriation

The Netherlands, especially the city of Rotterdam, has proved to be a steady source of innovation with regard to addressing the increased complexity of the growing metropolis. Partly this is due to the culture of the country, essentially progressive and technologically oriented, but it is also due to the very real problems of density and growth since the end of the second world war. The work of OMA has certainly played a role in the advance of new approaches toward urbanism; recently a younger generation of designers also has begun to make its

Fig. 8. Aerial view, terraces and surfaces, Vall d'Hebron, Barcelona. Eduard Bru, 1982.

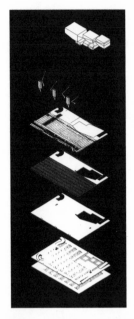

mark. Foremost among these is landscape architect Adriaan Geuze and his practice, West 8.[20]

The work of West 8 exemplifies the claims that landscape architects may absorb urban design into a newly synthetic practice of landscape urbanism. Rotterdam's industrial context and Geuze's particular aptitude for large-scale strategic thinking have contributed to the making of projects that support a diversity of uses and interpretations over time. Geuze prefers "emptiness" to overprogramming and argues that urban dwellers are more than able to create, adapt to, or imagine whatever they want to. In designing for indeterminate futures, he argues, new urban consumers may create and find their own meaning in the environments they use. As Geuze writes:

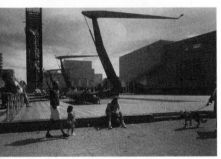

> The urbanite is self-assured and well-informed, finds his freedom and chooses his own sub-cultures. The city is his domain, exciting and seductive. He has proved himself capable of finding his way around the new landscape and of making places his own.[21]

If, in the traditional European city, the urban square was the place where civic and religious power was represented, then West 8's contemporary Binnenrotte market square and Schouwburgplein are zones where the public appropriates and modifies the very surface of the city. These surfaces are extremely simple and spare, yet they are designed in such a way that many different events can be supported. A range of services and equipment is embedded in the surface and can be appropriated at any moment. This is especially evident in the Schouwburgplein, completed in 1996 (Figs. 9, 10).

This great square is in the center of Rotterdam and is surrounded by theaters, restaurants, cafés, and a new cinema complex. As in many public spaces

Fig. 9 (top). Layered axonometric, the Schouwburgplein, Rotterdam. Adriaan Geuze and West 8, 1994–1997

Fig. 10 (bottom). View of the Schouwburgplein, Rotterdam. Adriaan Geuze and West 8, 1994–1997.

today, the presence of an underground structure—in this case, a car garage—imposes constraints with regard to weight and planting. Geuze turned this condition into a positive by replacing the existing heavy paving with a new lightweight metal and wood surface. Below this surface construction are a host of utilities and services, including lighting that produces a Milky Way of light across the floor at night. The square is also fitted with fence- and tent-post holes, enabling temporary structures and coverings to be erected. The principal theatrical elements on the site are four 35-meter-high lighting masts, whose crane-like forms echo the great structures along Rotterdam's docks. By dropping a coin into a machine, people can cause the light to move up or down according to their needs or whimsy.

243

Flow and Surface

A similarly conceived urban surface is the project for the Yokohama Design Forum produced by Koolhaas and OMA in 1992.[22] The site is at the nexus of road, rail, and shipping traffic and is dominated by two large market-halls and car-parking levels. Here, a careful analysis of the existing use patterns of the site, including vehicular and population volumes, revealed that the site was really occupied only between the hours of four and ten in the morning; the rest of the time, the site was empty. To maximize the use of the site over longer periods of time, the design had to address the problem of inventing new programs and provisions. Thus, the surface is itself folded or warped in order to create a continuous field that is then impregnated with new elements and structures. This concept enabled the design team to propose a twenty-four-hour use chart to show a more heterogeneous mix of functions and activities throughout the day (Fig. 11). The space of form is here replaced by the space of events in time.

Another scheme in Yokohama, this time for the International Port Terminal and designed by Foreign Office Architects in 1996, also produces a continuous yet differentiated surface as a means of reconciling the complexity of the program.[23] The various floors of the pier are folded and rolled one into the other through a building technology that allows for the construction of continuously convex and

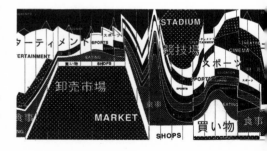

Fig. 11. Assemblage of programs over twenty-four hours, Yokohama, Japan. Office for Metropolitan Architecture, 1992.

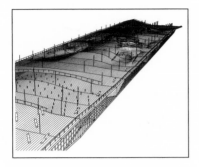

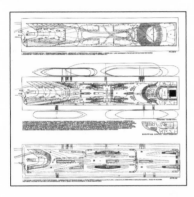

concave floors (Figs. 12, 13). This form is intended to mediate between the competing dimensions of the program—the differences between land and sea, natives and foreigners, city and harbor, and public and private. Moreover, the changeable character and size of ships docked along the pier is accommodated in a scheme that is both flexible and open. Rather than a typologically defined building with discrete enclosure and limits, the design provides a field that creases and warps to allow for alternate uses and needs. The designers provided the city with a project that is at once private and secure *and* public and open, "a model that is capable of integrating differences into a coherent system; an unbounded *landscape* rather than an over-coded, delimited *place*."[24]

Surface Strategies

The projects considered above are all located in previously built sites, whether open space—as in la Villette and the Schouwburgplein—or infrastructure, as in Ronda de Dalt or the Yokohama terminal. Even the projects of Melun-Senart, Vall d'Hebron, and the St. Denis–Bobigny tramline incorporate and link existing contexts. Rebuilding, incorporating, connecting, intensifying— these words describe not only the physical character of these projects but also their programmatic function. They are instruments, or agents, for unfolding new urban realities, designed not so much for appearances and aesthetics as for their instigative and structuring potential. Their strategies are targeted not only toward physical but also social and cultural transformations, functioning as social and ecological *agents*.[25] It is possible to summarize the more productive principles and strategies for designing the urban surface as follows.

Thickening. At the Schouwburgplein, West 8 conceived of a thickened, multi-layer surface that solved not only technical problems, such as drainage, struc-

Fig. 12 (top). Aerial view, Yokohama International Port Terminal, Japan. Foreign Office Architects, 1995.

Fig. 13 (bottom). Plans, Yokohama International Port Terminal, Japan. Foreign Office Architects, 1995.

ture, and utilities, but also brought a greater dramatic effect to the square while multiplying its range of uses. The expansion of inhabitation of subterranean networks in cities such as Montreal and Tokyo, and of aerial passageways in cities such as Atlanta and Minneapolis, effectively multiplies the number of public ground-planes. The multilevel movement of people, together with the connector flows of elevators, moving stairs, ramps, and so on, creates a marvelous spectacle in the city. This is the thickened surface, continuous, multiple, and dynamic.

Folding. Cutting, warping, and folding the surface creates a kind of smooth geology that joins interior and exterior spaces into one continuous surface. At the new port in Yokohama, Foreign Office Architects adopted a continuous, folded surface, as in a multilayered laminate wherein each floor "rolls" into others. Sectional joining and definition varies as the program demands. Consequently, the flows of people and goods combine in newly visible ways, as traditional zonal separations become more fluid and interactive.[26]

New materials. Developing new and synthetic materials brings a welcome diversity to the pedestrian realm. At the Vall d'Hebron, the use of asphalt, rubber tires, wood, and metal in new ways expresses and provokes new activities. The appearance of graffiti, skateboarders, and boom boxes does not necessarily mean that the park is in any way compromised; on the contrary, the presence of these everyday features acknowledges certain trends in youth culture while extending the range of uses typically associated with parks.

Nonprogrammed use. Equipping the surface with services and furnishings that can be appropriated and modified by the public enables a diverse and flexible range of uses. Instead of comprising elements serving only one function, a design that can accommodate many functions is both economical and enriching of social space. Eduard Bru and Adriaan Geuze are two designers who are especially interested in making things and places that are indeterminate in their functions and thereby allow their users to invent and claim space for themselves. Such investment by the users subsequently ensures a long and affectionate occupation of public space.

Impermanence. Program and function are, perhaps, the most changeable aspects of any city. Needs and desires can change overnight, and city administrators must be able to respond quickly without massively overhauling entire tracts of

245

land. Designing to create an indeterminate and propitious range of affordances replaces the traditional fascination of designers with permanence with that of the temporal and dynamic. The OMA projects at la Villette and Melun-Senart offer not only a designed landscape but also a framework capable of absorbing future demands without diminishing the integrity of the project. Indeed, the integrity of the project is predicated upon such changing demands, juxtaposing conditions as a great montage of effects.

Movement. In popular culture, the instruments and spaces of mobility—especially the automobile and the freeway—have provided new sites of collective life. A real challenge to urban design is to accept that infrastructure is as important to the vitality and experience of the contemporary metropolis as the town hall or square once was. At the Ronda de Dalt, Bernardo da Sola exploited the section of the site to create a new and public type of urban corridor, collecting, distributing, and connecting a great range of users and functions. As we move into the twenty-first century, one of the primary roles of urban design will be the reworking of movement corridors as new vessels of collective life.

246

Conclusion

The projects and ideas discussed above address the complexity and density of reconstructing cities and landscapes today. The emphasis is on the extensive reworking of the surface of the earth as a smooth, continuous matrix that effectively binds the increasingly disparate elements of our environment together. This synthetic form of creativity draws from all of the traditional disciplines of landscape architecture, architecture, urban planning, and engineering. The conditions these practices engage—mobility, density, congestion, instability—demand new techniques of practice, new modes of representation, and new kinds of discussion and conceptualization. Such activities can no longer be said to apply only to peripheral and derelict sites, as now even the most traditional city centers involve the same issues. Cities everywhere are competing to retain investment, capital, tax base, population, infrastructure, and amenities. The function of design is not only to make cities attractive but also to make them more adaptive, more fluid, more capable of accommodating changing demands and unforeseen circumstances.

We are witnessing a recovery of certain landscape themes and techniques that seem to have particular applicability to these problems. First, of course, landscape is the horizontal and continuous surface, the field that is best apprehended in maps and plans. Here, plans are of particular significance because they organize the relationships among parts and activities; all things come together on the ground. But a second use of landscape is the attention it draws to processes of formation and thus to issues of temporality, efficacy, and change. That many landscape architects study and are inspired by ecology is especially significant here, for ecology addresses the interrelationships of parts and dynamic systems.[27]

Also, landscape architects are taught early on to appreciate larger regional scales (watersheds, ecosystems, infrastructures, and settlement patterns, for instance) as well as understanding smaller, more intimate places as part of the larger framework. The surfaces they see are not just visual patterns but more mutable and thickened topographies, systemic and alive. If landscape architecture has been thought of as merely an art of amelioration, of secondary significance to buildings and urban planning, then today it finds itself assuming a more relevant and active role in addressing the regional and ecological questions that face society—questions about place, time, and process.

In the aftermath of the 1980s building boom, the potential and significant field of action today is less the design of monuments and master plans than the careful modification and articulation of the urban surface. The surface is manipulated in two ways: as planar folds and smooth continuities, and as a field that is grafted onto a set of new instruments and equipment. In either case, the surface becomes a staging ground for the unfolding of future events. The surface is not merely the venue for formal experiments but the agent for evolving new forms of social life.

The projects described above suggest how the surface may support future buildings and programs. Perhaps the synthesis of landscape, architectural, and urbanistic skills into a hybrid form of practice may allow for the invention of newly supple and reflexive built fabrics, new landscapes.[28] Such dynamic surface structurings may be the only hope of withstanding the excesses of popular culture—restless mobility, consumption, density, waste, spectacle, and information—while absorbing and redirecting the alternating episodes of concentration and dispersal caused by the volatile movement of investment capital and power.

Notes

I would like to thank James Corner for his many suggestions in finalizing this essay.

1   Many of the themes surrounding the shift from object to surface were presented and discussed in a symposium and exhibition called "Cityscape: The Urban Surface,"

organized by Alex Wall at the Graduate School of Fine Arts, University of Pennsy
vania, in April 1994. Participants included James Corner, Bill McDonald, Sulan
Kolatan, Laurie Olin, Susan Nigra Snyder, Steve Kieran, and Bob Geddes.

2   I draw this formulation from James Corner, "Field Operations," (unpublished lecture notes). See also Rem Koolhaas, "Whatever Happened to Urbanism?" in
S,M,L,XL (New York: Monacelli Press, 1995), 958–971; and Stan Allen "Infrastructural Urbanism," in *Scroope* 9 (Cambridge: Cambridge University Architecture
School, 1998), 71–79.

3   See J.S. Adams, ed., *Association of American Geographers Comparative Metropolitan
Analysis Project: Twentieth-Century Cities*, vol. 4 (Cambridge, Mass.: Ballinger, 1976);
and David Harvey, *The Condition of Postmodernity* (Cambridge, Mass.: Blackwell,
1989).

4   See David Harvey, *Justice, Nature, and the Geography of Difference* (Cambridge,
Mass.: Blackwell, 1996).

5   See Rem Koolhaas, "The Generic City," in *S,M,L,XL*, 1238–1264; and Joel Garreau,
Edge Cities: Life on the New Frontier (New York: Doubleday, 1991).

6   See Gilles Deleuze and Felix Guattari, "Rhizome," in *A Thousand Plateaus: Capitalism and Schizophrenia* (Minneapolis: University of Minnesota Press, 1987), 3–25; and
Corner, "Field Operations."

7   See Vittorio Gregotti, "La Strada: Tracciato e Manufatto / The Road: Layout and
Built Object," in *Casabella* 553–554 (January–February 1989): 118.

8   Victor Gruen, "Cityscape-Landscape," in *Arts and Architecture* (September 1955):
18–37.

9   Superstudio and Moryami Studio, eds. *Superstudio and Radicals* (Tokyo: Japan Interior, 1982), 9–86.

10   See Archigram, "Instant City," in *Archigram*, ed. Peter Cook (London: Studio Vista,
1972), 86–101.

11   See Marianne Barziley, ed., *L'Invention du Parc: Parc de la Villette, Paris, Concours
International* (Paris: Graphite Editions, 1984).

12   See Koolhaas, *S,M,L,XL*, 894–939; and Jacques Lucan, ed., *Rem Koolhaas/OMA*
(New York: Princeton Architectural Press, 1991), 86–95.

13   See Koolhaas, "Whatever Happened to Urbanism?"

14   See Koolhaas, *S,M,L,XL*, 972–989; and Lucan, *Rem Koolhaas/OMA*, 114–117.

15   Gregotti, "The Road," 118.

16   See Antonio Font, "Edges and Interstices: The Ordering of the Borders of the New
Barcelona Ring Road," *Quaderns* 193 (1993): 112–119.

17   See Jacques Lucan, "A Grand Boulevard for the Outskirts," in *Lotus* 84 (1995):
88–101; and Alessandro Rocca, "Chemetoff's Inter-Suburban," in *Lotus* 84 (1995):
86–87.

18   Eduard Bru, "Untested Territories," *Quaderns* 193 (1993): 82–85. See also Josep
Parcerisa Bundo, "Vall d'Hebron: Metamorphosis of a Park," *Lotus* 77 (1993): 6–17.

19   Bru, "Untested Territories," 83.

20   See Adriaan Geuze, *Adriaan Geuze/West 8* (Rotterdam: 010 Publishers, 1995); see also
Bart Lootsma's essay "Synthetic Regionalization" in this collection.

21   Gerrie Andela, "Challenging Landscapes for Explorers: Estrangement and Reconcil-
iation in the Work of West 8," *Archis* 2 (February, 1994): 38–49.

22   See Koolhaas, *S,M,L,XL*, 1210–1237; and Sanford Kwinter, "The Reinvention of
Geometry," *Assemblage* 18 (1996): 83–112.

23   See Foreign Office Architects, "Yokohama Port Terminal Competition," *AA Files* 29
(1995): 17–21.

24   Ibid., 7.

25 See James Corner, "Ecology and Landscape as Agents of Creativity," in *Ecological Design and Planning*, eds. George Thompson and Frederick Steiner (New York: John Wiley & Sons, 1997), 80–108.

26 See Greg Lynn, "Architectural Curvilinearity: The Folded, the Pliant, the Supple," in *Architectural Design Profile* 102: *Folding in Architecture* (1993), 8–15; see also Peter Eisenman, "Unfolding Events," in *Zone* 1 / 2 (New York: Urzone, 1986), 423–427.

27 See James Corner, "Ecology and Landscape," and also "The Agency of Mapping," in *Mappings*, ed. Denis Cosgrove (London: Reaktion, 1998).

28 See Lynn in *Architectural Design Profile* 127: *Architecture After Geometry* (1997) and *Architectural Design Profile* 133: *Hypersurface Architecture* (1998).

Chapter 16

Synthetic Regionalization:
The Dutch Landscape Toward a Second Modernity

Bart Lootsma

Since the late 1980s, global economic developments and the effects of new technology, especially with respect to mobility, communication, and new media,
have completely reshaped the world. These forces of globalization have
resulted in a blurring of national borders, increased congestion in cities, new
pressures on landscape and environment, and the fragmentation of society into
countless subcultures. With respect to these events, the sociologist Ulrich Beck
writes:

> The West is confronted by questions that challenge the fundamental
> premises of its own social and political system. The key question we
> are now confronting is whether the historical symbiosis between capi-
> talism and democracy that characterized the West can be generalized
> on a global scale without exhausting its physical, cultural and social
> foundations.[1]

Beck sees opportunities in emergent contemporary conditions for achieving a new society, one that offers individuals a more significant role on numerous levels while enabling them to form a new image of the mass collective of
which they are part. This has a number of consequences, not only political and
social but also ecological and aesthetic. Beck calls this process "reflexive modernization." As he describes it, "This concept does not imply 'reflection' but
self-confrontation."[2] Beck is interested in a new form of politics, what he calls
"sub-politics," in which society takes shape from the bottom up. He writes,
"The 'instrument of power' in sub-politics is congestion (in the direct and the
figurative sense) as the modernized form of the involuntary strike. The phrase
that Munich motorists can read at a typically congestion location: 'You are not
in a jam, you are the jam,' clarifies this parallel between strike and congestion."[3]

These themes of congestion, reflexivity, subpolitics, and the relationship of
the individual and the collective are especially relevant in the Netherlands.

Fig. 1. Oostelijk Flevoland. A typical example of the modern Dutch polder landscape as seen from
the air. Photograph courtesy of Topografische Dienst.

This is particularly true for a number of recent landscape, architectural, and urban planning offices, where issues such as these mentioned form a fundamental point of departure. Many Dutch offices of design and planning have turned Beck's notion of self-confrontation into a method. During the design process, these designers continually confront the parties involved with the extreme consequences of their respective desires in order to trigger a process of negotiation that leads to the design's realization. The landscape plays a crucial role in this process, not only because the traditional openness of the Dutch landscape is under enormous pressure but also because it functions as a kind of operational metaphor for these new design practices. In what follows, I discuss these ideas as well as the recovery of landscape architectural and urbanizing strategies in the Netherlands today. First, a brief history.

252

A Recent Past

The Netherlands is undergoing a period of great expansion. In 1986, the Stichting Wonen—a foundation for the study of housing and planning problems and one of the institutions to form the Netherlands Architecture Institute in 1990—estimated that 70 percent of the built environment in Holland dates from after World War II. Today, ten years on from this report, the number is probably around 75 percent, with a population density comparable to that of Japan. This can be seen in countless new large-scale districts and towns built from scratch on the virginal plains of the polders (Fig. 1). To remedy the housing shortage brought about by war damage, the cessation of building production and maintenance, and the large number of families and resulting postwar population growth, the government financed and subsidized new construction on a large scale from the 1950s through to the early 1980s. Consequently, most of the built environment in the Netherlands is less than fifty years old.

The larger part of the Dutch landscape is very recent also. The reclamation of the Zuiderzee, now the IJsselmeer, was made possible in 1918, before the end of World War I, in which the Dutch held a neutral position. Whereas the first Zuiderzee polder was reclaimed in 1930, the Noordoostpolder and Flevoland were developed after World War II. After the flooding of the Zeeland province, the Delta Act of 1953 led to the completion of not only numerous dikes and water barriers but also substantial works on the Zeeland coast as well. The Land Consolidation Law of 1945 changed the organizational and usage patterns of whole agrarian areas, involving much of the Dutch countryside. As a consequence, the traditional Dutch landscape changed dramatically.

Another postwar phenomenon is the remarkable increase in mobility and communications technologies. New motorways, railways, and other large-scale infrastructures have given rise to new concentrations of settlement and employment. This has had significant consequences for the development of the Randstad—the ring of cities in western Holland that includes Amsterdam, Utrecht, Rotterdam, The Hague, and Haarlem—which encloses a mostly agricultural and natural area known as the Green Heart. Increased mobility around this ring, together with Holland's strategic situation at the delta of the Rhine and the Meuse, has led to the port of Rotterdam becoming the world's largest.

These developments occurred in the exceptionally optimistic period of postwar reconstruction. During this time, ambitions were far greater than mere recovery from the war and occupation. The idea was to rebuild the whole of society and bring an end to poverty, inequality, and other social ills. New instruments for spatial planning were introduced at national and provincial levels as well as in cities and villages. Collective self-discipline and solidarity led to considerable prosperity and the organization of an extensive social facilities system. Despite these efforts, however, genuine social and cultural renewal (in the sense of increased participation and intellectual freedom) has failed to materialize. Events such as the rise of the PROVO movement in the 1960s and the oil crisis of 1973 began to erode this period of optimism. In recent years, the mechanisms that made reconstruction possible have stalled and a more radical cultural swing has emerged under the influence of European unification and globalization.

Today, the Netherlands is becoming more congested and inchoate, and the traditional spatial relationship between town and countryside is almost reversed. This is especially the case with the Randstad and the Green Heart. Whereas government policies are agreed on the preservation of the Green Heart, this area continues to be pressured and compromised, especially since the economic base of agriculture eroded. Countless small initiatives and intrusions are silting up the open clarity of this space. Further, some now argue that the Randstad should be treated as one big metropolis instead of a conglomerate of many cities and villages, where every larger urban scheme has to be negotiated among municipalities. While it has proved easier to create borough councils in the larger cities, it has been difficult to form larger administrative planning units. Even the formation of a city-province around Rotterdam Harbor—a crucial proposition for the port's strategic efficacy in the future European and world markets—has proved very difficult.

Planning and Market

In 1988 the Dutch government drafted a new building program for use until the year 2005. This is called the *Vierde Nota Ruimtelijke Ordening* (Fourth Memorandum on Spatial Planning) and is supplemented by the *Vierde Nota Extra*, known as VINEX, in which locations are identified and allotted to realize the plan. Both memoranda are based on the philosophy that the environment should be respected and that individual mobility should be reduced in favor of public transportation. On the other hand, the plans also call for the strengthening of infrastructural and economic strategies for favorably positioning the Netherlands within a modernizing Europe.

While these plans may sound good, the government has not been effective at following through on them. For instance, in 1994 the state ceased all subsidies to public housing in an attempt to stimulate new economic development and private investment. The debts of housing corporations were remitted in one swoop; in return, they are now obliged to compete in the free market unassisted. In taking this action, the state deprived itself of an important planning instrument: power. At the same time, the government's memorandum on planning and VINEX require eight hundred thousand to a million new homes before the year 2015. In this situation, the market will be decisive; it calls for low-rise development, which uses up a great deal of land. Because of rising prices of land and the investments needed to clear it for construction, and because the Dutch suddenly seem to have a collective desire to keep their countryside open and flat, the new developments will be characterized by unprecedented housing density and compactness. These estates will drastically change the appearance of the Netherlands, despite heroic plans for a new city of fifty to a hundred thousand homes off the coast of Rotterdam and The Hague, and for a new development near Amsterdam of thirty thousand homes on an artificial island in the IJ-meer near Amsterdam. Notably, the traditional concept of landscape as something distinct from the city is under pressure.

In 1993, within the framework of the Architecture International Rotterdam initiative for Alexanderpolder (AIR-Alexander Manifestation, 1993), Rem Koolhaas and the Office for Metropolitan Architecture (OMA) produced a controversial proposal that triggered a discussion about the existing policies for treating new settlements as mere city extensions.[4] OMA presented two alternatives for the future urbanization of the Netherlands: *Point City* and *South City* (Figs. 2, 3). *Point City* turns the arc of the Randstad into the periphery of a new center in the Green Heart, with an efficient new infrastructural network and—

to echo Koolhaas—"finally" truly urban conditions. This plan would greatly reduce the pressure of contemporary demands that the Randstad cities were never intended to meet. Thus, they could finally assume their historical status, encircling the new capital like a string of jewels.

In the other model, *South City*, all new construction would be concentrated in the southern half of the country. Here, the entire urbanized region of Holland would be physically closer to the most active zone of Europe, the so-called blue banana that runs from London to Milan and Turin. Both proposals were combined with a restrictive policy for the rest of the country. This policy vacated the land to create a reservoir of "emptiness" devoted to nature, leisure, history, and tourism. Koolhaas and OMA effectively took the underlying philosophy of VINEX (that had, in their opinion, become weak and diluted) to the extreme scenario, and thereby challenged the government to take more substantial and visionary measures.

Adriaan Geuze and West 8 Landscape Architects designed a similar demonstration of extreme scenarios in 1995. They built an enormous model of eight hundred thousand small individual houses on the floor of the arcade of the Netherlands Architecture Institute (Figs. 4, 5). The result was stunning and shocking: an almost endless sea of houses so vast that the individual layout of the parts was completely submerged in the whole. Traditional urban design made no difference any more; instead, a vast urban *landscape* appeared, as in a massive textural field.

The effect of Geuze's installation was enhanced by a book in which he documented 120 existing low-rise urban extensions from the postwar period in the western part of Holland.[5] This is a region wholly dedicated to housing, a massive and anonymous place where no one really goes unless they live there or are

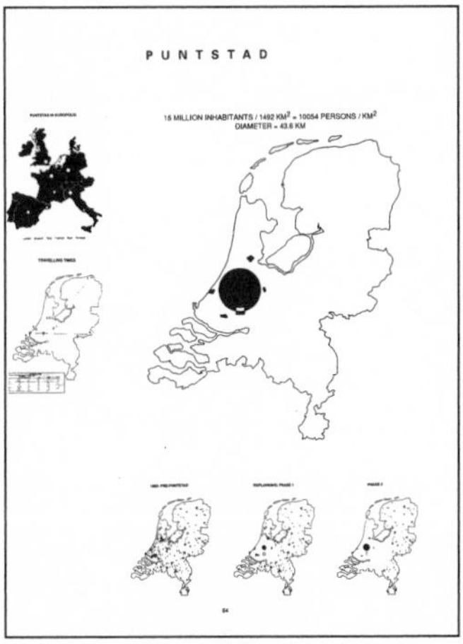

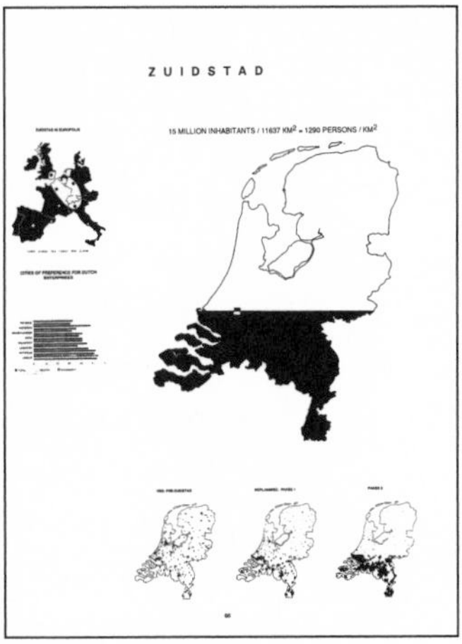

Fig. 2 (top). *Puntstad* ("Point City"). Rem Koolhaas and OMA, 1993.

Fig. 3 (bottom). *Zuidstad* ("South City"). Rem Koolhaas and OMA, 1993.

visiting somebody who does. Moreover, these places, and the people who frequent them, have never been of interest to the typical architectural press or theoretician. Geuze's model showed that while many designers have tried to produce schemes that emphasized the individual, unique aspect of each settlement, the differences blur, almost disappear, and become indistinguishable in the whole.

Still, the government did not respond to the proposals of OMA and Geuze. Instead, the Association of Dutch Urban Designers produced a map of the Netherlands in 1997. This, too, was conceived as a provocation to the government, intended to prompt a rethinking of policies and planning agendas. This map was an enormous undertaking and showed all current planning across the country. Not only did it reveal the sheer magnitude of new planning and development in the Netherlands today but it also pointed to a need to coordinate separate initiatives. The question, however, was—and still is—*how* such coordination can be accomplished.

One way to at least initiate a process of collective coordination is through establishing mechanisms for these topics to be debated and discussed on both local and national levels. To do this, the government has founded institutions—such as the Netherlands Architecture Institute—and provides funds to support a range of initiatives (through agencies such as the Netherlands Architecture Fund—Stimuleringsfonds voor Architectuur en Stedenbouw—for example). Competitions, publications, exhibitions, and manifestations that develop new ideas for dealing with the situation in the Netherlands over the next two decades will be subsidized by these funds. Plans that are made for these manifestations—such as the earlier mentioned AIR-Alexanderpolder and the Rotterdam 2045 initiative—often function as prototypes for later developments. Consequently, realized plans are often almost as extreme and exciting as their prototypes. This has led to a situation in which the Dutch debate is about

Fig. 4 (top). View of the installation "In Holland Stands a House," a model of eight hundred thousand houses, by Adriaan Geuze and West 8, 1995. Photograph courtesy of West 8.

Fig. 5 (bottom). Detail of the installation "In Holland Stands a House," a model of eight hundred thousand houses, by Adriaan Geuze and West 8, 1995. Photograph courtesy of Jannes Linders.

urbanism, landscape, and planning rather than architecture per se. Moreover, it is less about philosophy, theory, and aesthetics and more about how the visionary and the pragmatic may be combined in creative and paradoxical ways.

Market Democracy

The new market democracy has consequences for everybody, but especially for landscape architects, architects, and urban planners. The field in which they must work is becoming more and more complex and unstable. The process that leads to a design and its eventual realization involves an increasing number of parties: clients and their representatives, the local council, technical advisers, building contractors and subcontractors, and any number of social and environmental advocacy groups. Some of these players sit around the negotiating table with the architects, while others operate in the background, appearing at the most unexpected moments in the hope of disrupting or interfering in the project. In addition to these social interactions, design and planning has come to entail countless numbers of rules, regulations, codes, standards, and legislative measures. These too have an enormous impact on the work of architects and planners, overriding the imaginative will and authority of the individual designer.

257

Many architects find it difficult to operate in this new market democracy. In the 1980s, many designers cherished the idea that they could resist these developments and that the only way of saving architecture was to regard it as an autonomous discipline. Research was directed to the historical definition of the discipline and at its language. For these architects, the new rules and norms governing architecture and urbanism were merely obstacles to the achievement of their ideals. More pessimistic was a belief that the new situation would admit only a limited number of building typologies and the creative role of the architect be confined to aesthetic adviser or stylist. This impending homogenization was parried in the official architectural debate with an incredibly rapid succession of stylistic developments. In large urban design projects—the eastern docks area (Oostelijk Havengebied) in Amsterdam, Almere and Kattenbroek in Amersfoort, all realized in the past ten years—this spate of stylistic approaches has led to rather bizarre patchworks of development lacking in continuity. With market influences strengthened by the removal of government subsidy and planning, design has increasingly come to be regarded as a consumer item rather than as an inventive agent in creating public spaces. People now want their own highly individual home, one that not only houses them but also expresses their identity. This has led to a situation in which, as the Dutch urbanists and architects MVRDV put it, "Everything can be made, every object is imaginable and nothing seems strange or extravagant any more."[6]

This situation offered those designers who cherished an autonomous and "artistic" position the opportunity to "brand" their work. This was mirrored by an avalanche of publications, promotional literature, lectures, and exhibitions, each emphasizing the creativity of the individual architect—a form of commodification, if you will. On the other hand, the relatively marginal character of this movement led to a reconsideration of the architect's role in society. To come to terms with and to gain greater efficacy in cultural affairs, the architect had to find ways to engage with the influences surrounding a project and abandon the idea of individual genius.

Rem Koolhaas and OMA realized this situation as early as 1980, when they were commissioned to develop an urban scheme for the IJ-plein in Amsterdam-North.[7] In the design process, they took the desires and demands of the participatory committees seriously but confronted them at the same time with the consequences. For that purpose, OMA developed a handbook in the form of a suitcase that contained analyses of a series of classical urban schemes. These analyses were shown as plans, aerial views, density studies, figure-ground and land-use percentages, and, where possible, photographs of the built work. By means of this handbook, the designers could easily point out the possibilities and restrictions of certain demands. They could also overlay a number of approaches from the handbook in order to produce a "negotiated" scheme.

This method took the classical design process of working with typologies to its absolute limits. Even though Koolhaas later became critical about the results (excluding them from his book *S,M,L,XL*), the method was a breakthrough. The difficulty today, of course, is that cities have changed to such a radical degree, and with such new pressures of mobility, congestion, and service economies, that new typologies have to be developed.[8] Together with the complexity of forces surrounding architectural and urban production, the need to develop new typologies has led the Dutch architect Ben van Berkel to write:

> The field of architectural space is too vast for one architect to comprehensively formulate in a new terminology. I would go further and claim that it is now in any case impossible to undertake an architectural project in isolation. Even within the limitations of just one project the architect can no longer practice architecture on his own. Architec-

ture is changing in a direction where it involves other disciplines in an intensive way. These disciplines, whether they be structural engineers, acoustics or project management, are not hired in as consultants within a hierarchical structure with the architect on top. Often it is a primary activity to talk with structural engineers, with other experts. No longer do architects try to dream up the best possible solution alone in the studio, only to have it stripped later on in the process, as more and more essential information trickles down. The information has to be instrumental earlier on in the process.[9]

New Typologies

Many of the new typologies emerging in landscape and urban design in the Netherlands today deal with densification. This involves designing a compactness that leaves the surrounding landscape intact. The surrounding open space is then developed in various ecological, scenic, and recreational ways as compensation for the lack of public space in the building complex. The compactness of the building development is often realized by reducing gardens to enclosed patios and allowing for multiple ground use. Another important feature of these plans is that they take the cohesion of the landscape as a whole into account; hence, it is of little surprise that landscape architects play a crucial role in their design.

There is nothing particularly new about this, as landscape architects in the Netherlands have been intensively occupied in the design of urban environments since World War II. What is new, though, is that, in recent years, landscape architects have developed techniques to design complete urban schemes *as* landscapes. Adriaan Geuze and West 8 are forerunners in this field, which includes Winy Maas, a former collaborator of OMA and one of the founders of MVRDV, and others as well. And this is not limited to the younger generation, as older practitioners such as Riek Bakker—the driving force behind developments as the Kop van Zuid, in Rotterdam, and Leidsche Rijn, near Utrecht—has also been active in developing new approaches to design and planning. According to Geuze, the recent success of landscape architects in urban planning is explained by their natural ability to deal with unstable situations. He writes:

Architects and industrial designers often see their designs as a final product of genius, whose aesthetic entirety originated in their minds. A design like that is thrown off by the slightest damage. Landscape architects have learnt to put that into perspective, because they know that their designs are continually adapted and transformed. We have learned to see landscape not as a *fait accompli*, but as the result of countless forces and initiatives.[10]

A key project in the development of new, denser urban typologies with landscape qualities is the urban plan designed by Geuze and West 8 for Borneo and Sporenburg, two peninsulas in the eastern part of the Amsterdam docks (Fig. 6). Begun in 1993, this project will be completed in 1999. The original brief called for this large-scale dockland area to be developed as 2,500 new low-rise dwelling units. This translates to a density of 100 units per hectare. As is traditionally the case with Dutch towns around the IJsselmeer, such a settlement had to be related to the water and to the large, open qualities of the site. Taking these contrasting points of departure seriously presented a fascinating and unique opportunity for an urban experiment.

West 8 sought the solution in developing new types of three-story ground-accessed houses. These deviated from the usual terraced house in being strongly oriented to the private realm—in this case, enclosed patios and roof gardens. The design is, in fact, a variant of the traditional Dutch canal house, though with improved light penetration and privacy. A great deal of what normally would be designed as public space is incorporated into the individual plots, thus creating space within the walls of the buildings. By repeating this type in a great variety of dwelling modes (from public housing to exclusive apartments) and with maximum architectural variation (expressed in the special concern for entry zones), an animated street elevation emerges with a fine focus on the individual. The public space consists of streets 11 meters wide with quays overlooking the harbor basins. At the scale of the area as a whole, a balanced relationship exists among the repetition of individual dwellings, the articulated roofscape, and the great scale of the docks, between the intimate containment of the houses and the vast endlessness of the

Fig. 6. Model of Borneo/Sporenburg, Eastern Docklands, Amsterdam. Adriaan Geuze and West 8, 1993–1998. Photograph courtesy of Peter de Ruig.

water. Three immense sculptural blocks sited according to sightlines across the surrounding landscape break up the repetition of the housing layout. These new buildings and spaces offer their occupants a spectacular view while serving as highly visible landmarks.[11]

A similar project, in terms of new typologies, is *City Fruitful* by urban designer Ashok Bhalotra and architect Kas Oosterhuis, initiated in 1992. This project for an extension of the town of Dordrecht combines glasshouse cultivation with housing in a highly artificial landscape configuration. The design pushes the existing artificiality of the Dutch landscape to the maximum. The new typology here places the glasshouses on top of patio houses; thus, both soil and energy have double functions—first, the house is insulated in winter and shaded in summer, and, second, the carbon dioxide produced by the house is transformed in the glasshouse into oxygen that is, in turn, cycled back into the house. All of this is possible because the climatization system used in modern glasshouses is much more sophisticated than the ordinary air-conditioning systems ordinarily used in houses. But beyond technical innovation, this project is significant for its reformulation of a living environment, an exotic place where an inhabitant may look one way into a private garden with sky and horizon and another to the agri-horticultural beds of hybrid plants such as blue pepper and yellow cucumber, the pride of Dutch industrial design.[12]

261

A number of other approaches try to "save" landscape (in the form of greenery). These are the opposite of densification strategies, seeking instead to enlarge the private realm, the space of the garden. Again, a key project in this direction was developed by Adriaan Geuze and West 8 in their polemical 1993 proposal for the Alexanderpolder, in Rotterdam.[13] Here, the designers proposed to "colonize" the Green Heart with individual homes on large plots of gardens—a kind of Los Angelization (Figs. 7, 8). The approach was immediately embraced by developers as precisely the right the thing to do.

MVRDV developed this idea further in their town planning study for 13,500 dwellings in the IJsselmonde island that was originally designed for the Rotterdam 2045 project.[14] They called their concept "light urbanism," referring to "thin" forms of settlement—thin in terms of density and materiality as well as meaning and permanence (Figs. 9, 10). Consequently, the design called for houses made of light materials, grass roads, septic tanks instead of sewers, no gas pipes—only electricity, mobile phones and aerial receivers instead of cabling for telephone and TV, and call-up buses instead of trams and coaches. As the designers describe it:

The economy provides an amazing range of choice, allowing us to develop in all sorts of different ways within the same budget: either large gardens round the houses, enabling a villa-like environment to be created for the normal price for such a dwelling at a density of 7–10 dwellings per hectare, or a super-communal space that can be set up as a wood or a nature reserve. Two urban styles can be envisaged: "Campingland" and "Villageland."[15]

Because light urbanism is experimental and temporal in nature, MVRDV's vision might provide a countermodel to both densification (as in OMA's *Point City*) and supersprawl (as is much the case today).

Architecture as Landscape

Many other new typologies treat architecture and urbanism themselves as extensions of the landscape or, better, as extensions of the "skin of the earth," to use architect Raoul Bunschoten's term.[16] This synthetic approach finds its origins in the work of Rem Koolhaas and OMA. Ultimately, Rem Koolhaas's goal has always been to project an architecture that is physically absent, one that dissolves itself through channeling and supporting the processes of social group formation. This is evidenced in the 1983 competition proposal for the Parc de la Villette in Paris, in which the scenario mapping of programs and events led to the formulation of a multilayered design strategy. The overlaying of program structures has been developed since by many landscape architects and urbanists in the Netherlands, not only for designing parks but urban fabrics, too. While this technique may appear novel, it has its roots in the Dutch modernist tradition of town planning of the 1930s, wherein programs and services were rationally distributed over an area according to statistical research.

Koolhaas is fascinated by the dictum of Raymond Hood, architect of New York's Rockefeller Center, that the plan is the primary instrument in design.

Fig. 7 (top). *Justification of the Green Heart*, an experimental concept for the Randstad's empty space. Adriaan Geuze and West 8, 1993.

Fig. 8 (bottom). *Emptiness*, an experimental concept for the Randstad's empty space. Adriaan Geuze and West 8, 1993.

"The plan is most significant because all of man's activities take place on the ground," writes Hood. Koolhaas interprets this statement as a plea for "a 'functionalist' architecture which is not obsessed with form, but which conceives of and creates structures for human activity in previously nonexistent juxtapositions and catalysing combinations on the floor (meaning on the surface of the earth)."[17]

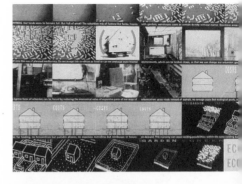

Thus, the building is conceived as a frame composed of floors, and the stack of floors may be considered a continuation of the ground. In designs by OMA, such as the competition entry for Yokohama (1992), the Jussieu Library in Paris (1993), and the Educatorium in Utrecht (1997), this attitude is especially evident in the folded continuity of the floor slabs as upward, "topographic" extensions of the landscape. Moreover, the floors are made from materials that recall the ground: stone, concrete, wooden parquet or screed (underlayment).

Preference is reserved for bare concrete, sometimes painted monochromatically, as in the Rotterdam KunstHal (1992). In earlier designs, asphalt-paved paths with painted lines moved from the street to the interior of the building. The typical, changing contours of desert sand play a key role in the 1990 design for a congress center in Agadir. Furthermore, a number of designs use water, which can also be considered a natural material for rendering surfaces. It plays an important structural role, especially in the famous floating swimming pool (1977) as well as in designs for private residences.

The approach toward building as a folded continuity of landscape is also evident in projects by MVRDV, notably the VPRO office and studio building (1993–1997). The VPRO is a public broadcasting organization that occupies a critical and progressive position in the Dutch public broadcasting system. In

Fig. 9 (top). *Light Urbanism: The City Center of Rotterdam Taken Over by Nature*, town planning study for the IJsselmonde Island, Rotterdam. MVRDV, 1995.

Fig. 10 (bottom). *Light Urbanism: The City Center of Rotterdam Taken Over by Nature*, town planning study for the IJsselmonde Island, Rotterdam. MVRDV, 1995.

recent years, this system has come under strong pressure from the growing number of commercial broadcasters beamed at the Netherlands. On top of this, the company needed to adapt to and capitalize on the potential of modern media technologies. To speed up and intensify this process, the VPRO decided to bring all its employees together in one building in the interests of greater exchange and contact. The company's aim was to create an open and adaptive environment so as to better respond to a changing and uncertain future. The site is a magnificent location in Hilversum, on the edge of forest and heath, close to a lake—the same site as the studios of the Netherlands Broadcasting Services Corporation (NOB). MVRDV's solution is a compact building of five floors that intrudes minimally on the landscape and even gives back a bit of nature in the form of a roof garden.

Inside, the building manifests itself as an uninterrupted continuation of the landscape surfaces (Fig. 11). The smoothly folded floors accommodate a range of office arrangements. All the floors are linked to one another by ramps (hills and slopes) and superstaircases—theatrical stairs that can also be used as

seating. Beginning with a general form, the designers systematically subject the building to diverse layers of differentiation. Infrastructural conditions, such as utilities, circulation, and furnishing, literally underpin the location and definition of individual elements. These elements are called *mini-buildings* and are distributed within the overall structure as offices, meeting rooms, and so on. Niches for the use of nonconformists emerge between the folds and slopes of the folded ground-plane. This mini-city is furnished partly with existing furniture from the many previous offices of the VPRO and partly with new furniture by designers from different periods. The effect is a radically inchoate differentiation of highly personalized workspaces.

Other Dutch architects have taken up the strategy of the building as an extended landscape as well. Van Berkel & Bos did this in their highly complicated urban-infrastructural proposal for the Arnhem Station Area (Fig. 12). Here, a continuously folded landscape surface channels the flows of traffic and pedestrians in an unprecedentedly smooth, uninterrupted way. Lars Spuybroek considers his H_2O Pavilion in Zeeland a "rolled-up square," and in several of

Fig. 11. Villa VPRO, Hilversum. MVRDV, 1993–1997. Photograph courtesy of Hans Werlemann.

Wiel Arets's schemes, levels are made to "float" to allow for different organizations and continuities.

But there is also the opposite strategy, in which the landscape becomes a vertical building, a skyscraper, or even or a city of high-rises. Adriaan Geuze and West 8 introduced such an idea in their competition entry for the Riem Park in Munich from 1995. This occurred alongside their *Green Manhattanism* manifesto, in which they proposed four new vertical parks in New York City.[18] In a similar vein, MVRDV introduced stacked parks in their competition entry for the Leidsche Rijn Park near Utrecht in 1998 (Fig. 13), and also in their Dutch Pavilion project for the Expo 2000 in Hanover (1997).[19]

Mapping

It is a marvelous paradox that the unstable conditions of the market democracy in the Netherlands today makes possible the development of highly unusual and exciting designs. Most of these projects are proposed by younger practices that see the new situation as both promising and challenging. This may be because some of the changes in architecture and urban planning have taken place within the last five years or so—a relatively short time. The strength of many of these young practitioners seems to be a critical pragmatism. They are able to transform—or recover—the original forces of large-scale functional logistics. To draw from Koolhaas, they are essentially occupied with "the maintenance and assimilation of the so-called 'functionalist' tradition." As this tradition appears to be faced with its own limits, these designers return to its original driving force: "a functionalism which is in fact a campaign in favor of the programmatic notion that architecture might exercise a direct influence on the content of a culture that is based on density, technology and social instability."[20]

Offices such as OMA, West 8, Kees Christiaanse, MVRDV, Neutelings Riedijk, Van Berkel & Bos, CHORA, and, more recently, Max-1, NL Architects,

Fig. 12 (top). Model of Arnheim Station. Ben van Berkel and Caroline Bos, 1996–1999. Photograph by Jan Derwig.

Fig. 13 (bottom). Aerial view of model for the competition design for Leidsche Rijn Park. MVRDV, 1998. Photograph courtesy of MVRDV.

Buro Schie, and Hans Venhuizen try to deal with the new situation by simply diving into it with a kind of masochistic pleasure. They analyze it rationally and without prejudice, and try to find the potentials hidden in the ruling system. Unlike for the older generations, the start and maybe the most important part of the design process is an extensive mapping of all internal and external forces that could possibly play a role in the genesis of a project. Often, projects are presented such that the layers of mapping almost automatically seem to generate the plan, although, as a result, it looks quite different from what anyone had expected. As Koolhaas writes:

> If there is a method in this work, it is a method of systematic *idealization*—a systematic overestimation of what exists, a bombardment of speculation that invests even the most mediocre aspects with retroactive conceptual and ideological charge. To each bastard, a genealogical tree; the faintest hint of an idea is tracked with the obstinacy of a detective on a juicy case of adultery.[21]

Consequently, some of the most important threads running through the work of Adriaan Geuze and West 8, for example, are such apparently uninteresting things as traffic laws and the civil code, things often seen as annoying obstacles by designers who put their own creativity first. According to West 8, however, such laws and codes contain rules that offer the firmest ground for public space. Everyone knows them or is expected to know them. By accepting the application of these rules, the designer of public space commits a genuinely public act in which everyone can participate and perhaps even subvert.

Techniques of mapping are especially important in this regard and mappings can become projects unto themselves. In Lucus Verweijs's and Buro Schies's *Randstad Street Map*, for instance, the image confirms the hypothesis that the Randstad is, in fact, already one large metropolis. The graphic character of the map (depicting the country as if a town street-map) changes people's perception of the Randstad as a somewhat quaint collection of separate and distinct towns and prompts them to reconsider the actual integrated metropolitan condition. As Buro Schie puts it:

> The map's design leads to a different way of looking that in turn affects the way this area is imagined. The street map introduces the Randstad Ring (a ring road created by linking up existing pieces of motorway)

that connects up all the Randstad districts. Because only those bits of greenery open to the public are marked as town parks and all development is shown (including ribbon villages and stray farms), the Green Heart is revealed to be a *fata Morgana*: housing density in this area is actually above average.[22]

The street map is accompanied by a set of postcards: one depicting tourist attractions from different cities in the Randstad, one of the Randstad railway system depicted as an urban transport map (Fig. 14), and one of the night trains. In changing and supplementing representational convention and technique, the world is shown in new and eye-opening ways.[23]

267

Mapping especially influences how decisions are made and how plans are realized. The development situation is complicated today, with government and industry establishing one set of practices and special interest groups operating under other rules. Apart from legislative and democratic procedures, the more empirical laws that investors develop on the basis of economic analyses and prognoses exercise a considerable effect on the direction in which society is steered. In an effort to appear as objective and as reasonable as possible, all of these various parties use "scientific" research in constructing their arguments. At the same time, these groups use the same techniques to dispute one another's methods and findings.

The only thing they have in common is that their studies are presented in the form of numbers, statistics, and charts. Even when instinctive or emotional arguments play a role in the decision-making process, they can nearly always be quantified—as in a poll or vote, for example. Such is a market democracy. Quantities are the new language of this international form of government. The computer is not only the tool used to manipulate quantities, it also, as a means of communication, serves to enforce this language as the new international standard. Consequently, mapping becomes instrumental in constructing arguments, presenting a case, and getting projects built. It is a rhetorical art form.

Fig. 14. Randstad City Trains Map. Buro Schie and Lucas Verweij, 1996.

Van Berkel & Bos carried out their first experiments with mapping and computers in developing the design for the Erasmus Bridge in Rotterdam (1990–1996). The bridge is the first link between the two halves of the center of Rotterdam, and it is also the first bridge that ships coming from the sea must pass under. With a height of 139 meters, the bridge is a new symbol for Rotterdam. It is also a remarkable sculpture that takes on a totally different character depending on the angle of viewing. The importance accorded the design of the bridge derives from a political desire to upgrade the southern part of the city, which has always had less standing than the city center on the north bank.

The bridge's unusual asymmetrical form derives from a desire to physically express the force field of the construction, in which tension and balance are combined. The first sketches for this bridge were done by hand, interpreting all the "mobile forces" that were at play in the genesis of the project and bringing them into an almost expressionist synthesis.[24] But in the course of the process, computers were introduced to make it possible to communicate clearly with all the parties involved—from the client to the structural engineers to the site foremen. The computer enabled a sharing of information and expertise so that the complexity of the project would not get out of hand. It also enabled the use of new computerized construction technologies in the fabrication and construction of this unusual design.

In their project for the Arnheim station area (1996–1999), Van Berkel & Bos take this method several steps further by introducing the computer in a much earlier stage in the design process. Here, the flows of pedestrian, car, train, and bus traffic are mapped and inventoried. In doing so, the designers discovered that the flows from and to the trains were not, in fact, dominant; instead, the flows between regional and local buses were shown to be much more important. By depicting the flows as "tubes" in the computer and exposing them to force fields representing the desires of the different parties involved, the design evolved in an almost natural but formally spectacular way. This made it possible to radically rethink the concept of the station and the square, and to actually save the project after other architects had tried for years to recreate a classical and monumental train station and public space.

Synthetic Regionalization

Throughout the 1980s, people believed that the globalizing tendencies of capital and technology would lead to an increasingly homogenous built environment.[25] Yet, in recent years, more and more architects have been arguing quite

the reverse. Alejandro Zaera Polo, for instance, argues that globalization actually leads to "the enhancement of diversification and heterogeneity by increasing our awareness of differences, the particularities of a location and its
specificities...we witness an artificial regionalization, an artificially enhanced
nature, where the local flavor becomes synthetic."[26]

This point is picked up by Adriaan Geuze in his analysis of the contemporary city, which he describes as "a well-aired metropolis of villages, urban cen-
tres, suburbs, industrial areas, docks, airfields, woods, lakes, beaches, reserves
and the monocultures of hi-tech farming."[27] This is a heterogeneous landscape
that, until recently, was simply called the *periphery*, or the middle landscape.[28]
These areas have since become so pervasive that they are now the predominant
condition in which most people live. They form mosaiclike enclaves and patchworks that accommodate the most disparate of functions. Geuze has long been
fascinated by the surrealistic nature of this landscape. In 1987, he described the
cemetery as "an urban fringe phenomenon on the same footing in society as
vegetable gardens, breakers' yards and gypsy encampments" and wrote about
"the analogy between graves and tended vegetable beds, mortal remains and
wrecks of cars, corpses and social outcasts."[29]

The ultimate concentration of such functions Geuze found on the
Maasvlakte, near Rotterdam. On this gigantic offshore dockland, an "impressive assemblage of orphans" have assumed residence. As Geuze describes it,
this area comprises:

269

> ...a twenty-five meter high artificial dune-land to hide the oil drums
> from the beach at the Hook, a uranium ore terminal, a dozen experi-
> mental wind turbines, a tidal gully with port dredging depot, a chemi-
> cal waste dump, a container terminal, a detonation zone for explosives,
> even a trout farm. The most bizarre program, however, is the World
> Disaster Center, an area where fake blocks of flats, an oil platform, a
> train, trucks, a refinery, storage tanks and such are built and set on fire
> with natural gas. Firemen and disaster teams from all over the world
> come to train here twenty-four hours a day.[30]

But that's not all. During weekends and vacations, hordes of people stream
to the Maasvlakte to engage in new, adventurous, and sometimes dangerous
forms of recreation, the like of which the designers of parks and leisure neither
dreamed of nor made provisions for in their designs. Visitors to Maasvlakte "see

the expanse of sand as a place to practice sledding or scrambling, the dredging depot as a hang glider runway, the wall of blocks as fossilized rocks, the saltwater sand reclamation pit as a place for deep sea diving."[31] And even here, Geuze neglects to mention the Maasvlakte as the venue for the largest techno-party ever held, with loud, electronic dance music and extravagant light shows attracting the alternative youth culture from all over Europe.

Datascapes

MVRDV holds with those unconvinced that the world is heading toward increased homogeneity. Instead, they believe that it is possible to identify various "gravity fields" or hidden strands of logic in the apparent chaos of contemporary development that ensure the differentiation of whole areas. They write:

> These gravities reveal themselves when sublimated beneath certain assumed maximized circumstances or within certain maximized constraints.... [For instance,] because of tax differences, the borders between Belgium and the Netherlands are occupied with vast numbers of villas generating a linear town along the frontier. Market demand has precipitated a "slick" of houses-with-a-small-garden in Holland. Political constraints in Hong Kong generate "piles" of dwellings around its boundaries.... Monumental regulations in Amsterdam limit the demand for modern programs, generating "mountains of program" invisible from the street behind the medieval facades.... In La Defense in Paris, to avoid the high-rise rules massive programs manifest themselves as ziggurats with 18 meter high accessible "steps" so that offices can be entered by the maximum length of the fire ladders. Psychological issues, anti-disaster patterns, lighting regulations, acoustic treatments. All these manifestations can be seen as "scapes" of the data behind them.[32]

Datascapes are visual representations of all the measurable forces that may influence the work of the architect or even steer or regulate it (Fig. 15). These influences may be planning and building regulations, technical and economic constraints, natural conditions such as sun and wind, or legislative measures such as minimum working conditions. There is also the increasingly complex array of divergent interest groups, political pressures, and competing agendas. Each datascape carefully maps only one or two of these influences at a time, revealing their influence on the design process by show-

ing their most extreme effects. As sites are typically governed by multiple forces and conditions,
the designers may have to map multiple datascapes, analyzing the various forces in all of their
complexity.[33]

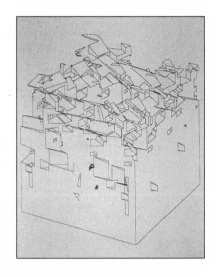

Datascapes are, in fact, visualizations of what
the sociologist Anthony Giddens calls "expert systems" and "abstract systems."[34] These are scientific
procedures adopted by bureaucracies to make
decisions. Because of the assumed expertise and
objective methodology used by those who produce
such systems, these systems are taken to be true
and neutral. Of course, the status of experts in one
system says nothing about their status in another.
Consequently, the information produced by expert systems is open to dispute.

Contemporary society is governed by a multiplicity of such abstract systems. Datascapes capitalize on the force and efficacy of such systems, analyzing
conditions so as to guide new development and accomplish desired ends.
Moreover, as the above quotation suggests, datascapes can literally generate
spatial propositions that come close to being architectural projects themselves.
But datascapes are not architectural projects. As Detlef Martins comments:

> What makes datascapes wholly unlike the "normal" architectural proj-
> ect today is their deliberate denial of the endless negotiation between
> competing forces, regulations, planning criteria familiar as the plan-
> ning-procedure by which all space is administered today: in the sense
> that Tafuri has written, [datascapes accomplish] a complex managerial
> task that largely characterizes the profession of architecture and
> defines its principal forms of labor.[35]

In other words, the visualization of the often contradictory forces and
dynamics that play a role in a project's creation marks the start of a negotiation
process that involves all the concerned parties. This process may finally lead to

Fig. 15. *Claustro City, Datascape*, city of 100 x 100 x 100 meters based on a combination of current fire regulations and direct sunlight delivered into emergency facilities at moments of
expected use. These parameters generate a fluid and connective space, where every possible
claustrophobia induced by monotony and repetition is avoided. Sven Grooten and Chris Rankin
(Berlage Institute) and MVRDV. Courtesy of MVRDV and Berlage Institute.

the project itself or at least help to show what is possible. The superimposition of multiple datascapes—each of which may have totally divergent consequences—gives rise to a complex spatial envelope that reflects not just the restrictions but also the possibilities and outer limits of the design.

MVRDV's "light urbanism" project, discussed earlier, is an example of a plan that both derives from and redirects prevailing norms and rules. More paradoxical, perhaps, is that this scenario can go hand in hand with an almost total surrender of architecture to market forces. Winy Maas has described their project as providing maximum choice and flexibility, a framework wherein:

> ...a "country" of smaller and larger plots emerges where individuals and groups are free to find a place in cottages, Belgian fermettes, Swiss chalets, New Hampshire homes, farmsteads and colonies. The result is one big family camp-site. It picks up on the camping spirit proclaimed over and over again in the media as where domestic life is heading.[36]

The president of the Association of Dutch Architects (BNA), Carel Weeber, immediately seized on MVRDV's scenario and suggested that the architect become an industrial designer producing standardized components from which future residents can assemble their houses as in a kind of do-it-yourself supermarket.[37] But this is an unfortunate misinterpretation of the more radical aspects of MVRDV's concept; not only does it reduce the entire framework to small and homogenized plots but also it fails to appreciate the necessary "structuring" of the ground conditions so that more heterogeneous and open-ended effects may be supported.

What MVRDV, Koolhaas, Geuze, and others recognize is that in structuring new conditions of the space in between, the picture of a society of free and active agents who do their own organizing and express themselves in new communities gradually emerges. This is, perhaps, the difficulty of light urbanism, for when the idea circulates in an unstable public sphere, with many different parties and interest involved, it is easily reduced to a lowest common denominator. Here, we shift from "light" to "lite," as in diet soda and beer. By contrast, and returning to Ulrich Beck's observations at the beginning of this essay, the power of the ideas discussed above lies "first, in their disembedding and, second, in their re-embedding of industrial society's ways of life by new [situations] in which individuals must produce, stage, and cobble together their biographies themselves."[38]

Datascapes and other design and planning techniques emerging in the

Netherlands today clearly show how complex the contemporary landscape has become. Apart from its immediate visual appearance, many invisible forces govern the processes and dynamics that give it shape. The synthetic regionalization of the Dutch landscape involves not only designers' complete immersion in the real world of market democracy and global forces but also their critical and creative capacity to realign those conditions toward more socially enriching ends. Besides, as the invisible envelopes of electronic and communications space, or as the equally invisible corridors of air travel, these conditions may even form new spaces and landscapes, high above in the air.

Notes

1   Ulrich Beck, "The Reinvention of Politics: Towards a Theory of Reflexive Modernization," in *Reflexive Modernization: Politics, Tradition and Aesthetics in the Modern Social Order,* Ulrich Beck, Anthony Giddens, and Scott Lash (Cambridge, England: Polity Press, 1994), 1.

2   Ibid., 5.

3   Ibid., 23.

4   See Rem Koolhaas, "New Urban Frontiers," in *Alexanderpolder: New Urban Frontiers*, ed. Anne-Mie Devolder (Bussum, Netherlands: THOTH, 1993), 60–61. See also Architecture International Rotterdam, *The Alexanderpolder: New Urban Frontiers* (Rotterdam: Rotterdam Arts Council, 1993).

5   See Adriaan Geuze, *In Holland staat een huis / Model of 800,000 houses* (Rotterdam: Netherlands Architecture Institute, 1995).

6   Winy Maas, "Datascape," in *FARMAX: Excursions on Density*, Winy Maas, Jacob van Rijs, and Richard Koek (Rotterdam: 010 Publishers, 1998), 100.

7   The IJ is a large water body in the middle of Amsterdam. The IJsselmeer, the former Zuiderzee, is a large lake in the middle of the Netherlands. Its name derives from the river that feeds it: the IJssel. The IJ-meer is a narrower part of that between the IJ and the IJsselmeer. The IJ-plein is a section of Amsterdam to the north of the IJ.

8   See Rem Koolhaas and Bruce Mau, *S,M,L,XL* (New York: Monacelli Press, 1995).

9   Ben Van Berkel, "Mobile Forces," lecture delivered at AnyBody Congress, Buenos Aires, June 1996.

10   Adriaan Geuze, "Interview with Olof Koekebakker: Verzoening met het eigentijdse landschap," in *Items* (July 1994): 46.

11   See Adriaan Geuze, *Adriaan Geuze/West 8* (Rotterdam: 010 Publishers, 1995), 68–73.

12   In 1987, such designer produce was prominently featured at the exhibition "Holland in Vorm." See Ivan Ginneke, "Land-en tuinbouw: een stille revolutie," in *Holland in Vorm*, eds. Gert Staal and Hester Wolters (Gravenhage, Netherlands: Stichting Holland in Vorm, 1987), 112–119.

13   See Adriaan Geuze, "Wildernis," in *Alexanderpolder: New Urban Frontiers*, ed. Anne-Mie Devolder (Bussum, Netherlands: THOTH, 1993), 96–105; and Geuze, *Adriaan Geuze/West 8*, 60–61.

14   See Winy Maas, et al., *FARMAX*, 34–51; "Light Urbanism," *Archis* 2 (February 1997) 74–79; and "A Conversation with Winy Mass, Jacob van Rijs, and Nathalie de Vries," in *El Croquis* 86: *MVRDV* (1998): 6–25.

15   Maas, "Light Urbanism," 75.

16   See Raoul Bunschoten, "The Skin of the Earth: A Dissolution in 15 parts," in *Forum* 36/1 (November 1992), 58.

17   Rem Koolhaas, "The New Sobriety," in *Rem Koolhaas/OMA*, ed. Jacques Lucan

(New York: Princeton Architectural Press, 1991), 153.

18 See Geuze, *Adriaan Geuze/West 8*, 28–31; and Bart Lootsma, "Connecting Nature/Disconnecting Nature," *Daidalos* 65 (1997): 104–109.

19 See *El Croquis* 86: *MVRDV*, 158–167.

20 Lucan, *Rem Koolhaas/OMA*, 153.

21 Ibid., 155.

22 Buro Schie, "Randstad Street Map," in *Nine + One: Ten Young Dutch Architectural Offices*, ed. Marijke Kuper (Rotterdam: Netherlands Architecture Institute, 1997), 92.

23 See James Corner, "The Agency of Mapping," in *Mappings*, ed. Denis Cosgrove (London: Reaktion, 1999), 213–299.

24 Ben van Berkel, *Mobile Forces/Mobile Kraft*, ed. Kristen Feireiss (Berlin: Ernst und Sohn Verlag, 1994); see especially Bart Lootsma, "Ambidexterity and Transgression," 19–27.

25 See David Harvey, *The Condition of Postmodernity* (Cambridge, Mass.: Blackwell, 1989); and Rem Koolhaas, "The Generic City," *S,M,L,XL*, 1238–1264.

26 Alejandro Zaera Polo, "Order out of Chaos: The Material Organization of Advanced Capitalism," *Architectural Design Profile* 108: *The Periphery* (1994): 24–29.

27 Geuze, *Adriaan Geuze/West 8*, 12.

28 See Peter Rowe, *Making the Middle Landscape* (Cambridge, Mass.: MIT Press, 1991); and also *Architectural Design Profile* 108: *The Periphery*.

29 Adriaan Geuze and Anja Guinee, "Vormgevingsargumenten voor de nederlandse begraafplaats" (postgraduate research paper, Wageningen Agricultural University, 1987).

30 Adriaan Geuze, "Accelerating Darwin," in *Modern Park Design*, eds. Martin Knuitt et al. (Amsterdam: THOTH, 1993). 16.

31 Ibid., 52.

32 Maas, "Datascape," 101–102.

33 Over the last two years, MVRDV has developed a catalog of datascapes in collaboration with students from the Architectural Association in London and the Berlage Institute in Amsterdam. See note 6.

34 See Anthony Giddens, "Living in a Post-Traditional Society," in *Reflexive Modernization: Politics, Tradition and Aesthetics in the Modern Social Order*, Ulrich Beck, Anthony Giddens, and Scott Lash (Cambridge, England: Polity Press, 1994), 56–109.

35 Detlef Martins, memo to Winy Maas, 21 June 1997. See also Stan Allen, "Artificial Ecologies," in *El Croquis* 86: *MVRDV*, 26–33.

36 Winy Maas, "Midden IJsselmonde, Lichte Stedebouw, Smitshoek en de toekomst van de Nederlandse uitbreidingswijk," in *Rotterdam 2045*, ed. Ole Bouman (Rotterdam: Manifestatie Rotterdam, 1996), 98–101.

37 See Bernard Hulsman, "Het Wilde Wonen, Carel Weeber wil af van het rijtjeshuis," in *NRC Handelsblad: Cultureel Supplement* (April 1997): 1.

38 Beck, "Reinvention of Politics," 26.

Afterword: What Is Public in Landscape?

Alan Balfour

The preceding essays offer a varied and provocative view of landscape practices and landscape thought as the close of the twentieth century approaches. They reflect marked differences between Europe and America, particularly in the idea of what constitutes a public landscape. This is especially evident in the examples of Dutch practice; in the Netherlands, over many years and in widely varied settings, landscapes have been formed to enhance public life. This is not simply an extension of shaping land reclaimed from the sea—it is a political expression of the need to give form to the idea of community and collective life. Apart from the high taxation that such projects demand, they might be viewed from America as reflecting too much public interference with individual choice. Though America shows little interest in using landscape in such an overt and singular way, the production of American landscapes—in all their splendid and confused variety, both good and bad—contain political and public agendas that need better understanding.

Landscape architecture[1] is a relatively new art form that from its inception was intended to provide an entertaining demonstration of political power by the privileged and for the privileged. It is an art of the artificial, bending nature to mankind's order. No matter with what degree of seriousness we now approach the poetic content of the great parks and gardens of eighteenth-century Europe, these were no more than flattering confections toying romantically with the idea of the classical world—paintings made real.

Landscape gained favor as an art form not simply because it embellished the land—the primary asset of the privileged—but for its ability to make palpable the romance with the classical world, offering a poetic engagement with nature. For the cultivated tastes of the eighteenth century, to discover in the woodland glade a "sacred grove," seemingly shaped by the forces of nature, was to experience paradise regained.[2]

Eighteenth-century English landscapes were created for sublime effect, often in imitation of paintings, such as the influence of Poussin on the compositions of landscape artist and architect William Kent. Lancelot (Capability) Brown, the most influential of the English makers of landscape, condemned such artificiality as a disgusting display of art and shaped his parks and gardens to appear natural and informal, to the great satisfaction of English society.

In America this recreation of the natural led Jefferson to write, in 1806, that the new nation should look to England *as a model for this art.*[3] Jefferson, ever the idealist, saw an analogy between the creation of a rich and varied landscape, sustained and renewed by natural laws, and the maintenance of a democracy continually being refined and developed with the guidance of equally unchanging laws.

The American patrons of landscaped realities are no longer the landed gentry and the new rich but the federal government and commercial enterprise, and landscapes have evolved from artifacts of public order and private pleasure to a boundless, untidy mix of ordered grandeur, individualism, and mass consumption.[4]

276

Landscapes of Popular Desire

Essentially, three public and political landscapes have evolved and persist in American culture: the front lawn that unites so much of the domestic landscape, the surviving nineteenth-century city parks, and the state and national parks. One should add others, of course—the landscape of the highways, the visual impact on the land of the powerful technologies of farming, and the vast public projects of the Corps of Engineers. The latter, through engaging the most complex technologies and commanding vast resources, offers powerful tools to contemporary practices of landscape architecture.[5] Still, the discipline of landscape architecture is more traditionally identified with the first-mentioned three landscapes.

The front lawn is perhaps the most American expression of the public realm, framing the idea of community within nature. Leaving the lawn unfenced, unenclosed, and consciously modest in its plants and ornaments, remains a popular practice across the nation, creating a continual field in which ideas of individual property and neighborliness are symbolized.

Public parks were, from the beginning, under municipal control and had strict regulations for use, including the discouragement of political activities. They were created by paternalistic city governments to provide release from the harshness of city life and as instruments of social control. However, out of such a constrained beginning the public park evolved into an art form that enhanced civic life in the United States well into this century. It greatest achievement, New York's Central Park, emerged out of the works of Lancelot Brown and Thomas Jefferson and the dominant figure in nineteenth-century English landscape architecture, Joseph Paxton.[6] It was, of course, the great creation of Frederick Law Olmsted and Calvert Vaux.[7] Central Park was and continues to be American landscape architecture's supreme achievement and defines to this day the political and social potential of the discipline. Subsequently, in parks from New York and Boston to San Francisco, Olmsted's influence transcended landscape, enhancing and giving form to the very idea of civic life. He became, by many measures, the nineteenth century's most influential political and public artist.

Yet this very success has created difficulties for the current-day practice of landscape architecture. With the demise of the public park as an essential complement to civic life, landscape architecture has lost the public context through which to demonstrate its worth, and it has also lost the public visibility and celebrity that attended great public works. Sadly, the field has been increasingly marginalized in the modern world, and its practitioners must now work hard to find new ways of reinserting landscape into the larger imagination and public domain.

Olmsted's parks brought nature to the city, but the automobile was able to take people into nature, into the wilderness, preserved in the national and the state parks. These vast areas of unspoiled land are America's antidote to an overstimulated world. From coastal beaches and forests to mountains and lakes, being and playing in semiwilderness is much more a conscious part of American life and experience than that of any other developed country. The raw wilderness, in all its danger and unpredictability, is a compelling state of harmonic chaos that demands design and management to sustain its appearance, seemingly unspoiled, while supporting its exploitation for whatever use.

Changing Perceptions of Reality

Private lawns and public parks, whether city, state, or national, should be the significant public landscapes of America,[8] yet there are perhaps two segments of the landscape profession for whom these are not necessarily the primary sites of attention. As James Corner outlines in his introduction to this volume, one group instead draws on the recent rise of ecology and environmentalism, often with the best of intentions but also, and unfortunately, neglecting to pay sufficient attention to the cultural imagination and to public life, especially in cities. The other group retreats into the projects and concepts of art practice, much in evidence in several recent books on landscape. This is a division that echoes the eighteenth-century arguments between Kent and Brown, between seeking to form landscapes from painterly concepts or by improving on nature. The roots lie in landscape architecture's long-standing relationship with fine art and with changes in the perception of reality.

In the nineteenth century, the physical distance and distinction between the object of contemplation and the eye of the witness was clearly recognized. In the case of landscape, the pleasure for the individual was essentially pictorial—a pleasure of being within a natural setting, albeit idealized. As the first quarter of the twentieth century made fetishes—certainly among the fashionable—of self-knowledge and the uncovering of the subconscious in the production of art, the felt distance between the individual and the object began to close. It moved closer and closer as the century progressed until, finally, the actual object became less significant, in fact, than its place in the mind and imagination—the significance residing in the idea, not in the actual.

278

This had a transforming effect on those art forms based on illusion—such as cinema—extending invention in ways not possible without such a shift. However, landscape architecture is work in reality, complex reality continually changed by natural forces. Overemphasis on the conceptual has confused the relationships among natural forces and cultural ways of life. For a discipline that acts on a vast scale and over generations of time, such conceptualization has led, at best, to some refreshing and peculiar invention and, at worst, to episodic and contrived practice, with little interest in actual plant material or the sense of time and the passage of the seasons.

The difference between such practice now and in the eighteenth century is the absence of an informed public clearly desiring such entertaining and inventive landscapes. The result is a diminution of influence. It is a paradox that while the most ambitious intellectual practice in landscape risks marginalization through overly conceptual practice, our highly commercial culture conceptualizes landscape for equally self-serving reasons, but with much more influence and success.

The Commodification of Landscape

In anticipating the future uses and forms of landscape, the unprecedented power and private purpose of corporate culture must be recognized. Landscape has always been shaped by the power elite and, given declining support for public programs, corporate domination will increasingly affect and mold reality in all forms.

Corporate agendas and corporate visions increasingly manipulate the formation of significant, productive realities around the world. They call for landscapes to aid in the consumption of goods and services, landscapes formed to enhance themed or trademarked realities. Most national and international producers and retailers invest in elaborate fantasy packaging to reinforce the illusion of lifestyle embodied in their product, be it clothing, perfume, or household accessories. Malls assume a carnival spirit as they orchestrate the performances of the retailers. They will soon have to employ stage managers to interweave the various stages and plays together to gain the best advantage (in terms of consumption).

The corporate clients who are the major producers of landscapes of illusion show less and less interest in the security of place. For them, place increasingly is a liquid asset held only as long as it enhances profit. Being held in place is something corporations seek to avoid. In all their actions, they become increasingly light on the ground, always prepared to shift their offices and factories to take advantage of new markets and lower wages, avoiding union interference. Apart from those in the landscape-based recreation and entertainment industries, most corporations have neither the time nor the place for landscape. Yet these same corporations employ the imaginations of a creative army dedicated to the creation of imagined places, landscapes formed from dream-fulfillment scenarios that enhance the consumption of their products and the functioning of their enterprise.

Coca-Cola created a museum in Atlanta. At its center, a picture gallery exhibits art that the company has commissioned since the end of the last century—art that has, decade after decade, related the consumption of Coke to images of ideal social and family life. With great skill, Coca-Cola has anticipated and manipulated shifts in the social landscape. Though commercial, this art reflects a prescient understanding of the importance of landscape to the popular imagination.[9]

Consider the dominance of landscapes in all advertising. A count of advertising in a recent issue in *Architectural Digest* shows that more than a third of advertisers establish the identity and value of their product through landscape. Yet on the nation's magazine rack there is not a single publication on landscape, save perhaps *House and Garden* and *Martha Stewart Living*. From automobiles to fashion, landscape helps to sell.

Eddie Bauer has moved from being a retailer of clothes to being a prop master of lifestyle. Beyond clothes and home furnishings, they now plan to complete the lifestyle experience by adding travel packages and may even create landscaped artificial destinations in which to play out the image embedded in the clothes and the name. Such events will increasingly be bundled with the products of other manufacturers to allow the consumption of apparently complete realities. These will cover all aspects of life and lifestyle, from food to dress to health to social performance, with all the necessary props—furniture, architecture, sun, landscape—to go with them.

Sega has moved beyond video games to pioneering virtual theme parks called Sega World in several major world cities. Enter one and rise by escalator alongside the screams of willing victims of the free-fall ride. Arrive at the top of four levels of simulated pulsating action driven by the deafening sound of technobeat. Each level presents the most advanced simulation games. Imagine being in a small room sitting on a mechanized bleacher subjected to instant terror. Consciousness of the room dissolves as the illusion begins. Within seconds it compels and captures your every sense. You believe you are traveling out of control across vast landscapes, rocketing into space, charging down volcanos, narrowly avoiding a rock face that you *know* is real. This is happening just to you. Your life is in danger as you careen across endlessly elaborate and cunning landscapes conceived by armies of digital landscape architects competing to satisfy an unquenchable thirst for the new.

Commercial fantasies are only as successful as their ability to touch or stimulate individual desire and, as such, they are both constrained and responsive. Yet demands for such consumable illusions will continue to cause anxiety for those who believe that there can be some authenticity to the artifice with which society constructs reality. However, prevailing realities are formed by dominant economic forces, and the illusions of Sega's world, Eddie Bauer's world, and Disney's world are different only in form, not intent, from many of the created landscapes and parks of history.

Disney's World

Celebration, the new town being developed by the Disney Corporation in Florida, is the most ominous of all these themed and bundled synthetic landscapes. It is the most striking example of the power of the corporation to manufacture and manipulate reality.

Disney has created Celebration as the fullest illusion of American democracy within a legal arrangement that is explicitly antidemocratic. A charmingly landscaped town center with plantings of mature trees and shrubbery convey a sense of cultivation, of rootedness, an illusion of establishment, carefully, and with conscious political intent, *controlled*. Disney's designers have engaged in a deceptive consumption of the authentic. The form of the ideal American small town is here shaped into the packaging for a controlled product—co-opting the public realm, franchising myth.

How should the landscape architect react when the most authentic elements of our cultural heritage—small-town America, front yards, tree-lined streets, and neighborhood parks—become mere corporate packaging?

Celebration's compliant consumers sign charters and covenants that, while politically correct, seem to impose constraints on freedom of action, freedom of association, freedom to allow new social formulations to emerge. *Compliant consumers* is not an idle name; the tenants of the pretty little houses that form the American streets of Celebration agree to allow their family lives to be used in the testing of new products. Celebration is itself a product made out of the illusion of the quintessential American reality—the small town democratically formed around the city hall, a town structured by laws, not people. But the city hall in Celebration houses not the mayor but the property managers for the Walt Disney Corporation, for whom the just society is only of value to the extent that it enhances the profitability of the company.

Just as the evolution of major cities will become increasingly dependent on corporate enclaves, the creation of franchisable product lines such as Celebration will accelerate the fragmentation of society. Those who can pay the price of admission remain contented behind the borders of their private world. This may increase the divide between the haves and the have-nots, increase the divide between society as compliant consumer and society as a collection of free wills. Architecture and landscape architecture will evolve into little more than packaging and imaging practices of consumable realities.

On one issue Walt Disney was clear from the beginning: the so-called citizens of his town would have no rights to the land. In 1967, he wrote:

> It will be a city that caters to the people as a service function. It will be a planned, controlled community, a showcase for American industry and research, schools, cultural and educational opportunities. In EPCOT there will be no landowners and therefore no voting control. No slum areas because we will not let them develop. People will rent houses instead of buying them, and at modest rentals. There will be no retirees. Everyone must be employed.[10]

Novelist E.L. Doctorow summed up the project of Disney:

> What Disneyland proposes is a technique of abbreviated shorthand culture for the masses, a mindless thrill, like an electric shock, that insists at the same time on the recipient's rich psychic relation to his

country's history and language and literature. In a forthcoming time of highly governed masses in an overpopulated world, this technique may be extremely useful both as a substitute for education and, eventually, as a substitute for experience.[11]

Yet all our realities are, in essence, fictions. What is revolutionary is the threefold change from their definition by an autocratic elite for their own pleasure to their formation by paternalistic authority in the name of public culture to, increasingly, their appropriation by manufacturers creating illusions of reality, manipulating mass desire for commercial gain. However, satisfying mass desire requires as much understanding as manipulation. There is an implicit public dimension to this exchange. What emerges may be far from the polite civic performances that Europe excels in, but what emerges will order the landscapes of the future.

Agendas

The ongoing project of recovering landscape cannot afford to be nostalgic for either past vistas or past societies. Instead, the field must continue to develop new forms of theory and practice that will influence and shape the forms of landscape and emerging popular desires, both real and virtual. The desire for new landscapes of transformation and engagement dominate both the cultural imagination and the corporate agenda of flexible accumulation of capital, especially landscapes of recreation, sports, tourism, and entertainment. Can the discipline develop a rich and substantial appreciation of the role landscape plays in the popular imagination and the public realm? Can the field adequately develop a critical understanding of the many public roles for landscape, encouraging diversification and enrichment of opportunities? Can landscape architects recognize and act on the autonomous strength and character of things natural and wild?

The essays collected in this book provide useful and important beginnings to finding and articulating answers to these questions. It is my belief and hope that these ideas will find their way into larger sectors of practice and built reality. In a rapidly changing world, landscape architecture has unequalled opportunity to not only represent the constancy and profundity of humankind's relation to nature and to others but also to create and effect new modes of relationship.

Notes

1 The *Oxford English Dictionary* still carries a rather nineteenth-century aristocratic definition of the phrase *landscape architect*, making no distinction between gardener and architect: "landscape gardener (architect): a person who plants the layout of landscapes, especially extensive grounds." *Webster's*, on the other hand, recognizes a separate definition for *landscape gardener*, first used in 1763, at the height of privileged garden making, and *landscape architect*, which dates from 1863. This is defined as "one whose profession is the arrangement of land for human use and enjoyment involving the placement of structures, vehicular and pedestrian ways and planting"—quite a public definition.

2 Christianity has shown little or no interest in landscape, except in death and in the cloister garden. It is the *char bagh,* or fourfold garden, the most powerful creation of Islamic culture, that has sustained the most ancient idea of the garden: a consciously ordered frame displaying the cycles of the seasons and the beauty of plant life, depending on water and on a cosmic harmony. This paradise garden became the cloister garden later embraced by Christianity.

283

3 "Thither without doubt we are to go for models of this art." Letter from Thomas Jefferson to William Hamilton, July 1806.

4 See James Corner and Alex S. MacLean, *Taking Measures Across the American Landscape* (New Haven, Conn.: Yale University Press, 1996); and J.B. Jackson, *A Sense of Place, A Sense of Time* (New Haven, Conn.: Yale University Press, 1997).

5 See Corner and MacLean, *Taking Measures*.

6 Architect of the Crystal Palace in London, and also of the great leisure-park created around the relocated Crystal Palace at Sydenham.

7 Many other influences helped shape Central Park, including a mood of transcendentalism and Vaux's English education, but Olmsted—farmer, journalist, then landscape architect—was deeply impressed by Paxton's achievements in the making of Birkenhead Park.

8 The spiritual pleasure in nature is now a major topic in popular writing from garden making to travel, and the pleasure and satisfaction mass America takes in being in nature, being in the wilderness, should alone give significance to those who help maintain and shape it. Compared with Europe, the modest attempts at landscape gardens' specific beautification are devoid of awareness of the rich tradition such activities belong to. If Beatrix Farrand had influenced popular gardening in the United States the way that Gertrude Jekyll changed the English garden, things might have been otherwise. Individuals do make a difference.

9 As a conceptual aside, Coca-Cola appears to play on almost every urban landscape in the world, but nowhere more dramatically than in Shanghai at this time. Shanghai's Fifth Avenue is Nanjing Road, 6 kilometers in length and, in 1998, for two-thirds of this, Coca-Cola. With mathematical precision, Coca-Cola placed its iconic logo on every lamp post on both sides of the street, forming a rippling band of red that receded into the distance. At midpoint, however, there is an almost imperceptible change: the color remains but instead of "Coca-Cola," the disks read "Raise the flag for Deng Xiaoping."

10 Walt Disney, cited in Stephen M. Fjellman, *Vinyl Leaves: Walt Disney World and America* (Boulder, Co.: Westview Press, 1992), 116. From a press conference given by Walt Disney in 1966.

11 E.L. Doctorow, *The Book of Daniel* (New York: Random House, 1971), 289.

Contributors

Alan Balfour, dean and professor of architecture at Rensselaer Polytechnic Institute, is the author of *Berlin: The Politics of Order, 1737–1989* (New York: Rizzoli, 1990), editor of *Berlin, World City* (London: Academy Editions, 1995), and past chairman of the Architectural Association, London.

Anita Berrizbeita, assistant professor of landscape architecture at the University of Pennsylvania, is a practicing landscape architect based in Philadelphia.

James Corner, associate professor of landscape architecture in the Graduate School of Fine Arts at the University of Pennsylvania, is author, with Alex S. MacLean, of *Taking Measures Across the American Landscape* (New Haven, Conn.: Yale University Press, 1996) and is a practicing landscape architect based in Philadelphia.

Denis Cosgrove, Alexander Von Humboldt Professor of Geography at UCLA, is author of *The Palladian Landscape: Geographical Change and Its Cultural Representations in Sixteenth-Century Italy* (State College: Pennsylvania State University Press, 1993) and *Social Formation and Symbolic Landscape* (Reprint, Madison: University of Wisconsin Press, 1998). He is also the editor of *Mappings* (London: Reaktion Press, 1999) and, with Stephen Daniels, of *The Iconography of Landscape* (London: Cambridge University Press, 1988).

Georges Descombes, professor of architecture at the University of Geneva, is author of *Georges Descombes: Shifting Sites*, Giordana Tironi, ed. (Roma: Gangeme Editore, 1988), and is a practicing architect based in Geneva.

Stanislaus Fung, Director of the Asian Architecture Research Unit at the University of New South Wales in Sydney, has written extensively on Chinese garden and landscape art.

Christophe Girot, professor and director of the landscape architecture program at the École Nationale Supérieure in Versailles, is a practicing landscape architect based in Paris.

Adrian Hemming is a painter and fine artist based in London; his work has been exhibited internationally.

Steen A.B. Høyer, professor and director of the landscape architecture program at the Royal Danish Academy of Fine Arts, is a practicing landscape architect based in Copenhagen.

David Leatherbarrow, professor of architecture at the University of Pennsylvania, is author of *The Roots of Architectural Invention: Site, Enclosure, Materials* (London: Cambridge University Press, 1993) and, with Mohsen Mostafavi, of *On Weathering: The Life of Buildings in Time* (Cambridge, Mass.: MIT Press, 1993).

Bart Lootsma, critic and guest professor in architectural theory at the Berlage Institute for Architecture in Amsterdam, has written extensively on contemporary Dutch urbanism.

Sébastien Marot, director of the cultural department of the Société Française d'Architecture, is also a landscape and architectural critic at l'Ecole d'architecture de la ville et des territoires, Marne-la-vallée, and the Institute of Architecture at the University of Geneva.

Anuradha Mathur, assistant professor of landscape architecture at the University of Pennsylvania, is a practicing landscape architect based in Philadelphia.

Marc Treib, professor of architecture at the University of California at Berkeley, is author of *Space Calculated in Seconds: The Philips Pavilion, Le Corbusier and Edgard Varèse* (New York: Princeton Architectural Press, 1996), and *Sanctuaries of Spanish New Mexico* (Berkeley: University of California Press, 1993). He is coauthor, with Dorothée Imbert, of *Garrett Eckbo: Modern Landscapes for Living* (Berkeley: University of California Press, 1997), editor of *Modern Landscape Architecture: A Critical Review* (Cambridge, Mass.: MIT

Press, 1990), and coeditor, with Therese O'Malley, of *The Regional Garden in the United States* (Washington, D.C: Dumbarton Oaks, 1995).

Charles Waldheim, associate professor of architecture and director of the landscape urbanism program at the University of Illinois in Chicago, is a practicing architect based in Chicago.

Alex Wall, professor of urban design and architecture at the University of Karlsruhe, Germany, has written extensively on contemporary urbanism and is a practicing architect based in Karlsruhe and Philadelphia.

287